Aspar and the Struggle for the Eastern Roman Empire, AD 421–71

Also available from Bloomsbury

Boethius' Consolation of Philosophy as a Product of Late Antiquity,
Antonio Donato
Corinth in Late Antiquity, Amelia R. Brown
Rome at War AD *293–696*, Michael Whitby
The Roman Army, David J. Breeze

Aspar and the Struggle
for the Eastern Roman Empire,
AD 421–71

Ronald A. Bleeker

BLOOMSBURY ACADEMIC
LONDON · NEW YORK · OXFORD · NEW DELHI · SYDNEY

BLOOMSBURY ACADEMIC
Bloomsbury Publishing Plc
50 Bedford Square, London, WC1B 3DP, UK
1385 Broadway, New York, NY 10018, USA
29 Earlsfort Terrace, Dublin 2, Ireland

BLOOMSBURY, BLOOMSBURY ACADEMIC and the Diana logo are trademarks of
Bloomsbury Publishing Plc

First published in Great Britain 2022
Paperback edition published 2024

Copyright © Ronald A. Bleeker, 2022

Ronald A. Bleeker has asserted his right under the Copyright, Designs and Patents Act, 1988, to be identified as Author of this work.

Cover design: Terry Woodley
Cover image © *Missorium*, large silver plate, of consul Ardabur Aspar. Diameter 42cm.
Photo By DEA / G. NIMATALLAH/De Agostini via Getty Images

All rights reserved. No part of this publication may be reproduced or transmitted in any form or by any means, electronic or mechanical, including photocopying, recording, or any information storage or retrieval system, without prior permission in writing from the publishers.

Bloomsbury Publishing Plc does not have any control over, or responsibility for, any third-party websites referred to or in this book. All internet addresses given in this book were correct at the time of going to press. The author and publisher regret any inconvenience caused if addresses have changed or sites have ceased to exist, but can accept no responsibility for any such changes.

A catalogue record for this book is available from the British Library.

Library of Congress Cataloging-in-Publication Data
Names: Bleeker, Ronald A., author.
Title: Aspar and the struggle for the eastern Roman Empire (A.D. 421-471) / Ronald A. Bleeker.
Description: New York : Bloomsbury Academic, 2022. | Includes bibliographical references and index.
Identifiers: LCCN 2021052181 | ISBN 9781350279261 (hardback) | ISBN 9781350279308 (paperback) | ISBN 9781350279278 (ebook) | ISBN 9781350279285 (epub) | ISBN 9781350279292
Subjects: LCSH: Aspar, Flavius Ardaburius, –471. | Generals–Byzantine Empire–Biography. | Statesmen–Byzantine Empire–Biography. | Politicians–Byzantine Empire–Biography. | Leo I, Emperor of the East, –474. | Byzantine Empire–History–To 527. | Byzantine Empire–Politics and government–To 527. | Rome–History–Empire, 284-476. | Rome–Politics and government–284-476.
Classification: LCC DF564 .B57 2022 | DDC 355.0092 [B—dc23/eng/20220105
LC record available at https://lccn.loc.gov/2021052181

ISBN: HB: 978-1-3502-7926-1
PB: 978-1-3502-7930-8
ePDF: 978-1-3502-7927-8
eBook: 978-1-3502-7928-5

Typeset by RefineCatch Limited, Bungay, Suffolk

To find out more about our authors and books visit www.bloomsbury.com and sign up for our newsletters

Contents

List of Illustrations vi
Preface vii
Genealogies ix

1 Why Does Aspar Matter? 1
2 "Barbarians" and "Heretics" 7
3 Aspar's Antecedents 17
4 Ardaburius the Elder and Aspar: Persia and Italy (421–5) 33
5 Aspar in Africa: The War with the Vandals (431–5) 51
6 Aspar and Attila: The Wars with the Huns (440–50) 65
7 Aspar and the Choice of Marcian (450–7) 93
8 Aspar and the Choice of Leo (457) 111
9 Beginnings of the Struggle with Leo (457–65) 119
10 The Rise of Zeno (465–7) 131
11 Leo's African Gamble (467–8) 141
12 Aspar's Apogee and Defeat (469–71) 157
13 Aftermath (471–91) 177
14 Conclusions 195

Bibliography 209
Index 225

Illustrations

Map

1 Map of the Roman Empire *c.* 400 AD   xii

Figures

1	Family of Theodosius I	ix
2	Family of Aspar	x
3	Family of Leo I	xi
4	Silver *missorium* of Aspar	19
5	Detail from *missorium* of Aspar showing Ardabur the Elder and Plinta	20
6	*Solidus* of Aelia Pulcheria	34
7	Cameo of Galla Placidia and her children	42
8	*Solidus* of Theodosius II with a young Valentinian III, *c.* 425	48
9	*Solidus* of Valentinian III showing his marriage to Licinia Eudoxia, with Theodosius II as *pronubis*, *c.* 437	83
10	*Solidus* of Anthemius with Leo I, *c.* 468	147
11	*Solidus* of Aelia Ariadne	192

Preface

This book has an unusual genesis. Many years ago, I discovered that my law school library had a complete collection of the *English Historical Review*. In my few leisure moments, I was able to explore that resource and it was then that I discovered the world of late antiquity. In particular, I began to read about the eastern Roman empire, "the Rome that did not fall", and to ask myself the question "why not?". It was this that led me to the crucial fifth century and to Aspar.

The initial result of my reading was my short article on "Aspar and Attila," published in 1980. However, the subsequent demands of career and family prevented me from further historical writing for many years, although I continued to study new works in this field. While many of them mentioned Aspar, and some discussed his role in the succession crises of 450 and 457, none presented a full assessment of his long life and central role throughout the fifth century. It was not until my retirement in 2015 that I at last had the time to write a book that tries to do so.

In reflecting on how the book became a reality, I wish to express my appreciation and thanks to several people. It was my good fortune to become acquainted with the Georgetown University Classics Department. In particular, I would like to express my appreciation to Professor Josiah Osgood, an inspiring teacher and gifted writer, who was generous and encouraging to a retired lawyer with an unusual interest in late antiquity. A Georgetown seminar on "Selling the Roman Empire" by Professor Zach Herz (now University of Colorado, Boulder) enriched my understanding of sources and methods. In addition, I would like to thank two scholars of late antiquity who were kind enough to review early drafts of this book, Professor Jonathan Arnold (University of Tulsa) and Dr. Jeroen Wijnendaele (University of Ghent). In getting the book published, it has been a pleasure to work with the team at Bloomsbury, most notably Alice Wright and Lily Mac Mahon, as well as the two anonymous reviewers who provided extremely helpful comments. Any failings in the text are of course my own.

Finally, I would like to thank my wife, Nancy (whose interests rarely include the fifth century, but who over many years has consistently encouraged me) and my son, Andrew (whose keen grasp of people and politics is accompanied by his admirable empathy and humanity).

Ronald A. Bleeker
McLean, Virginia
September, 2021

Genealogies

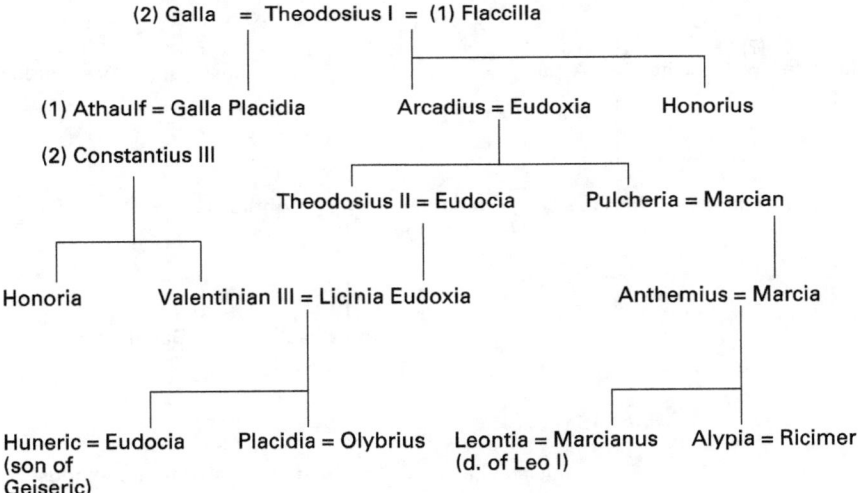

Figure 1 Family of Theodosius I.

x *Genealogies*

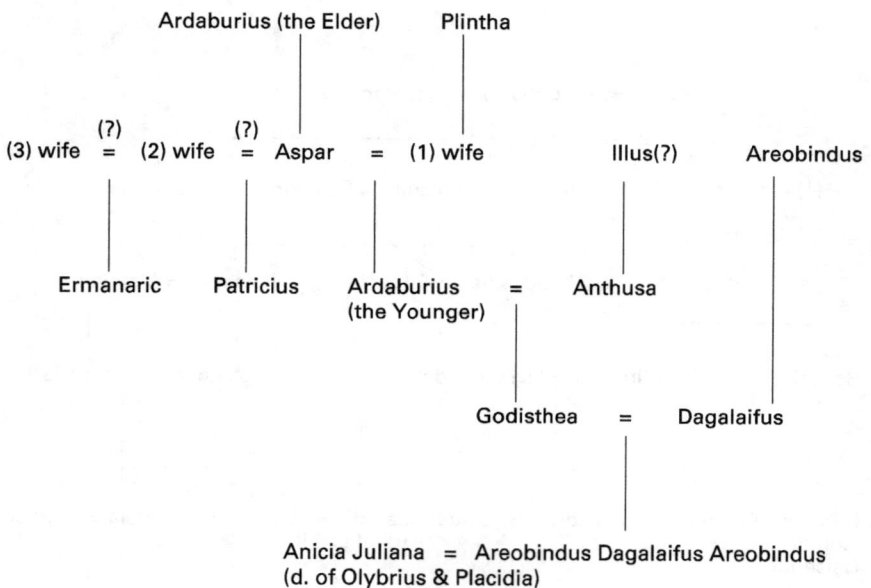

Figure 2 Family of Aspar.

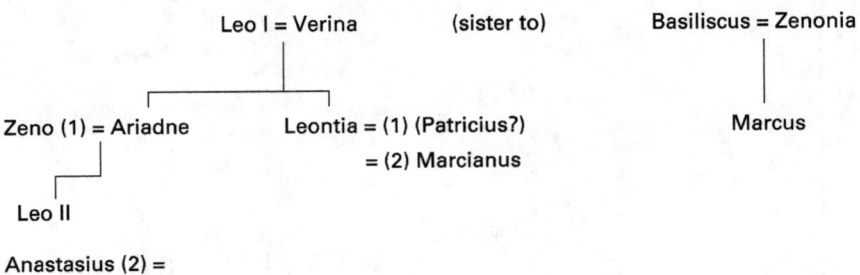

Figure 3 Family of Leo I.

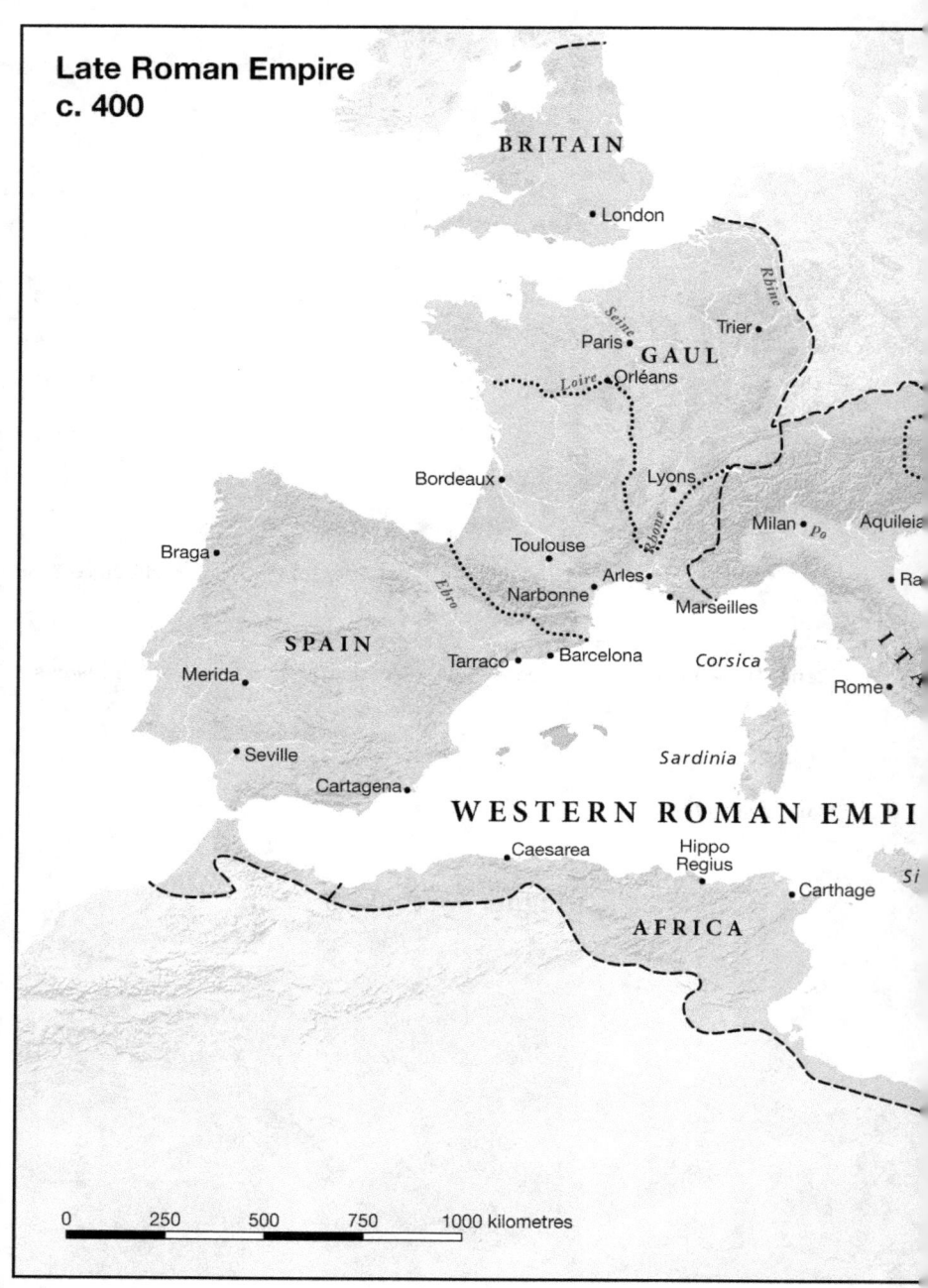

Map 1 Map of the Roman Empire *c.* 400 AD (Craig Molyneux at CartDeco).

1

Why Does Aspar Matter?

Theodosius I, a strong military leader, was the last person to rule all of a Roman empire with essentially the same borders as the empire established by Caesar Augustus some four hundred years earlier. When Theodosius died at Milan in January 395, the management of this empire was divided territorially between his two young and very underwhelming sons.[1] The older son, Arcadius, age eighteen, was given responsibility for the eastern provinces. The younger son, Honorius, age ten, was given responsibility for the western provinces (i.e., everything west of the Balkans and of Egypt). It was not the first time that administration of the empire had been divided in this way, but it would be the last.[2]

Despite this division of management, the concept of a unified empire remained intact. On occasion, the two parts cooperated in military efforts (e.g., in 431, 440, and 468 against the Vandals). Other forms of cooperation included coinage, acceptance of laws (e.g., the Theodosian Code), and (usually) the reciprocal recognition of emperors and consuls.[3] However, separate courts in separate capitals inevitably led to the development of as much rivalry as cooperation. Since the task of running each part of the empire rested with the emperor's advisers (initially Rufinus in the east and Stilicho in the west), each of the young emperors depended on men who jealously guarded their own power and often competed with the other camp for prestige and military resources.[4] Given these diverging interests, historians of the early fifth century refer to "eastern Roman" and "western Roman" states, even though in theory they both remained part of one Roman empire.

Yet, by the last quarter of the fifth century, this picture had dramatically changed. The western Roman empire had essentially ceased to exist, and its

---

[1] All dates are AD unless otherwise noted.
[2] Valentinian I and Valens had done it in 364. Kulikowski 2019:37, 118; Drijvers 2015:82–95; Salzman 2021:13–21.
[3] Basic & Zeman 2019:109–21; McEvoy 2010:175–8, 2014:245–7; Kaegi 1981:3.
[4] Zosimus 5.1.1–2; Omissi 2018:292; C. Kelly 2004:168.

territory was now ruled by several "barbarian" kingdoms.[5] In contrast, the eastern Roman empire had been battered but remained vibrant and Roman—and it would survive as a Roman state for another thousand years.[6]

Historians of late antiquity tend to fall into two camps—those who see these changes as a "catastrophe" as a result of invasions by hostile "barbarians," and those who see a more gradual "transformation" in which the empire's internal factors played a larger role and where the influx of "barbarians" was part of an ongoing and often less violent process.[7]

But why did the outcomes differ in the two parts of the empire? While there has been considerable study of the fall of the west, this book will focus on the survival of the east, and particularly on the role of military officers of "barbarian" descent in the politics of imperial succession during the fifth century. In that arena, no one of "barbarian" descent played a more important role for as long a time as the general, senator, consul, and patrician, Flavius Ardaburius Aspar.

Aspar's story stands at the intersection of two major issues in the Roman world in late antiquity. One was the evolving concept of imperial succession; the other was the role of "barbarians" in the Roman state. This is not to suggest that these were the only issues that have been advanced.[8] However, the question we will consider is how did the incorporation of "barbarians" into the Roman state (and particularly the Roman military) affect imperial succession in the mid-fifth century? On several occasions, this question became central to the differing fates of the empire's two parts. Our focus will be on how Aspar's life illuminates matters. However, it also leads to further questions—e.g., who was a "barbarian"? who was "orthodox"? how did these concepts affect who could be emperor?[9]

Looking at the first issue, there had always been a surprising lack of clarity about the Roman imperial succession.[10] While there was a continuing preference for dynastic succession, legitimacy could also be based on acceptance by the senate and/or the army. Without this, the result was often civil war. Nonetheless, in the fourth century, relatively stable dynasties were established by Constantius I, followed by Valentinian I and then Theodosius I. Moreover, Theodosius'

---

[5] On the controversial term "barbarian," see ch. II, *infra*.
[6] Kaldellis 2019a; Wickham 2016:22.
[7] Mathisen 2019:138; Arnold 2014:3–5; Lee 2013:xii.
[8] Demandt 1984:638–9, 719, listed 227 reasons that have been proposed for the "fall of Rome." Recent scholarship has highlighted environmental and epidemiological factors. Harper 2017.
[9] McEvoy 2013:325–9; MacGeorge 2002:96 n. 62, 262–8; O'Flynn 1983:ix; Lee 2013:94–102; Lee 2000:33–4; Williams & Friell 1999:75; Ferrill 1986:83 ff.; F. Lot 1927:218.
[10] Börm 2015:239–64; Beard 2021:69–70, 218.

dynasty was connected by marriage to the previous dynasty, since his second wife was Galla, the widow of Valentinian I.[11]

However, the glaring weakness of a dynastic approach to succession was that a successful transfer of power depended on having a suitable male heir. In addition, a Roman emperor had come to be viewed as a "soldier-emperor" who confirmed his legitimacy through military victories.[12] This could be a problem if the available dynastic candidate was unable or unwilling to fill this role.

The problem became real in the late fourth and early fifth centuries when on several occasions the dynastic heir was a young child who had received the imperial title of "Augustus." Nonetheless, these "child-emperors" were accepted as legitimate rulers. This often involved having a guardian (usually a military officer) run matters until the child came of age.[13] In some cases, this "partnership" continued after the child became an adult.[14] McEvoy persuasively suggests that this arrangement would not have been successful without a "transformation of the imperial office" in which the role of the emperor no longer required actual military leadership but instead became primarily ceremonial (and distinctly Christian) in nature. However, while McEvoy refers to this as an "infantilization," she recognizes that an adult might simply lack the interest or ability to take a more active role. Nor did it preclude the possibility of partnership between a military leader (e.g., Ricimer) and a soldier-emperor (e.g., Majorian).[15] This development occurred roughly simultaneously in both halves of the empire, with ceremonial practices at Constantinople influencing its evolution in the west.[16]

However, the use of "child-emperors" broke down in the mid-fifth century, when both the eastern and western branches of the Theodosian dynasty faced succession crises due to the complete absence of a male dynastic heir.[17] The western Roman empire never recovered from its crisis. However, the eastern Roman empire saw peaceful transitions in 450, 457 and 491. As we will see, it was Aspar, a second-generation general of "barbarian" descent, who played a key role in the first two transitions.

---

[11] *PLRE* 1, Theodosius 4.
[12] On military victory and legitimacy, Heather 2018:28; McEvoy 2010:159; Angelova 2004:6.
[13] McEvoy 2013:9–12, 143, 2010:159, 162; "guardian" because the Romans did not have the formal position of "regent."
[14] e.g., Honorius/Flavius Stilicho (*PLRE* 1) and Valentinian III/ Fl..Aetius 7 (*PLRE* 2).
[15] McEvoy 2010:191–2. On Christian piety and legitimacy, Soz., 9.1.2; Harries 2013:70; McCormick 1986:47–8.
[16] McEvoy 2010:175–8.
[17] While a "child-emperor" was created in the east by Leo I in 473/474 to transfer power to his grandson, it did not result in a permanent transition. Nor did the brief reign of the last west Roman emperor, Romulus, in 476. See ch. XIII, *infra*.

A main thesis of this book is that Aspar essentially expanded the concept of a "ceremonial ruler" by recognizing that the emperor could be a non-dynastic adult so long as he was agreeable to a "partnership" with his military leader and could perform his ceremonial duties. Although not limited to religious matters, "ceremonial" also meant someone who was sufficiently orthodox and could be acclaimed as "pious." Although this had previously (and unsuccessfully) been attempted in the west, it was something new in the eastern empire.[18]

However, the dynastic preference remained strong.[19] In 450 and 491 the choice of a non-dynastic candidate was buttressed by the new emperor's marriage to an Augusta from the prior dynasty. However, in 457, Aspar's non-dynastic candidate was selected over a strong claimant with dynastic ties. Since the continued success of a "partnership" required concurrence between the emperor and his military partner, trouble could arise if the interests of the two diverged.[20] Recognizing this, Aspar attempted to bind the new emperor's interests to his own by creating a dynastic bond between them. We will see how this turned out.

In addition to the issue of succession, external pressure on the empire had increased by the fifth century. On the eastern frontier, the Parthian state had been replaced by the stronger and more aggressive Sassanid Persian state. Along the Rhine and Danube frontiers, centuries of interaction between the Roman state and its "barbarian" neighbors had resulted in larger "barbarian" entities that were also more militarily proficient. In part, this was the result of the increasingly heavy Roman reliance on "barbarian" troops in late antiquity, which tended to equalize military quality.[21] In addition, new peoples from the Eurasian steppe (notably the Huns) added to the pressure on the frontiers.

This has often caused the fifth century to be characterized as an age of "barbarian invasions." It is true that the gradual collapse of the empire's Danube and Rhine frontiers in the late fourth and early fifth centuries resulted in the entry of several large "barbarian" groups who settled (with or without imperial approval) on Roman territory.[22] However, this is only part of the picture.

---

[18] For western examples, see Eugenius and later John, both adult civil officials with military backers. Omissi 2018; McEvoy 2010. Aspar's candidates in 450 and 457 were adults with military experience, although their most important qualification was prior service with Aspar's family.

[19] Croke 2014 (rev. Croke 2021:30).

[20] For earlier western "partnerships" involving maturing child-emperors that did not end well, see Valentinian II/Arbogast, Honorius/Stilicho, Valentinian III/Aetius. Omissi 2018:251–3, 294–5; McEvoy 2013:86–102, 153–86, 251–304.

[21] Kulikowski 2019:8, cf. Goffart 2006:30–1, on military proficiency. See Lenski 2002:118–20, 371, on the porous frontier. For archaeological evidence, see Whittaker 1994, esp.196; Harper 2017:147.

[22] This was not true of the Huns, who were essentially raiders. Nor (in this period) was it true of the Persians.

It is important to recognize that the empire not only transmitted its influence and culture to its neighbors, but also served as a magnet attracting them to its wealth and opportunities.[23] Both literary and archaeological evidence suggest that the porosity of the frontiers had long allowed *individual* "barbarians" to settle within the empire, enter imperial military service, and in some cases rise to high ranks. Aspar's father was one such "barbarian."

However, a full picture of the "barbarian" impact on the late Roman world needs to take into account *both* of these processes—the violent invasions by large "barbarian" groups, and the more peaceful incorporation of individual "barbarian" soldiers, farmers, and their descendants into the Roman state.[24] In the case of Aspar, his family had become very "Romanized" by the mid-fifth century, with three generations having served as Roman consuls. However, a full understanding of Aspar needs to explain how and why he also developed important ties with non-Romans, particularly the Thracian Goths and perhaps the Vandals, as well as other members of the east Roman "barbarian" military aristocracy.

In the mid-fifth century, the combined result of these two issues led to very similar political crises in both parts of the empire. The "child-emperors" had a dynastic claim to legitimacy, but in 450 (east) and 455 (west) there was no male Theodosian who could make this claim. Moreover, the increasingly "ceremonial" role of the emperor, coupled with the empire's greater dependence on an army that now comprised a large number of "barbarian" troops led by generals of "barbarian" origin or descent gave increasing power to the military partner.[25] In the late fifth-century west, that military leader was Ricimer, a fully "barbarian" general who never sought the throne for himself, but who made and disposed of several emperors.[26] In the east, and at the very same time, a similar political supremacy was achieved by Aspar—and yet the outcome of Aspar's story was different.[27]

Previous studies have focused on key military figures in the government of the western Roman empire of the fifth century, who have been variously described as "generalissimos" or "warlords."[28] In contrast, the politics and

---

[23] Halsall 2014:515–32; Geary 1988:vi–x.
[24] Mathisen 2019:141–2 questions the use of the term "invasion" at all, since many of the barbarian "invaders" eagerly sought salaried positions in the Roman military. See also Wijnendaele 2019b; Arnold 2014:63, 152–3; MacGeorge 2002:301–2; O'Flynn 1983:53, 57–9.
[25] Börm 2015:263–4; Wickham 2009:96–9; Averil Cameron 1993a:30 ff.
[26] *PLRE* 2, Fl. Ricimer 2. His father was a Sueve, and his mother a Visigoth.
[27] MacGeorge 2002:266–7; Harries 1994:56–7; Lot 1927 (Harper ed. 1961:218).
[28] Mathisen 2019; Wijnendaele 2015a; McEvoy 2013; MacGeorge 2002; O'Flynn 1983.

evolution of government in the eastern empire have received less attention.[29] As to Aspar, while some excellent studies have focused on his late-career role in the accession of the eastern emperors Marcian and Leo I, there has been much less consideration of his earlier life and the shifting degree of his political influence in the east over the course of his long career.[30] As a result, assessments of Aspar and his opponent, Leo, vary widely.

The purpose of this book is to explore the full scope of Aspar's career against the broader background of the Roman world of the fifth century. By exploring these issues, we may come to better understand both Aspar and the reasons for the survival of the eastern Roman empire.

---

[29] Croke 2021 and 2005; McEvoy 2016; Kelly (ed.) 2013; on Theodosian empresses, Angelova 2015; Herrin 2013; Holum 1982.
[30] Stewart 2014; Roberto 2009; Croke 2021 and 2005.

2

"Barbarians" and "Heretics"

The concept of "identity" is central to Aspar's story—both in the sense of how he perceived and represented himself to others, and how others saw and sought to define him.

There has been considerable modern debate on what "identity" meant in late antiquity. Studies have mainly focused on how a group (e.g., the Vandals) came to have an understanding of itself as distinct and to identify the qualities that differentiated its members from "others." However, "identity" becomes complex when applied to individuals such as Aspar, since an individual might emphasize different facets of their identity (e.g., ethnic v. religious) in different situations.

With respect to Aspar's identity, there are two important terms that will recur throughout this book.

The first is "ethnicity," which will for convenience be framed as the distinction between "Roman" and "barbarian."[1] This seems to have been a meaningful distinction in Aspar's world, although the limits of each term were often difficult to define. While phrased here as a dichotomy, it is perhaps better viewed as a spectrum since individuals such as Aspar combined elements of both. Moreover, they sometimes found ways to use each of these elements to their advantage in different situations. Geary has even suggested that "ethnicity" is better defined by "subjective" or "situational" factors, rather than by the usual "objective" factors such as one's origin, customs, language, or applicable law.[2]

It is important to stress that this is not about "ethnogenesis," the highly debated process by which new "national identities" were formed among the various peoples who established post-Roman states in the west.[3] Instead, the

---

[1] Kulikowski 2019:201; Mathisen 2013, 2006:1021; Brather 2002:171; Gillett 2002a; Geary 1988: vi–viii. Croke has questioned whether the modern term "ethnicity" had the same meaning or significance to Aspar's contemporaries. Croke 2021:53, 102.

[2] Geary 1983:18, 21; cf. Kaperski 2015:218–25; Halsall 2014:515–32; Haynes 2013:21 ff. (on "bricolage"; by distinguishing between this process and "Romanization," he allows for the possibility of multiple ethnic identities). See also Arnold 2014:5–7; Merrills & Miles 2010:86–7; Wood 2008; Brather 2002:171; Amory 1997:13–42.

[3] Arnold 2014:4–5; Conant 2012:6–9, 58–66; Merrills & Miles 2010:83–108; Amory 1997:34–9, 306–7.

focus is on a particular type of fifth-century *individual*—"barbarian" generals who had a "Roman" identity as well as a "barbarian" one. We can further distinguish between "first-generation" men of this type (such as Alaric, Gainas, Ricimer, or Gundobad) and "second-generation" generals, i.e., men with a "barbarian" father (or, in some cases, grandfather) who had been raised within Roman society (such as Stilicho and Aspar). In the later fifth century, a third category may be provided by the two Theoderics, basically leaders of a "barbarian" people who also had extensive experience living and holding office in the Roman world.[4]

The second key concept in Aspar's identity is religion, in particular the idea of Christian "orthodoxy" as opposed to doctrinal variations. In Aspar's time, this can be framed as the distinction between followers of the Orthodox Church in Constantinople, and those who held one of the many religious views which that church regarded as heterodox and sometimes officially condemned as "heretical."[5] Unlike the more fluid concept of "ethnicity," and despite the many differences among Christians during the fourth and fifth centuries, this was usually a sharp distinction in Aspar's Constantinople. The point is important because Aspar was a Christian who subscribed to the Arian creed, a confession which was regarded by the Orthodox Church of his time as heterodox and came to be condemned as "heretical."

Ethnicity: "Romans" and "Barbarians"

The evolution of the term "barbarian" in Roman minds has been explored in greater depth elsewhere.[6] The point to emphasize here is that it usually had a negative connotation in Roman life, political discourse, and imperial propaganda. In the fifth-century world of Aspar it was a way in which the imperial government and Roman "traditionalists" defined and slandered

---

[4] See ch. XIII, *infra*. Several leaders of "barbarian" troops in the early fifth century sought imperial commands, Wijnendaele 2019b (Alaric and Sarus); see also Gainas, Fravitta in ch. III, *infra*. This multivalency is not limited to "German" officers, but included "internal barbarians" from border regions, such as Gildo in Africa (Kulikowski 2019:130), and those from Isauria (e.g., Zeno, Illus). The term "German" is an anachronism that would have had little meaning to Aspar. Goffart 2006:4–9, 187–8.

[5] On heresies, see *C. Th.*16.5; Escribano Pano 2009:39–41.

[6] Halsall in Arnold 2016:173–99; Halsall 2014:515–32; Goffart 2006:3–5, 31; Burns 2003:1–41, 365–6; Williams 1998:10; and the debate between Goffart and Halsall in *J. Late Antiquity* 3:1 (Spring, 2010), 65–112.

"barbarians" as "the other," i.e., as a person or group who threatened the Roman empire and its way of life.[7]

The idea of the "barbarian" was a useful element of imperial rhetoric. Imperial legitimacy and divine approval had long been connected and were best demonstrated by military success over the empire's enemies. These concepts were readily adapted by the Christian empire.[8] In addition, the need to defeat "barbarians" could also be used to justify heavy military expenses.[9]

However, the term "barbarian" took on a new life in Roman writing and politics in the late fourth century as the empire struggled to survive. For example, the military handbook of Vegetius urged the exclusion of "barbarian" recruits and a return to a more "Roman" army.[10] Similarly, Synesius, in his *De Regno*, lamented the elevation of barbarians at court and the accommodating treatment they had received from Theodosius I.[11] Such tracts have been described as "anti-barbarism as a political policy."[12] Similarly, the propaganda campaign that Leo I later used against Aspar has been described as playing "upon the traditional Roman distrust of non-Romans in positions of authority."[13]

Roman fears of the "barbarian menace" date back many centuries.[14] In the fifth century they would include the Goths, Vandals, and Huns. Yet this ingrained fear of "barbarians" competed with an equally ancient tradition—the idea that Rome welcomed and incorporated immigrants who could contribute to its growth and success. Goffart succinctly described this dichotomy: "Instinctive Greco-Roman hostility to barbarians co-existed with a long and proud Roman tradition of openness to outsiders."[15] The result was a strange disjunction in attitudes towards "barbarians" in the late empire. On one hand, greater daily familiarity with "barbarians" led to their increasing acceptance as an exotic (if sometimes dangerous) but normal part of the Roman world. Their fashions, habits and culture began to undergo the same blending (with local variations) that had occurred earlier as the Romans incorporated Gauls, Greeks, etc. into their daily lives.[16] Yet this process co-existed with the lingering idea that there

---

[7] However, alleged barbarian virtues could sometimes be contrasted with Roman failings. See, e.g., Salvian, *On the Governance of God*; Halsall 2014:515–20; Cf. Hebblewhite 2020:83–4, 137.
[8] Soz. 9.1.2; Heather 2018:28; Lenski 2016:52–6; Angelova 2004:6; Harries 2013:70; James 2001:1656; McCormick 1986:47–8. On victory titlature, Lenski 2002:29, 126, 138–9.
[9] Mathisen & Shanzer:24–7, 133–7 (Sogno), 199–212 (Ziche).
[10] Flavius Vegetius Renatus, *Epitome Rei Militaris* (N. P. Milner, trans.), 1993.
[11] Synesius, *De Regno*; Mathisen & Shanzer 2011:199–222 (H. Ziche).
[12] Alan Cameron & Long 1993:323 ff.; cf. Lenski 2002:349–50; Southern & Dixon 1996:46.
[13] Stewart 2014:9.
[14] Livy 5:39–49; Dio.Sic. 14.115–16; Beard 2015:156–7.
[15] Goffart 2006:191; Gruen 2011:346; Mathisen 2006:1015, 2013:191.
[16] Geary 1988:4–5.

was something distinctive about being "Roman," and a prejudice against "barbarians" at all levels of society, even though the Roman elite was marrying prominent barbarians.[17]

The process of assimilation was especially evident in the Roman military. The separation of Roman citizens from non-Romans in the imperial army gradually eroded as a result of demographic changes and the army's constant need for new sources of manpower.[18] As the focus of recruitment gradually shifted from Italy to the once-"barbaric" frontier provinces, many "provincial" recruits may in fact have originated outside the empire.[19] They were either "barbarians" who had crossed the frontier in search of new opportunities in the Roman army or the immediate descendants of such immigrants.[20] The numbers enlisted became much greater after the heavy Roman losses at the Battle of Adrianople in 378. Needing troops, Theodosius I had little choice but to increase the recruitment of "barbarian" soldiers as individuals or (in some cases) in groups.[21] To say, as Roberto does, that after Adrianople "the Roman army was predominantly composed of barbarians, commanded by other barbarians" may be an exaggeration.[22] However, the reaction of Romans such as Synesius and Vegetius suggests that the number of "barbarian" soldiers in the Roman army noticeably increased in the two decades before Aspar's birth.[23]

As their numbers increased, some of these recruits rose to senior ranks in the Roman army.[24] In a few cases, they rose even higher. A very early example is Maximinus, who in 235 briefly became emperor of Rome. He is known to us from his birthplace as Maximinus Thrax, "Maximinus the Thracian." That nickname was not a compliment, at least in the hostile, pro-senatorial third-century sources that we have.[25] Kulikowski is right to note "the spurious imputation of barbarism that it still connotes."[26] However, Maximinus presaged

---

[17] Kaldellis 2019a:45, 125, 261; Arnold 2014:121–9, 139–41; Croke 2014 (rev. Croke 2021:30, 32); Demandt 1980.
[18] Haynes 2013:1–2, 63, 271–2. On the citizenship issue, Mathisen 2013:191–217.
[19] Kulikowski, "Regional Dynasties and Imperial Court," in Weinand (ed.) 2015:135–50.
[20] Lenski 2002:117; Kulikowski 2019:41–4. Halsall 2014:515–32 refers to archaeological evidence for the "circular career-migration" of Germans to the Roman army and home again.
[21] Goffart 2006:35, 238; cf. Geary 1988:13.
[22] Roberto 2009.
[23] Ibid.
[24] Goffart 2006:188–9; Potter 2013:251–2; on barbarian generals under Constantine, Liebeschuetz 1990:7–47.
[25] Cassius Dio, 79.1; Herodian, 6.8.1–8.8.8; Moralee 2008:58–62.
[26] Kulikowski 2016:112. A similar "barbarian" charge was made against the early fourth-century emperor Galerius because his mother was born outside the empire, although the real objection was his religious views. Lactantius 9.2 13; Eusebius, *HE*, 8.3; Gaddis 2005:31 n. 4. Note also Lactantius' use of the "*semibarbarus*" tropes against Maximinus Daia. Lact.18.13; Waldron 2021:41.

Aspar in several ways—he was not born outside the empire, and was allegedly the son of a Gothic/Alan couple who had settled within the empire.[27] Similarly, he had lived his life as a soldier in the Roman army. While it may go too far to say that Maximinus was "the first emperor to be fully barbarian," he definitely set a precedent. Significantly, while Maximinus' "barbarian" ancestry may have been perceived as an embarrassment by the Roman senate, it apparently did not disqualify him from the job of emperor.[28] Maximinus reigned for less than three years, killed in an army mutiny in 238.

In the fourth century, as more "barbarians" rose to senior Roman commands, there were a few more instances where a "barbarian" became an Augustus. Unlike Maximinus, the scope of their authority was limited, and they were quickly suppressed. They included the general Magnentius (son of a Frankish father and British mother) who in 350 overthrew the emperor Constans and ruled the western half of the empire for several years,[29] and the second-generation Frankish general Silvanus who briefly ruled along the Rhine in 360.[30] For a limited time and in a limited area, both of these "barbarian" generals of Rome assumed imperial power, demonstrating the difficulty of defining "barbarian."[31]

In the late fourth century, as McEvoy has shown, a different pattern developed in the west, with "barbarian" generals overthrowing emperors and ruling through a Roman "child-emperor" rather than assuming the throne themselves. In some cases, the position was reinforced by the general's marrying (or having one of his children marry) into the imperial family.[32] The outstanding example was Stilicho, the leading general of Theodosius I, the son of a Vandal father (who had served in the Roman army) and a Roman mother.[33] He married a favorite niece of the emperor Theodosius I and in 395 was appointed as a "guardian" for the emperor's sons (at least for Honorius).[34] Stilicho never sought to be emperor himself, but instead pursued a marital strategy, a model which Aspar would later

---

[27] Moralee 2008:60–1; Bachrach 1973:13–15 (critique of Syme:14 n. 28, 15 n. 44). Maximus' mother was said to be an Alan (as was Aspar's father) and Maximinus' father who was also a Goth (as Aspar's mother may have been). Both Aspar and his descendants would also marry into Gothic families.

[28] McEvoy 2013:141; Wickham 2009:96–9; Wickham 2005:158, 165–6.

[29] Mathisen 2006:1028. Magnentius' wife Justina was related to Constantine, which may have helped his claim. Humphries 2019:13–27; Woods 2004:325–7. See also Drinkwater 2000; on use of "barbarism" by his enemies.

[30] *PLRE* 1, Bonitus; Omissi 2018:169, 180–1; McEvoy 2013:141; Williams & Friell 1994:83.

[31] Kulikowski 2016:291.

[32] McEvoy 2013, 2016a; Wickham 2009:96–9; MacGeorge 2002:8; O'Flynn 1983:59–61.

[33] *PLRE* 1, Fl. Stilicho; Matthews 1975:258; Moralee 2008:68–9 (on criticism of Stilicho as a "barbarian").

[34] However, this claim was rejected by the eastern court of Arcadius. Claud. *VI. Cons. Hon.*; Omissi 2018:293; Blockley in *CAH* XIII:113.

follow.³⁵ His two daughters were (sequentially) married to the western emperor Honorius and he planned to have his son marry Honorius' half-sister, Galla Placidia. Nonetheless, Stilicho could never entirely escape the charge of "barbarism." For example, Jerome called Stilicho a "half-barbarian traitor."³⁶ Averil Cameron has suggested that "[a]s a Vandal, Stilicho was always suspect because he was of barbarian origin."³⁷ For all his ties to the imperial family, Stilicho's career had a dark ending—he was killed in 408 by a courtier of Honorius.

The early fifth century shows increasing evidence of intermarriage between the Roman imperial family and its "barbarian" generals or their children. In the west, Galla Placidia (the abducted younger sister of the emperor Honorius), married her Gothic captor, the Gothic leader Athaulf, in a Roman ceremony. They even had a son who they named Theodosius, although he died in infancy. Sivan speculates that, if he had lived, this child might have become "the first half-barbarian to rule Rome as its lawful emperor."³⁸

Even more telling is the case of Eudoxia, the daughter of the Frankish general Bauto, who had been one of the "guardians" appointed by Theodosius I for the young Valentinian II. Although Bauto had died earlier, in 395 Eudoxia married Arcadius, the elder son of Theodosius I and the legitimate emperor at Constantinople. In 400, she received the imperial title of Augusta. Thus, the entire eastern branch of the Theodosians was thereafter of partial "barbarian" descent. As Wickham points out, "[t]his genealogical heritage makes a nonsense of cultural difference, at least at the imperial or royal level."³⁹

These examples show that the "barbarian" ancestry of Maximinus, Magnentius, Silvanus, Bauto, and Stilicho was not a bar that stopped them from becoming an emperor, choosing an emperor, or having children who married into the imperial family. As McEvoy asked with appropriate exasperation, "Just how 'barbarian' did a man have to be to be totally barred from the throne?"⁴⁰ Nonetheless, the "barbarian" charge was still made against all of them.⁴¹ It would be no different with Aspar.

---

³⁵ It has been suggested that a law *c.* 370 forbade marriage between a "barbarian" and a Roman. *C.Th.* 3.14. Modern scholars believe that this law was limited to certain classes of soldiers. Lee 2013:133; Mathisen 2009b:140–55. However, even the general Fravitta apparently had to ask for permission. Eunapius fr. 59 (*FCH*:87).
³⁶ Jerome, *Ep.*123.16.2; Moralee 2008:69.
³⁷ Averil Cameron 1993:140.
³⁸ Sivan 2011:133.
³⁹ Wickham 2009:96–9; Traina 2009:76.
⁴⁰ McEvoy 2013:141.
⁴¹ Cameron 1993:140.

Even if "barbarian ancestry" was not an absolute bar, what may have mattered was a person's ability to "play the Roman."[42] By this I mean participating in activities expected from a Roman general, senator, or senior civilian official. This included not only military success, but holding high civic office, acting as a patron for other officials, corresponding with civil and religious leaders throughout the empire, and engaging in acts of civic and religious munificence (e.g., the construction of public works or churches). This was more typical of "second-generation" types than people who were born outside the empire. Stilicho did all of this, and so would Aspar.[43]

An important development in this process of assimilation for "barbarian" generals occurred in the mid-fourth century when senior military commanders (*magistri militiae*) were given senatorial status. This was probably more significant in the senate that was created at Constantinople, which had more "new men" and fewer "old families." It enabled military officers to take on aspects of the lifestyle of the civilian senators, and vice versa, and perhaps provided a common ethos of imperial service.[44] For individuals who were born and raised in the empire, and could "play the Roman," there was a better chance that they would not be viewed as "barbarian."

However, "playing the Roman" did not mean that a person necessarily gave up all of his "barbarian" heritage.[45] While Aspar held high civil and military rank in the empire, he also developed close relations with the "barbarian" Thracian Goths and apparently married into their "royal" family later in his life.[46] We also know that he retained another important element of his "barbarian" identity—his religious beliefs as an Arian Christian. We will come back to this important point.

Finally, a development which may have caused concern among some Romans was the formation of an intermarried military aristocracy among the empire's "barbarian" generals, particularly in the east.[47] Aspar and his family were central figures in this network. In 420, two of the most senior generals in the east Roman army were a Gothic general named Plintha, and Aspar's father, Ardaburius the Elder. A key alliance was Aspar's marriage to a daughter of Plintha sometime

---

[42] Wickham 2005:158, 165–6.
[43] Mathisen 2006:1034–9; Mathisen 2013:213–15.
[44] Davenport 2019:598–9.
[45] Mathisen 2006:1035; Mathisen 2013:210.
[46] Arnold suggests that the holding of prestigious Roman offices and a connection to barbarian "royalty" mattered to "barbarians" as well as Romans. Arnold 2014:150 ff.
[47] Goffart 2006:195–7; Kulikowski 2019:32. Aristocratic Roman families, such as the Anthemii, eventually intermarried with the Romanized descendants of these "barbarian" generals. McEvoy 2019a:124, 2016:492–4.

prior to 421. This policy of *adfinitas* later included other "barbarian" military families, such as the Gothic family of Areobindus.[48] It was an "essential tool" in the integration strategies used by Aspar's family to extend their influence.[49] Nor (as Aspar himself showed) was it limited to "barbarians" in the Roman army but could include "barbarian" federates such as the Thracian Goths.

The growth of this "barbarian" aristocracy in the Roman military raised concerns among some Romans about loyalty. A subsidiary theme that had often existed in the "barbarian" trope was that barbarians were not only dangerous but also treacherous, unreliable, or "faithless."[50] As the empire began to fail in the fifth century, this particular aspect of the "barbarian" trope would be increasingly emphasized in our sources as an explanation for Roman defeats. As we will see, Aspar would be accused of collusion with the Vandals.[51]

In short, "barbarism" was a charge that Aspar had to contend with throughout his career, although its relevance may have changed over time. It was likely raised against him in connection with east Roman campaigns against the Vandals in the 430s, 440s, and 460s, as well as after his defeats by Attila in the 440s. His connection to the Thracian Goths that developed in the 450s and after may also have encouraged this charge.

However, there was a related allegation that Aspar never overcame—the idea that a "barbarian" was often either a pagan or a "heretic" who did not subscribe to Christian orthodoxy. For although Aspar was a Christian, his faith was of the Arian variety.

Religion: Orthodoxy and Heresy

To understand east Rome in the fifth century, one needs to appreciate the era's pervasive and turbulent quest to define Christian orthodoxy or "correct faith." One also needs to understand the ways in which this issue became intertwined

---

[48] See ch. VII, *infra*; *PLRE* 2, Fl. Ardabur Aspar, Fl. Plintha. McEvoy 2016:492–4; Beers 2013; Wickham 2009:96–9; Goffart 2006:193ff, 238; Croke 2005:152–153.

[49] Roberto 2009.

[50] Cicero, *Pro Fronteio, In Catilinam* III:4–6, IV:12; Caesar, *Gallic War*, 5.26–37, and *Civil War*, 11.59–63; Tacitus on Arminius, who was "famous ... for treachery," *Annals* I.55; Procopius, *Wars*, 6.22.10; Gruen 2011:146–7, Lintott 2008:101–3. Oddly, the charge that barbarians were "untrustworthy" was also used as a justification for conquests. Procopius, *Wars*, 1.19.33; Conant 2012:257. Cassiodorus refers to protecting Italy from "barbarians whose oaths could not be trusted." *Variae*, 7.4.2–3; Arnold 2016:79; Kaegi 1965:23–53.

[51] e.g., Hydatius s.a. 468 regarding both Aspar and his son, Ardaburius the Younger. Ardaburius also intrigued with the Persians. See ch. X, *infra*.

with imperial politics. As with ethnicity, the object here is not to provide a comprehensive survey of Christian theology in the fifth century, but to show how terms like "Arian" and "heretic" (like "barbarian") became a way to define and condemn "the other." Our focus will be on Arianism, the variety of Christian confession held by many of the "barbarians" who lived in the Roman world in the fifth century. It is important here because it was the creed of Aspar and his family—but not of the imperial families that they served.

In essence, Arianism differed in its understanding of the relationship between the Father and the Son in the Trinity. The Orthodox Church in Constantinople believed that the two were of the same "essence" or "matter" (*ousia*). Hence, this position is sometimes referred to as "homousian," i.e., "sameness." In contrast, the Arian position (so called after its early exponent, Arius) was that the two were *homoios*, "alike" but not the "same." For the sake of simplicity, the terms "Arian" and "orthodox" will be used here.[52]

The ferocity of the dispute over these terms that ensued among the eastern bishops in the early fourth century caused the emperor Constantine I to convene an ecumenical council at Nicaea in 325, at which the homousian position was adopted.[53] Although some of Constantine's successors in the east (notably Constantius II and Valens) favored Arianism and persecuted non-Arian Christians, Theodosius I reversed course.[54] He convened the First Ecumenical Council of Constantinople in 381, that explicitly condemned Arianism as a heresy.[55] Throughout the fifth century his Theodosian descendants, as well as the subsequent east Roman emperor Leo I, issued increasingly stringent edicts which penalized Arians as "heretics" and suppressed Arian churches.[56] This would be a major issue for Aspar.

However, history is full of unintended consequences. As a result of fourth-century missionary activity, the Goths and other "barbarians" had been converted to the Arian creed. This became a problem when large numbers of these "barbarians" entered the empire and its armies in the late fourth and early fifth centuries because the empire was now ruled by the Theodosians, who viewed Arianism as a "heresy" but nonetheless needed barbarian soldiers.

---

[52] For modern usage, see Kulikowski 2019:20–3; Conant 2012:159–60, 182 n. 250; Stephenson 2022: 132–3; Salzman 2021:93, 154; Hebblewhite 2020:8, 11 n. 27.
[53] Kulikowski 2019:22–3, 177; Lenski 2016:264–7; MacMullen 2006:29–31 61, 70; Barnes 1993:202–6.
[54] Lenski 2004:93 describes Valens as "semi-Arian." When Theodosius I first arrived in Constantinople in 380, Greg. Nazianzus complained that Arians occupied all the churches. Arians were then restricted to churches "outside the walls." *Or.* 37.23; *Or.* 31; Escribano Pano 2009:41–4, 52.
[55] *C.Th.* 16.5.6 (Jan. 10, 381); 16.5.12 (Dec.3, 383); Escribano Pano 2009:41, 2016:241–62.
[56] *C.Th.* 16.5.65 (May 30, 428), 16.5.66 (Aug.3, 435), Jo. Malalas 14.41, Marcell. *comes*, s.a. 471.

This dilemma had two major results. First, much as they disliked it on theological grounds, the Theodosians were forced to tolerate the existence of at least some Arian churches within the empire. Prodded by the Orthodox Church, they made repeated efforts to apply social and economic pressure against Arians, but they could not eliminate them outright without damaging their own military base. Many of these barbarian soldiers (such as Aspar) held proudly to their Arian beliefs. In addition, in the fifth century both the Goths and Vandals were predominantly Arian.[57]

The persistence of Arianism in the fifth century also had a second effect—it further inflamed passions between Romans and barbarians. It became an additional way to define "the other," not just as a "barbarian" but as a "heretic," with all the passion and associated imagery that word conveys.[58] We will see evidence of this hostility in the overthrow of Gainas in 400, and in later riots in Constantinople incited by reports of Vandal persecution of the orthodox in North Africa.[59]

Although the combined term "barbarian heretics" is often used rhetorically, it is worth remembering that not all "barbarians" were "heretics" and not all "heretics" were "barbarians." We will see several dramatic (or pragmatic) conversions.[60] However, Aspar always remained firmly in the Arian camp. Because theology mattered passionately in the fifth century east, it is important to keep this in mind in explaining how religion was used by both Aspar and his opponents for political purposes. The strength of Aspar's faith is an issue we will need to consider in more depth when we come to his role in the events of 457.

---

[57] The Visigoths began as Arians but later switched to Catholicism, whereas the Vandals went in the other direction. When east Roman troops reconquered Vandal North Africa in the 530s, the east Roman government unwisely attempted to enforce anti-Arian laws. A.D. Lee 2019:286. See ch. V, *infra*.

[58] Roberto 2009. On Gothic v. Roman attributes, Arnold 2014:117–74; on Vandal v. Roman attributes, Conant 2012:47–66. The "barbarian" trope was earlier used by Christians against pagan persecutors. Eusebius, *HE*, 8.3; Lactantius *MP* 9, 13; Waldron 202:41; Gaddis 2005:31 n. 4.

[59] See ch. VI, XI, *infra*.

[60] Arians could convert to orthodoxy, and sometimes did, e.g., the Gothic general Jordanes and the (perhaps apocryphal) story of Galbinus and Candidus. Croke 2021:77–8; Crawford 2019:56. Conversely, the orthodox could convert to Arianism, e.g., the Vandal leader, Geiseric. Hydatius s.a. 428 79(89), *PLRE* 2, Geisericus; Conant 2012:185. See ch. V.

3

Aspar's Antecedents

In 1769, a large silver dish was discovered in the Tuscan countryside.[1] Near its center, the dish shows a bearded man dressed as a Roman consul seated on a curule chair. Along the edge, the name "Fl. Ardabur Aspar" is prominently inscribed, along with several Roman titles. It is the only pictorial image of Aspar that we have from his lifetime.[2] Slightly below is a smaller figure, wearing a toga, with the inscription "Ardabur Iunior Pretor." This is Aspar's oldest son, Ardaburius the Younger, named for his paternal grandfather and already holding the rank of *praetor*.

Above the figure of Aspar are figures of two other men who are also dressed as Roman consuls. The imagery suggests that they are ancestors of Aspar and his son. Their names indicate that although they were Roman consuls, they were of "barbarian" origin. Inscribed next to one figure is the name "Ardabur," indicating that he is Aspar's father, Fl. Ardaburius the Elder, who was an east Roman general and a consul in 427. Next to him is a figure with the name "Plinta" (or Plintha), another east Roman general of "barbarian," probably Gothic, ancestry who was a consul in 419.[3] Since Aspar's first wife is believed to have been Plintha's daughter, Plintha was also the grandfather of the younger Ardaburius.

When was this silver dish created and why? We know that Aspar became a consul in 434.[4] We also know that he received this honor at Carthage in North Africa, where he was commanding an east Roman force that was assisting the west Romans against the invading Vandals. The normal practice was for each half of the empire to appoint one of the two consuls for a given year.[5] However,

---

[1] Zaccagnino 2012:431ff.
[2] *PLRE* 2, Fl. Ardabur Aspar.
[3] *PLRE* 2, Fl. Plinta, says that he was a Goth, citing Priscus. But Priscus describes him as a "Scythian," which usually means Goths but can also mean Huns or others. Priscus, fr. 2 (*FCH*:225); Croke 2001:70–85.
[4] *CLRE*, 402–3.
[5] Basic & Zeman 2019:111–13; *CLRE*, 16–18. There were a number of exceptions.

Aspar's award was unusual in that he was nominated by the west Roman government even though he was an east Roman general.⁶ It is believed that this honor was in recognition of his military services in the Vandal campaign, as well as an earlier campaign in which he had helped restore the empress Galla Placidia and her family to the western throne.⁷ Therefore, it was probably made in or shortly after 434.

The silver dish, known as a "*missorium*," can be found today in the Mueseo Archaeologico Nazionale del Bargello in Florence. It is unique in that objects of this type are known to have been created by emperors, but no others are known that commemorate the consulate of an imperial general.⁸ It is also unusual in that a consulate was usually commemorated by ivory diptychs, which the new consul would commission and send to friends.⁹ Finally, the plate's iconography is striking in commemorating three generations of a consular dynasty.¹⁰

Why was the plate created? The standard and likely explanation, given the centrality of the figure of Aspar, is that it commemorates Aspar's consulate in 434. However, Alan Cameron believed that the presence of the figure of Ardaburius the Younger suggests that the dish could have been created to commemorate the young Ardaburius' giving praetorian games in Constantinople.¹¹ While possible, a similar *missorium* of Theodosius I shows his two sons but was made to celebrate his *decennalia* in 388.¹² Whatever the reason for the Aspar *missorium*, the point is the same—if Aspar commissioned this artifact, it shows how he saw himself and his family, and how he wanted to be seen by Romans. Even if not commissioned by Aspar, it reflects how the person who commissioned it saw Aspar and his family. It would be interesting if that person was the west Roman empress Galla Placidia, who is known to have sent similar gifts on other occasions.¹³ Or she might have been the recipient. In any

---

⁶ See ch. V, *infra*.
⁷ Zaccagnino 2012:443. See ch. IV and V, *infra*. However, Alan Cameron 2015:278 suggests that it may have also been arranged to balance the similar honor given that year in the east to his "rival," Areobindus. While possible, there is no evidence of such rivalry and the two families later intermarried.
⁸ Alan Cameron 2015:275; Zaccagnino 2012:438; Stephenson 2022:163–5; Hebblewhite 2020:86–7.
⁹ Ibid.
¹⁰ Ardaburius the Younger became the eastern consul in 447. *PLRE* 2, "Ardabur Iunior." Aspar's other two sons became consuls later under Leo I. *CLRE*:389, 453, 464–5.
¹¹ Alan Cameron 2015:279–80; Zaccagnino 2012:443.
¹² Elton 2018:144. Silver plates of his type were also exchanged between the Roman and Sassanian ruler. Canepa 2009:161–4.
¹³ She gave a silver dish to St. Germanus during his visit to Ravenna sometime between 437 and 448. Sivan 2011:167–8. He reciprocated with a wooden platter.

Figure 4 Silver *missorium* of Aspar (Getty Images).

case, as Roberto says, "The choice of iconography shows a strong desire to integrate these characters into proper society and the culture of the empire."[14]

Let us look further at the name inscribed on the dish—"Flavius Ardabur Aspar." Salway suggests that by the late fourth century the praenomen "Flavius" had become a "status *nomen*" associated with people of high rank in the Roman state.[15] Alan Cameron, however, takes the view that the "Flaviate" was a title received by all officers in the Roman military, regardless of their ethnic origin.[16]

---

[14] Roberto 2009.
[15] Salway 1994:137.
[16] Alan Cameron 1988.

Figure 5 Detail from *missorium* of Aspar showing Ardabur the Elder and Plinta (Getty Images).

Moreover, the fact that it was used by Aspar, his father, and his sons shows that it was hereditary, a distinction that was reserved for only "the most illustrious."[17] In sum, it tells us that Aspar chose to present himself and was known to others as a high-status Roman official.

Yet, despite the "Flavius" praenomen, his other two names are clearly *not* Roman. They are Alan names. "Ardabur" (or the Romanized "Ardaburius") was the name of Aspar's father; like Aspar, it is an Alan name.[18] So Aspar not only included his father's name in his own formal name, but he also named his oldest son "Ardabur," preserving a family naming tradition. It is unfortunate that we do not know the name or ethnicity of Aspar's mother. Some sources suggest that she was a Goth. If so, that could also explain Aspar's marriage to Plintha's daughter, as well as Aspar's later alliance with the Thracian Goths.[19] Modern historians refer to this multi-generational family as the "Ardaburii," emphasizing that this was not merely a family but a dynasty.[20] The *missorium* shows us this in a striking visual manner.

---

[17] Salway 1994:138; Mathisen 2006:1022.
[18] Bachrach 1973:98. See also Salway 1994:131, 136–7; Merrills & Miles 2010:95.
[19] *PLRE* 2, Fl. Ardabur Aspar cites Candidus (Alan), but notes Jordanes and Damascius/Photius call him a Goth. Cf. Wolfram 1998:32 (Alan) and 259–60 ("Alanic-Gothic descent" although here he may be referring to Aspar's son); Kaldellis 2018:11; Zuckerman 1994:170 ("the Alan Aspar"); Goffart 2006:38 ("Alan").
[20] McEvoy, 2019:123–5, 2016:483–4; Goffart 2006:299 n. 72. Similar Gothic examples from the sixth century are Areobindus Dagalaiphus Areobindus (*PLRE* 2, 143) and Fl. Amala Amalafrida Theodenanda (*PLRE* 3, 1236). My thanks to J. J. Arnold for the latter.

The mix of names also reflects the dual identity that will be a theme of this book—"Aspar the Roman" and "Aspar the Alan." Did one have to choose between these identities or, like many children of immigrants today, was this a way to assert their "Romanitas" while preserving links to their ancestral identity?[21]

What else do we know about Aspar's family? Over his long life of about seventy years, he is believed to have had three sons by three successive wives.[22] The three sons were named Ardabur (we will refer to him as Ardaburius the Younger), Patricius, and Ermanaric. He also had two daughters, of whom we unfortunately know little.

The names of Aspar's three sons are especially interesting. It is not surprising to see that the eldest was named for Aspar's father. Since he is shown on the *missorium* (c. 434) as already having praetorian rank, this suggests that he may have been born sometime around 415.[23]

The Roman name of the second son, Patricius, may suggest that Aspar's second wife was a Roman. Patricius is not shown on the *missorium*, which could either mean he was born after 435 or he was too young at that date to have held a curule rank. Alternatively, it has been suggested that the name "Patricius" could be connected to Aspar's elevation to the patriciate around 451. However, if that was his birth date, it would probably make Patricius extremely young for a consulate in 459. It is also possible that he was born with a different name that was changed around 451 to reflect his father's new status.[24] However, a birth date around 440 seems most probable for Patricius, since it would make him about nineteen at the time of his consulate. While this is still very young, it would make him closer in age to the emperor Leo's older daughter, Ariadne. This would fit better with a supposed understanding between Aspar and Leo in 457 that their children would soon marry. Ariadne was born shortly *before* Leo's accession in 457, and her younger sister Leontia was born shortly *after* his accession. Since Ariadne lived until 515, a birth date in the early 450s is reasonable. The girls were educated together by the same tutor, which also suggests that they were not that different in age.[25]

The third son was named Ermanaric, which had been the name of the great king of the Greuthingi Goths in the fourth century. He is believed to have

---

[21] Geary, in Bowersock et al. (ed.) 2001:107–29.
[22] Candidus, fr. 1 (*FCH*); *PLRE* 2, Fl Ardabur Aspar. Croke 2005:147 suggests that "three wives" means Aspar was "polygamous," but I think this unlikely since he was a Christian.
[23] Petronius Maximus became a praetor in 411 at age 15 or 16. Wickham 2009:27.
[24] My thanks to Prof. J.J. Arnold for this suggestion. The Isaurian Tarasicodissa changed his name to Fl. Zeno. *PLRE* 2, Fl. Zenon 7; Croke 2021:72. See ch. X, *infra*.
[25] *PLRE* 2, Aelia Ariadne.

been the son of Aspar's third wife, a Thracian Goth and possibly of royal blood (likely the sister of the Thracian Goth leader, Triarius).[26] Aspar may have married her in the 450s, when Aspar became a patron and ally of the Thracian Goths; indeed, the marriage may have been a part of this alliance. However, an earlier date for this relationship (and so an earlier birth date for Ermanaric that fits better with the fact that he held a consulship in 465) is possible. For that reason, Ermanaric's birth date may have been around 445.[27]

Arnold has suggested that the names of the three sons also seem to indicate that Patricius was intended by Aspar to eventually become part of the imperial family, whereas his brothers would follow Aspar as military leaders.[28] For example, Ardaburius could reasonably expect to become a *m.m. praesentalis* someday, whereas Ermanaric might have a special role with Gothic or other federates.[29]

The Alans

If the names of Aspar and his eldest son show that their Alan heritage had some meaning for them, then it is worth briefly examining what we know about the Alans.

The Alans were "a cultural entity composed of many peoples and not simply a linguistic or 'racial' group."[30] They were Iranian in origin, distinct from either the "Germanic peoples" (such as the Goths and Vandals) or the Asiatic Huns. However, racial or tribal concepts were very fluid, and intermarriage was common.[31] In the fourth century, the Alans lived a semi-nomadic life in the steppes north and east of the Black Sea.[32] The historian Ammianus Marcellinus knew of them and compared them (favorably) to the Huns, but Orosius put them in the same category as the Huns and Goths.[33]

---

[26] Malalas, 14.40 refers to Aspar's "concubine, a beautiful and rich Gothic girl." Perhaps the sources referring to a third "wife" are using a euphemism for "concubine," or else there may have been a Gothic wife who died and was succeeded by a "concubine."
[27] Croke 2005:155.
[28] Arnold 2014:159.
[29] In 484, he commanded Rugian soldiers in Zeno's campaign against Illus. *PLRE* 2, Herminericus. See ch. XIII, *infra*.
[30] Matthews 1989:332–42; Bachrach 1973:19. See also Arrian, *Acies contra Alanos*; Ammianus Marcellinus, XXXI.2; Goffart 2006:90–1.
[31] See ch. II, *supra*, re Maximinus.
[32] Alemany 2000:21, 13; Bachrach 1973:3–25.
[33] Ammianus Marcellinus, XXXI, 2; Orosius, I.16.2; Matthews 1989:334–42; Burgersdijk 2016:112–32.

In the late fourth century, the westward-moving Huns attacked the Alans. They absorbed some Alan groups while others dispersed widely.[34] As the Huns moved further into Europe, some Alans fled into Gothic and Roman territories.[35] In 376 there were Alans among the Goths who crossed the Danube into the empire, and they played an important role in the Roman defeat at Adrianople in 378. But other Alans joined the Roman army. Ardaburius the Elder, Aspar's father, may have been one of them.

Some Alans traveled further west, where they joined the army of the youthful western emperor, Gratian, around 380.[36] In the late 390s, additional Alans came to the west as part of the army led by Theodosius I against the usurper, Eugenius, and in the fifth century Alans fought for the western empire in the armies of Stilicho and Aetius, and many were settled in Gaul.[37] However, Alans also served in the Hun armies of Attila. As a result, Alans were fighting on both sides at the great battle in Gaul in 451.[38] While the Alans readily absorbed captives into their society, they also seem to have had an ability to easily assimilate into other cultures, whether the Huns, the Vandals, or the Romans. Claudian, the early fifth-century panegyrist, praised the western army's Alan units: "Alans, you have adopted the customs of Latium!"[39]

Apart from joining either the Roman army or the Huns, some groups of Alans became part of the great movement of the Germanic peoples through the provinces of the western Roman empire in the first two decades of the fifth century, crossing the Rhine in 406 in company with groups of Vandals and Sueves, and eventually getting to Spain by 408.[40]

By 410, these Alan groups had established a separate Alan entity in Spain under two "kings." Since the Alans received the largest share in the barbarian division of Spain, Goffart believes that they were the most powerful of the barbarian peoples in the peninsula.[41] Although the Alans offered to fight as federates for the west Romans, the Romans considered them the greater threat and instead hired the Visigoths to destroy them. The Alan survivors fled and

---

[34] Goffart 2006:91.
[35] Ammianus Marcellinus, XXXI, 3; Ambrose, *De fide*, II, 16, and *Expositio evangelii secundum Lucam*, X, 10. Maenchen-Helfen 1973:18–20, 71–2. See also P. Heather 2009:22–3; Wolfram 1998:136, 180; Thompson 1996:26–7; Errington 2006:31; Cromwell 1998:28–9.
[36] Zosimus, IV, 35, 2; Bachrach 1973:33 n. 21; MacGeorge 2002:230–1.
[37] Bachrach 1973:34–6; Goffart 2006:237. On the settlement of Alans by the west Roman government, see the Goffart/Halsall debate in *JLA*, 3:1 (2010), 65–112.
[38] *LRE*, vol. 1:185–8; Bachrach 1973:68; Wolfram 1997:136.
[39] Claudian, *De Con.Hon. IV*, II.485ff; Bachrach 1973; Kaperski 2015:235–9.
[40] Goffart 2006:91–6.
[41] Hydatius, s.a. 411, 418; Goffart 2006:80, 89.

amalgamated with the Asding Vandals in southern Spain. They may also have been joined by individual Sueves, Goths, and Hispano-Romans.

It is important to Aspar's story that we bear in mind that the Vandals now included a significant number of Alans. It is unclear whether these Alans maintained any sort of separate organization or identity within the group.[42] Some memory of their unique status seems to have been retained, as shown later by the occasional use of the Vandal royal title "King of the Vandals and the Alans." However, this title was not used by a Vandal king until Huneric, the son and successor of Geiseric, and after him not until Gelimer, the last Vandal king. It may have been used on occasion because it seemed more impressive.[43] It is a point to recall when we come to consider possible ties between Aspar and the Vandal king, Geiseric.[44]

A final point needs to be made about the Alans – while many had become Christians, they were predominantly Arian Christians. This was something that they had in common with many of the Vandals. Although some Vandals in Spain may have become Catholic (i.e., orthodox), the Alans appear to have been Arians.[45] When Geiseric became king of the combined Vandal/Alan people around 428 he made Arianism the official religion.[46] Geiseric's motives for this conversion are unknown. His mother may have been Roman, and, if so, she might have been Arian. Alternatively, his conversion might have been related to the addition of the Alans to the Vandal kingdom at this time. Thus, Aspar and Geiseric also had a religious tie. When Aspar confronted Geiseric in the 430s and later, this would become an irresistible ground for suspicion in orthodox Constantinople.

Ardaburius the Elder

To understand how Aspar's Alan family came to serve Rome, we should begin with his father, Ardaburius the Elder. In the wake of the Roman military disaster

---

[42] See the panegyric of Sidonius Apollinaris for Ricimer (Wallia's grandson), *Carm*, II, 363, 364, 379 as well as Hydatius, s.a. 418; Victor Vit., II, III. Also, Maenchen-Helfen 1973:22; Kulikowski 2019:267; Merrills & Miles 2010:96–7; *LRE*, vol. I:204; Jones 1964:188; Gibbon, ch. XXXI; Bachrach 1973:56–8; Jacobsen 2012:64–5.

[43] Kulikowski 2019:267 and Merrills & Miles 2010:96–7 note that Prosper uses it re Geiseric, but not that Geiseric himself used it. Prosper Tiro (*MGH AA*, IX 487); Merrills & Miles:274 n. 48, 49: Kaperski 2015:229–34. Gillett 2002:110 n. 31 says that it shows "some form of sustained separate identity of the Alani."

[44] See ch. V and XI, *infra*.

[45] Bachrach 1973:58–9.

[46] Hydatius s.a. 428, 79(89); *PLRE* 2, Geisericus; cf. Conant 2012:185.

at Adrianople, Theodosius I had to quickly rebuild the east Roman army.[47] He was therefore willing to recruit "barbarians," either individually or (and here we see a new development, or possibly an acceleration of a prior trend) as "federates," i.e., autonomous groups of "barbarians" under their own leaders who by treaty were paid to serve as Roman allies. Alan recruits appear to have been particularly welcome, probably as effective cavalry. The story of the Ardaburii may have begun with such a recruit.

We know that Ardaburius was a senior Roman general by 421 when he commanded Roman forces in a war with the Persians.[48] If so, then he was probably born sometime around 375–80. This would also be consistent with the fact that he appears to have remained active until about 435 and then disappears from our sources. It is possible that he or his family were among the Alans who crossed into Roman territory in the late 370s to escape the Huns. Whether he joined the Romans as part of a group or as an individual, he could have been part of the Roman army that Theodosius I led in his western campaign of 394. However, given the connections he seems to have developed at the court of Theodosius' successors, it seems more likely that he remained at Constantinople, possibly as part of a unit of Huns and Alans that served as a personal bodyguard for Rufinus, the eastern praetorian prefect and the leading figure in the east Roman court of Arcadius, the emperor's older son.[49]

This chronology would also suggest that Aspar, Ardaburius' son, was likely born in Constantinople sometime around the year 400. This birthdate for Aspar also fits with the following: (a) he likely accompanied his father in the Persian War of 421/22; (b) he was old enough and experienced enough to be given an important and independent command during the invasion of Italy in 424–5; and (c) when he became consul in 434, his oldest son had already achieved the rank of *praetor*.

If Ardaburius was serving as a soldier in Constantinople in the 390s, he likely witnessed the seizure of power by the Gothic general Gainas in 395, as well as the popular uprising that followed in 400. The story of Gainas is a very significant event in the history of east Roman/barbarian relations, although its consequences have often been misunderstood. It is worth studying in some detail because of what it tells us about east Roman attitudes towards "barbarian" soldiers at the

---

[47] Southern & Dixon 1996; Williams & Friell 1994:29–30, 89, 91–102.
[48] *PLRE* 2, Fl. Ardabur 3; see ch. IV, *infra*.
[49] Maenchen-Helfen 1973:50–1 cites Claudian's *In Rufinum*, II, 270–1, where the returning Gothic soldiers complain that Rufinus would make them "the slaves of the foul Hun or the restless Alan" as evidence that Rufinus had a Hun/Alan bodyguard. Bachrach 1973:42.

beginning of the fifth century, and its implications for the later career of Aspar and his family.

The Revolt of Gainas

The story of Gainas' revolt begins with the emperor Theodosius I's defeat of the western usurper, Eugenius, at the river Frigidus in late 394.[50] On the first day the battle did not go well for Theodosius, but on the second day a windstorm and a decisive charge by his Gothic cavalry carried the day.[51] While this victory was used to support Theodosius' claim of "divine favor," the Goths sustained heavy casualties and came away feeling that Theodosius had made them bear the brunt of the fighting. This grievance would fester among them.

When Theodosius I died in Milan in early 395, *de facto* control of the west and its military forces rested with the "barbarian" *magister militum*, Stilicho.[52] But Stilicho also retained command over those units of the east Roman army that had accompanied Theodosius to the west. In Stilicho's view, Theodosius' intent had been to make him the guardian of *both* his sons. This was disputed by the eastern emperor Arcadius, who had remained in charge at Constantinople, and his praetorian prefect, Rufinus. The increasingly bitter nature of this quarrel is evident from an invective delivered by Claudian, Stilicho's resident rhetorician at the western court, which is succinctly titled *In Rufinum*.[53] However, Rufinus also had enemies within the court at Constantinople, notably the eunuch chamberlain, Eutropius.

When a group of Goths led by Alaric (sometime Roman allies who had been settled in the Balkans) rebelled, Stilicho led his army against them and managed to corner Alaric in Illyricum. However, Illyricum was considered part of the east Roman empire. The east Romans demanded that Stilicho withdraw from their territory and return those east Roman units that he still retained. Stilicho could have finished off Alaric, and then obeyed the order, or he could have ignored the order completely.[54] Instead, he reached a truce with the Goths, and returned to

---

[50] On the background for Gainas, see generally, Eunapius (in Blockley, fr. 62, 64, 67(10, 12, 13), 69); *PLRE* 1, Gainas 1; *CAH XXIII* 116–17 (Blockley); Kulikowski 2019:125–6, 131–3; Alan Cameron 1993:323–31; Liebeschuetz 1990:90–125, Bachrach 1973:41–2.
[51] On the religious response to the battle, Ambrose, *Explan.Psalm* 36, 25.2–4 (*CSEL*, LXIV, 91); Alan Cameron 2011:93–131; Holum 1982:6–7.
[52] See ch. II, *supra*; *PLRE* 1, Fl. Stilicho.
[53] Claudian, *In Rufinum*; Alan Cameron 1970.
[54] A concern may have been that Stilicho's wife and children were in Constantinople for the funeral of Theodosius I. Blockley, in *CAH XIII*:114.

Italy.⁵⁵ However, he complied with the demand that he return some troops to Arcadius by sending the Gothic *comes* Gainas to Constantinople with a troop of Gothic soldiers.⁵⁶ This proved to be a poisoned gift.

As Gainas and his force neared Constantinople, the emperor Arcadius came out from the city to greet them, accompanied by Rufinus and other members of his court. Gainas and his soldiers approached the imperial party and then, in a shocking act of violence, slaughtered the imperial bodyguard and killed Rufinus in the presence of the emperor. Although many of the sources blame Stilicho, Eutropius also stood to gain. Indeed, Eutropius took the place of Rufinus as the dominant figure in the east Roman court, with the military backing of Gainas.⁵⁷

When Gainas and his soldiers marched into Constantinople they did not displace the badly frightened emperor Arcadius. Perhaps Gainas imagined that he could control the east through Arcadius, just as Stilicho controlled the west through Honorius. Or perhaps he thought he could rely on the chamberlain Eutropius to run the government for him. In either case, this would not turn out to be a successful long-term strategy.

Despite their general unpopularity in the city, Gainas and Eutropius managed to run matters in the east reasonably well for several years.⁵⁸ Gainas allegedly attended meetings of the senate at Constantinople in a toga, a sight which the anti-barbarian Synesius mocked but which the pagan historian Zosimus commended.⁵⁹ Eutropius even had a minor military success in which he personally led Roman troops. However, Eutropius became unpopular, especially after he briefly became consul for 399.⁶⁰ However, the immediate cause of his downfall stemmed from a revolt in 399 (perhaps instigated by Gainas) by a Gothic military unit in Asia Minor. Their leader, an officer named Tribigild, demanded that the emperor Arcadius remove Eutropius from office. Gainas, as the *de facto* head of the east Roman army, marched out to confront the rebels. However, although Tribigild was killed, Gainas instead joined forces with the rebels and led the combined force of Goths back into Constantinople. The

---

⁵⁵ Rufinus later made secret promises of promotion to Alaric and diverted him to Greece. Zosimus, 5.5. Stilicho may also have decided to return to Italy because of the revolt of Gildo. Wijnendaele 2017b.
⁵⁶ Maenchen-Helfen 1973:50–1 suggests Synesius' *Egyptian Tale* shows a rivalry in Constantinople between the Huns (and Alans?) and the Goths of Gainas. Cf. Alan Cameron 1993; Liebeschuetz 1990.
⁵⁷ Blockley, *CAH XIII*:114; McCormick 1986:48.
⁵⁸ Blockley, in *CAH XIII*:116.
⁵⁹ Synesius, *De regno*, 19/23C; Zosimus, 5.13.1; Mathisen 2006:1034; 2013:209–10.
⁶⁰ The idea of a eunuch consul apparently offended Roman sensibilities in both east and west. Claudian, *In Eutrop.* 1.8; *CLRE*, 333–4; Holum 1982:62; Blockley, in *CAH XIII*:116.

empire's eastern capital thus came under Gothic military occupation in 399—a full ten years before a different Gothic army captured Rome.[61]

The demand of the Goths for the removal of Eutropius was hard to resist, despite the emperor Arcadius' personal support for the chamberlain. Even the empress Eudoxia urged her husband to dismiss Eutropius.[62] Realizing that the game was up, Eutropius sought sanctuary in the great church of Hagia Sophia. The bishop of Constantinople (the famous John Chrysostom) negotiated his exile to Cyprus, but Eutropius was soon executed.[63]

Gainas lacked the political and administrative skills of Eutropius. Once back in Constantinople, he seemed uncertain as to what he should do. Meanwhile, the "Roman" elements in the city began to organize a resistance.[64] For once, the empress Eudoxia worked with John Chrysostom, since they were united by their common hatred of Arians.[65] Opposition also appears to have come from the survivors of Rufinus' Hun/Alan guard. Given later evidence of his close connection to the Theodosian family, it is tempting to suggest that Ardaburius the Elder was part of this group.

Rapidly losing control of the situation, Gainas pleaded illness, and abruptly left Constantinople in June, 400.[66] Surprised by this sudden decision, his Gothic followers attempted to follow him, creating gridlock at the city's gates. Seizing the moment, a popular uprising broke out in Constantinople during which many Goths were killed by citizens hurling stones and tiles. A large number of Goths (reputedly 7,000) took refuge in an Arian church, and allegedly died when the crowd set fire to the building.[67] The emperor Arcadius quickly regained control of the city, which suggests that he had retained command of at least some military forces, and loyal units of the army were ordered to pursue and destroy Gainas. This was accomplished, with an assist from the Huns, as Gainas tried to flee across the Danube.[68]

It is noteworthy that the pursuit of Gainas included some Goths in Roman service. It was led by an officer named Fravitta, who (like Gainas) was also a

---

[61] Crawford 2019:42.
[62] *Historia Ecclesiastica (HE)* of Philostorgius (Philost.). 11.6; *Historia Ecclesiastica (HE)* of Socrates Scholasticus (Soc.) 6.2.7; Holum 1982:62–3. This was even though she was a passionate champion of the orthodox against the Arian Goths. Soc. 6.8.1–9; Soz. 8.8; Holum 1982:54.
[63] *PLRE* 1, Eutropius.
[64] Holum 1982:68.
[65] Cameron 1993:98–100; Liebeschuetz 1990:147–8, 158–9.
[66] On Gainas, see Zosimus 5.13–5.22 (Ridley tr. and notes:210–12); Synesius, *De providentia*, 1.15–18 and 2.1–3; Philost. 11.8; Soz. 8.4; Theodoret, 5.30, 32; Soc. 6.5 ff; Marcell. *comes.*, s.a. 399–401; *PLRE* 1, Gainas.
[67] Croke 2001:84; Averil Cameron 1993b:149–50; Roberto 2009.
[68] McCormick 186:51.

Goth. Even the usually "barbarophobe" Eunapius speaks admiringly of Fravitta and of the high esteem in which he was received by the court after his victory.[69] In recognition of his success, Fravitta was given the honor of being named consul for 401.[70] However, Fravitta was executed not long after. He is said to have clashed with a supporter of the empress Eudoxia, perhaps for advocating a more cooperative approach with the regime of Stilicho. This could be interpreted in several ways, but if he was executed for taking this position it may reflect the strong feeling against barbarians that existed in Constantinople at this time.[71]

The story of Fravitta is a reminder that we should not view east Roman politics as an ethnic struggle between "Roman" and "German" factions. The use of the term "German" has itself been rejected by historians such as Goffart, who prefers "barbarian."[72] We are perhaps better advised to see a more nuanced struggle among individuals in Roman service, some of whom happened to have "barbarian" backgrounds and not all of whom were Arian.[73] We will see many further examples of such complex identities as we explore the career of Aspar.

Unfortunately, these stereotypes have too often caused Gainas' revolt to be misrepresented by some modern historians as the end of the "German threat" in the eastern empire.[74] This may be because we find evidence of "anti-barbarian" rhetoric in the east during and just after the career of Gainas.[75] Synesius of Cyrene's speech *De Regno* (whether or not actually delivered to Arcadius) summed up the political views of the "anti-German" faction that now controlled the government.[76] This attitude is also seen in Vegetius' handbook on military reform, which advocated a return to a more "Roman" army.[77]

However, it is an over-statement to maintain that there were practically no "Germans" in the east Roman army after Gainas. In addition to Fravitta, the Theodosians clearly had no hesitation in appointing officers of Gothic ancestry to high commands. This became quite common during the reign of Theodosius II (408–50). For example, Aspar's father held the highest rank of

---

[69] Fravitta was a pagan. Eunapius fr. 59, 69.4 (*FCH*:87, 111–12); *LRE*, vol. 1:135.
[70] *PLRE* 1, Fl. Fravitta; *CLRE*, 337. This honor had been intended for Gainas Ibid. Blockley 1992:120.
[71] Synesius, *De providencia*; Blockley 1992:100. Although there may have been a period of "limited de-barbarization" of the eastern military after Gainas, by 419 it was being led by Plintha and the elder Ardaburius. Crawford 2019:42–3; Cameron & Long 1993:311–36.
[72] Goffart 2006:187.
[73] Eunapius, fr. 69.2 and 69.4 (*FCH*:109–13).
[74] On "barbarians," see Averil Cameron 1993a:17; Geary 1988:13. On seeing this as the end of a "German" threat, see *LRE*, vol. 1:320; Brooks 1893; Lot 1927 (Harper ed:216).
[75] Crawford 2019:42–3; cf. Cameron & Long 1993:311–36.
[76] Synesius *De regno*; see also his *De providentia*; Kulikowski 2019:133; Blockley, in *CAH XIII*:117.
[77] Fl. Vegetius Renatus; Kulikowski 2019:133–4.

m.m. praesentalis by 422. Aspar's father-in-law, Plintha, was a Goth who received that rank even earlier (in 419) and held it for almost twenty years. He was succeeded by another Goth, Areobindus, who commanded the east Roman expedition sent to Sicily in 441; he and most of his principal lieutenants were Goths. And in the wars that broke out in the 420s, 430s, and 440s, the most important commands in the east Roman army were given to these men.[78]

Liebeschuetz is therefore right to conclude that "even during the period of debarbarization the Eastern army included soldiers of Gothic or Alan origin."[79] But if the defeat of Gainas was not the end of the "German threat" in the east, what was its relevance to the career of Aspar?

First, it may have had an important effect on the rise of Ardaburius the Elder and thus on Aspar. If Ardaburius the Elder was in fact a soldier in Constantinople at the time of the revolt, it is likely that he was among those who (like Fravitta) chose to support Arcadius over Gainas. This stance, and perhaps his proximity to members of the court, may have led him to become associated with the empress Eudoxia and her children, which could explain his subsequent promotion.[80] The repeated selection of Ardaburius the Elder (and later, of Aspar) to lead important military operations over the next two decades occurred while the empress Pulcheria (Eudoxia's daughter) was a major figure at the eastern court. It has even been suggested that Theodosian support of the Ardaburii was deliberate, since Arian generals may have been viewed as less likely to make a successful bid for the throne.[81]

Second, the career of Gainas may have taught Aspar what *not* to do. Gainas was neither a great general nor a subtle politician, and his efforts to use his Goths as a blunt military weapon to directly seize power in Constantinople failed. His story also shows the high level of opposition in Constantinople to military rule by a non-Roman, non-orthodox, military leader. In particular, the role of religion in the uprising demonstrates the power of the Orthodox Church and the growing popular antipathy to Arians.[82] If Gainas represents a failed model of *direct* "barbarian" political dominance in east Rome, then Aspar represents an *indirect* approach that allowed him to achieve and maintain a position of influence over a much longer period.[83]

---

[78] Bleeker 1980; McEvoy 2016:500 n. 99.
[79] Liebeschuetz 1990:130–1. Roberto 2009 suggests that the fall of Gainas marks the start of the rise of the Ardaburii.
[80] Wickham 2009:96–9; Traina 2009:76.
[81] C. Kelly 2013:12; J. Harries 2013:71–2; and D. Lee 2013:108, all in C. Kelly (ed.) 2013.
[82] See Averil Cameron 1993b:149–50.
[83] Liebeschuetz 1990:130–1; Roberto 2009.

Finally, although Aspar is normally perceived as a military leader, it is important to also stress his role in east Rome's civil government. This is the way he is portrayed on the m*issorium*—as a Roman consul, not as a general. Although a military man throughout his career, he simultaneously built a civilian identity in which he acted as a senior Roman senator and aristocrat. This ability to "play the Roman" was never a pretense—Aspar was born into the military aristocracy but grew up in the civil society of Constantinople and in the service of the Roman state. Blockley may therefore be correct when he suggests that "the most important result of the expulsion of Gainas was not the elimination of barbarians but the removal of the threat of military rule and the consolidation of civilian government in the east."[84]

---

[84] Blockley 1992:100. This may also explain the long reign of the non-military Theodosius II.

4

Ardaburius the Elder and Aspar: Persia and Italy (421–5)

In the decade after the suppression of Gainas, there were important changes in the government of the eastern empire. In October, 404 the empress Eudoxia died, followed in 408 by her husband, the emperor Arcadius. The new eastern emperor was their only son, the seven-year-old Theodosius II. Initially, the government was ably run by a civilian official named Anthemius.[1] However, Anthemius died or retired around 414; Holum suggested that Anthemius and his son may have been removed from office as part of a strategy to "close off" the Theodosian dynasty from their ambitious aristocratic family. The dominant figure at the eastern court now became Theodosius II's older sister, the devout and remarkable Pulcheria.[2] In a dramatic public ceremony in 413, Pulcheria and her two younger sisters had made vows of virginity, becoming "holy virgins."[3] In July, 414, Theodosius II formally gave the fifteen-year-old Pulcheria (but not her sisters) the title of Augusta.

Pulcheria played an important part in Aspar's career. While her role changed over time, and despite their religious differences, she was consistently Aspar's greatest political ally in the east Roman government until her death in 453.

Pulcheria and the Role of the Theodosian Empress

Modern scholarship has observed that a major change in the role and presentation of the empress occurred under the Theodosians in the late fourth and early fifth

---

[1] Along with the Theodosians and the Ardaburii, the Anthemii were a third great family contending for power in the east throughout much of the fifth century. McEvoy 2019a:117–18.

[2] Holum 1982:94–6; Van Nuffelen 2013:136–41. Anthemius was elderly and may have died around 414. *PLRE* 2, Anthemius 1; McEvoy 2019a:117–18; Holum 1982:96, n. 80.

[3] *CAH XII*, pp. 135ff; McEvoy 2016b:172 ff; Holum 1982:91–3. Pulcheria's vow of chastity may have been taken to keep her (and her sisters) from becoming pawns in the intrigues of the east Roman court. Soz., 9.1.3; C. Kelly 2013:15–16, 54; Harries 2013:70. A precedent had been created in the late fourth century by the three half-sisters of the emperor Gratian. While Galla became the 2d wife of Theodosius I (and the step-grandmother of Pulcheria), her sisters apparently took vows of virginity. McEvoy 2016b:172ff.

Figure 6 *Solidus* of Aelia Pulcheria (*RIC X* 226; wildwinds.com).

centuries.[4] Many ancient sources and modern scholars attribute exceptional influence to Pulcheria.[5] In part, this was due to her strong personality; in part, to the alleged weakness or disinterest of her younger brother, Theodosius II.[6]

However, the extent of Pulcheria's power, especially in the years 414–25, has been debated. Several sources describe her as the dominant figure in the east Roman government, as do many modern scholars. For example, Sozomen says that she "managed with extraordinary wisdom the business of the Roman government."[7] James observes that the placement of Pulcheria's statue in the Senate House at Constantinople in 414 alongside statues of the emperors "makes the point about Pulcheria's perceived significance in government."[8] Gibbon, who was perhaps overly impressed, says that "she alone, among all the descendants of the great Theodosius, appears to have inherited any share of his manly spirit and abilities."[9]

Recent scholarship has suggested a more nuanced role, giving greater weight to Theodosius II and emphasizing competing players and institutional factors in the east Roman government.[10] However, between 414 and 425 Pulcheria seems to have had a major influence on several important issues in the government of the eastern empire. This was the period in which the Ardaburii were first

---

[4] See e.g., McEvoy 2021:136; 2016b; Angelova 2004:3, 2015:199; Herrin 2013:2, 164–5, 174, 195–6, 307; James 2001:98; E.A. Clark 1998:1–31; Holum 1982:2–4.

[5] Holum 1982:79ff; James 2001:65–7; Beers 2013 (although I disagree that Pulcheria's return to power was *after* the death of Theodosius II in 450. See ch. VI, VII *infra*).

[6] Soz. 9.1; Soc. 7, 22, 4–6; Theodoret 5.36.4; Theophanes AM 5905.

[7] Soz. 9.1; Herrin 2013:2; James 2001:15, 169.

[8] James 2001:44. Pulcheria's grandmother, the Augusta Flaccilla, had also received this honor. McEvoy 2021:120.

[9] Gibbon, ch. XXXII. This comment ignores her aunt, Galla Placidia, discussed *infra*.

[10] C. Kelly (ed.) 2013, especially C. Kelly:14–15; J. Harries:67–89; also Liebeschuetz 1985:146–7.

advanced to the most senior military commands. Although Pulcheria's influence may have been somewhat tempered after her brother's marriage in 421 she continued to play a major role, especially in religious affairs. Her influence was also limited by the resurgence of her sister-in-law, the empress Eudocia, in the late 430s, and by the machinations of the eunuch Chrysaphius in the 440s. Things changed again in early 450 with her dramatic return to her brother's side and the fall of Chrysaphius. As a result, when Theodosius II unexpectedly died in July, 450, she and Aspar were able to play crucial roles in resolving the succession crisis. She would remain an important figure until her death in 453.[11]

A major source of Pulcheria's power among the people of Constantinople was her pious support of orthodoxy.[12] She was deeply involved in the Nestorian controversy that culminated in the First Council of Ephesus in 431. And while (due to the influence of Chrysaphius) she was unable to prevent the reversal of that victory at the Second Council of Ephesus in 449, she was a major figure in the re-establishment of Nicene orthodoxy at the Council of Chalcedon in 451.[13]

Military policy was the area in which an empress was at her weakest, since she could not lead an army.[14] Pulcheria needed generals who would be successful, but above all could be trusted to be loyal to her family. The choice of such generals also helped to guarantee military victories which, like acts of religious piety, were seen as evidence of divine favor that enhanced the legitimacy of the imperial family.[15] Although Pulcheria was deeply orthodox, she nonetheless supported the advancement of several Arian generals, including Plintha, Ardaburius the Elder, and Aspar. An important moment was the elevation in 419 of the Gothic general Plintha (probably Aspar's father-in-law) to the most senior rank of *magister militum praesentalis*. The Arianism of these generals does not appear to have been a bar to their advancement. Bury observed that "[Ardaburius] and his son Aspar were the ablest generals Theodosius had, and their devotion to the Arian creed did not stand in the way of their promotion."[16] This combination of a deeply orthodox imperial family with an Arian military leadership is surprising. It has even been suggested that the Theodosians may

---

[11] This is based on her *known* actions and influence with regard to matters of policy. We will never know what policies Pulcheria was able to influence in ways that were indirect or simply unrecorded. Beard 2021:238–9; Herrin 2013:2–5.
[12] James 2001:90–1; Holum 1982:130 ff, 147ff.
[13] James 2001:67–75; Herrin 2013:185, 195–6.
[14] James 2001:83–4, 88–9; Beers 2013; Holum 1982.
[15] Soz. 9.1.2; J. Harries 2013:70; James 2001:165; M. McCormick 1986:47–8.
[16] *LRE*, vol. 1:225.

have preferred this because an Arian general was less likely to mount a successful usurpation.[17]

It is probably no coincidence that Ardaburius the Elder rose through the ranks of the east Roman army at a time when Pulcheria's influence in government was strong. In 421, we have his first appearance in our sources—commanding Roman troops in a war on the Persian front that had been sparked by Pulcheria's religious zeal.

The Persian War (421–2)

The rise of Sassanid Persia is beyond the scope of this book, but there are two points to consider.[18] First, the Persians were a more formidable military threat to the Roman empire in the east than the Parthians had been. This was demonstrated by some spectacular Persian successes in the wars of the third and fourth centuries, although by the end of the fourth century an equilibrium had been established between the two empires.[19] Second, the vigor of the Persian state arose in large part from the close relationship between the Sassanid dynasty and the Zoroastrian priesthood.[20] This strong religious element in the Persian revival was paralleled by the growing integration of the Roman empire and the Christian Church.[21] Religious issues are particularly important in explaining the outbreak of war between Rome and Persia in 421, although there were other causes (such as the Roman failure to contribute to the joint upkeep of Caucasian defenses).[22]

At the start of the fifth century the Persian ruler, Yezdegerd I, was generally considered friendly to Rome and tolerant.[23] However, late in his reign, reacting to Christian attacks on Zoroastrian fire temples in Persia, he resumed persecution of Christians. Although Yezdegerd died in late 420, he was succeeded by Varahram V who intensified the persecution due to Persian political pressures.[24]

This concerned the Augusta Pulcheria (and presumably Theodosius II) who believed that a Christian Roman emperor should view himself as not only the

---

[17] A.D. Lee 2013:107–8 and Van Nuffelen 2013:138, both in Kelly (ed.) 2013. McEvoy cautions that a general could still change his religion for the sake of political expediency. McEvoy 2016:499 n. 115. See, e.g., Jordanes and Patricius in ch. X and XII, *infra*.
[18] In general, see Isaac 1992; Millar 1993, ch. 4 and 5; Kulikowski 2016, ch.8.
[19] *CAH XIII*:437–42 (Issac); Potter 2013:55–6.
[20] Kulikowski 2019:8; 2016:129–30, 203–5; *CAH XIII*, ch. 14:437–44.
[21] Potter 2013:13, 21–2; Whitmarsh 2015:193; Canepa 2009:100–3; Fowden 1993:31–6.
[22] *CAH XIII*:434–5; Crawford 2019:144–6.
[23] Blockley 1992:46–55.
[24] Schrier 1992:78; Blockley 1992:56–7; Holum 1982:102.

protector of Roman Christians, but also of Christians living outside the empire.²⁵ In addition, Pulcheria understood that nothing would be better than a military victory over the Persians in the name of Christ to enhance her gentle brother's hold on the throne.²⁶

When news of the Persian persecutions reached Constantinople, the empire began to prepare for war.²⁷ In fact, Roman preparations may have begun even earlier.²⁸ Since Yezdegerd's death triggered a brief Sassanid succession crisis, the Romans saw an opportunity and initiated the war by sending an army into Persian territory. That army was led by Aspar's father, Ardaburius the Elder.²⁹ The Persians were besieged in their fortress-city of Nisibis, but the Romans were soon forced to lift their siege on the approach of the main Persian army led by Vaharam himself. The Romans withdrew to their fortress of Theodosiopolis where they in turn were besieged.³⁰ However, the Persians soon lifted their siege, perhaps because of the failure of their Saracen allies to successfully invade Roman Syria.³¹ Fighting continued for another year until a settlement was reached.

If one were to only read the *Ecclesiastical History* of the fifth century historian Socrates Scholasticus, one might conclude that the Persians were quickly defeated and that the Roman "victory" was merely confirmed by the peace of 422.³² The Theodosian regime certainly celebrated the treaty as a great success for both church and state. A mid-fifth-century hagiography mentions a Roman officer named Vitianus "who looks back with pride on his part in the victory over Persia in 421/2."³³ There were also festivities in the Hippodrome at Constantinople attended by the emperor and his court. This provided an opportunity for the people to see the emperor's new wife, the highly educated Eudocia, who wrote a special panegyric for the occasion.³⁴

In reality, this war did not change much in the balance of power between Rome and Persia. However, it is important because it was the first military effort by the regime of Theodosius II, and it was seen and celebrated as a Christian

---

²⁵ Millar 2006:70. Even if some of these Christians might be heretics who had fled orthodox rule.
²⁶ Soz. 9.1.2; Kent 1960:129–32.
²⁷ Soc. VII.18.1–21.6; Millar 2006:73.
²⁸ Millar 2006:72; see also *CAH XIII*:443 (Isaac), 134–5 (Blockley).
²⁹ For the course of the war, Soc. VII, 18–20; Theodoret v.37.4–10.
³⁰ The location of this fortress is debated, as there were two with this name. Greatrex 1993:5–8; Schrier 1992:79–80.
³¹ Millar 2006:73
³² Soc. VII 18.1–21.6; Millar 2006:73; *CAH XIII*:443 (Isaac).
³³ *Miracles of St. Thekla*; Millar 2006:69. Vitianus served under Ardaburius the Elder. *PLRE* 2, Vitianus.
³⁴ Soc. VII 21.7–10; Millar 2006:73–4; Holum 1982; Tsatsos 1977.

Roman victory.³⁵ This was particularly important to Theodosius II, a distinctly non-military emperor, who was now coming of age and needed to support his rule with a claim to military and religious success.³⁶ This ability to claim a "success" may also have encouraged the regime to take an aggressive military posture when faced with its next crisis.

Which brings us back to Ardaburius the Elder and Aspar.

When the war with Persia began in 421, Ardaburius appears in our sources as a general who led troops from Constantinople to the empire's eastern border and then attacked into Persian territory.³⁷ His rank at the time is unclear. He may have been the Master of Soldiers for the east (*m.m. per Orientem*), or he may have received this rank sometime in 421–2. Alternatively, he may have begun the war having the most senior rank of *m.m. praesentalis*, but it is more likely that he received it around the end of the war.³⁸ He then returned to Constantinople to serve alongside the other *m.m. praesentalis*, his son's father-in-law, Fl. Plintha.³⁹

What did Ardaburius actually do in the war? After some initial successes, he was forced to withdraw to Roman territory where he was besieged at Nisibis, although the siege was unsuccessful. He is later said to have ambushed a Persian force, causing the death of seven Persian commanders.⁴⁰ The war then appears to have bogged down until the Romans initiated peace negotiations in 422. This may have reflected Roman concerns about a possible invasion of Thrace by the Huns, who understood that the Romans had shifted troops from the Danube frontier to their eastern front. The Persian king was receptive, since he had a similar concern about nomadic peoples who were invading his eastern territories. In the peace negotiations, the Romans were represented by the diplomat Maximinus, who is described as "an associate of Ardaburius, the commander-in-chief of the army."⁴¹ A contemporary source speaks of "Ardaburius who had greatly distinguished himself in the Persian War."⁴²

---

35 McCormick 1986:58; *CAH XIII*:443 (Isaac). Ironically, the treaty with the Persians contained a clause that resulted in the severing of relations with the Christians in Persia. Kulikowski 2019:173.
36 C. Kelly (ed.) 2013. Pulcheria was clearly instrumental in giving this war a religious cast. See her pre-war efforts to obtain a holy relic with military overtones from Jerusalem, as well as the post-war issuance of gold *solidi* that associated her with this relic. Holum 1982:103–5, 109–10; 1977:153–72; Kent 1960:129–32.
37 *PLRE* 2, Fl. Ardabur 3, 137 (believes he was *m.m. per Orientem* in 421, "probably" promoted in 422).
38 Ibid.; also *PLRE* 2:1291; Holum 1982:112. Cf. Greatrex 1993:2. Marcell. *com.* refers to him as "leading the praesental army" to the east in 421, which might mean he already held that rank, but a later date is more likely.
39 Thus, twenty years after the defeat of Gainas both of the top commands in the east Roman army were held by "barbarian" generals.
40 Soc. VII, 18; *PLRE* 2, Fl. Ardabur 3, 137.
41 Soc. VII, 20. Maximinus was on Ardaburius' staff. Later, his secretary was the historian Priscus.
42 Soc. VII, 23.

It appears that while the peace negotiations were in progress, the Persians attempted to secretly surround the Roman army, but were foiled by the fortuitous arrival of fresh Roman troops led by the *comes* Procopius. Later sources and some modern historians seem to give more credit to Procopius' role in ending the war than to Ardaburius.[43] Malalas recounts the arrival of Procopius as the occasion for the Persian king to offer peace if a Roman soldier could defeat a Persian champion in single combat.[44] The victorious Roman was Areobindus, who later became a *m.m. praesentalis* and a colleague of Aspar as consul in 434. Blockley comments that it was Procopius (not Ardaburius) who "brought [Vaharam] to terms."[45] Procopius was also promoted at the war's end, not to praesental rank, but as Ardaburius' successor as *m.m. per Orientem*. An emphasis on Procopius may reflect the difference between a source writing about Ardaburius in the 440s, and a source writing in the sixth century after the fall of the Ardaburii. The later source might have preferred an orthodox Roman hero from a distinguished family. Procopius was the son-in-law of Anthemius, the former praetorian prefect whose familial ambitions were supposedly of such concern to Pulcheria.[46] Although Procopius disappears from the sources after this promotion, and may have died, his son Anthemius became prominent under Marcian and Leo.

So, what does this suggest about Ardaburius, who is said to have "greatly distinguished" himself in this war? While he seems to have been a moderately successful general, there was no decisive battle. However, the sources celebrate the fact that Ardaburius "ambushed" a Persian force in which "seven commanders" were killed. Perhaps this is a trope or an exaggeration, but the term "ambush" and the role of his "associate" in the peace talks is suggestive. Does it imply that Ardaburius obtained results by negotiation and some timely intelligence rather than by military action? Given the stretched military resources of the east Roman state in the fifth century, this would have been a wise strategy, one that conserved military power while achieving desired diplomatic and political results.[47] Were these lessons absorbed by his son, Aspar?

---

[43] Jo. Malalas, *Chron.*, 14.23; *PLRE* 2, Procopius 2; *CAH XIII*:435; Kulikowski 2019:173.
[44] Jo. Malalas, *Chron.*, 14.23; Greatrex 1993:2. The incident is referred to, but not described, in Soc. VII, 18.
[45] *CAH XIII*:135 (Blockley).
[46] *PLRE* 2, Procopius 2; McEvoy 2019:122; Holum 1982:94–6. See ch. VIII–XIV, *infra*.
[47] On Roman losses: *CAH XIII*:435 (Isaac), 135 (Blockley). Note Blockley's comment that the "unsatisfactory progress of the war led to a decline in Pulcheria's power." This may also be related to the emergence of Procopius.

We cannot be certain that Aspar accompanied his father in the Persian War of 421. Nothing in the sources says that he did. However, if we are right that Aspar was born around 400, then he would have been of prime military age in 421 and it is very likely that he would have been actively serving with his father. Moreover, when the next crisis erupted in Italy in 424, we know that Aspar was considered competent enough to be a senior commander in the campaign, with responsibility for the western empress Galla Placidia and her son, the future emperor Valentinian III. A role of this importance would not have been entrusted to a junior officer without prior military experience, which may be the best argument that Aspar likely participated in his father's Persian campaign.[48]

The Expedition to Italy Against the Usurper John (424–5)

Galla Placidia was the most colorful of the children of Theodosius I. In addition to her adventurous youth, she was one of several empresses who played a large role in the history of the fifth century Roman empire. Her story provides the background to Aspar's campaign in 424–5.

Galla Placidia was born in 388/389. Her maternal grandmother, Justina, was related to both the emperors Constantine and Valentinian I.[49] Placidia was the daughter of Theodosius I by Galla, his second wife. This made her a half-sister to the emperors Arcadius and Honorius. Arcadius apparently disliked his stepmother, and it is likely that things in Constantinople only got worse for Placidia after Galla died in childbirth in 394.[50]

However, her father was apparently fond of her. On his deathbed in Milan in January, 395, he summoned his younger children, Placidia and Honorius, from Constantinople. Honorius became the new west Roman emperor, but Placidia was put in the care of Theodosius' niece, Serena (who was not only her cousin, but the wife of Stilicho, the western *magister militum* and effective ruler in the west). Initially, they lived in Milan, but they later moved to Rome.

The period from 395–408 saw the ascendancy of Stilicho in the west Roman empire. A domestic sidelight was his wife's growing wealth and political power in Rome. Placidia may have resented Serena's stature, perhaps feeling that she deserved the Augustal title that her two brothers had.[51]

---

[48] Liebeschuetz 1990:130.
[49] Humphries 2019:21; Woods 2004:325–7.
[50] On Galla Placidia generally, see Salisbury 2015; Sivan 2011; Holum 1982; Oost 1968.
[51] There was precedent for the emperor's sister to be given the title of "Augusta," e.g., Pulcheria; also Constantia, the sister of Constantine I.

However, in August, 408, courtiers of Honorius murdered Stilicho, the west's leading general. In October, 408 Alaric promptly led his Goths into Italy and were soon besieging Rome. Stilicho's wife, Serena, somehow became the subject of a rumor that she planned to betray the city to the Goths. Although there appears to have been no basis for this (other than the possible motive of revenge for her husband's murder), Serena was condemned by the senate of Rome (with Placidia's approval) and executed.[52] This may show the ruthlessness that Placidia was already capable of in imperial politics.[53] With Honorius having taken refuge in Ravenna in 402, Placidia became the senior member of the imperial family in the city of Rome.

A detailed account of the subsequent fifteen years of Placidia's life is beyond the scope of this book. However, just the highlights of the years 408–23 include: her capture by the Goths in 410; her marriage to the Gothic king Athaulf; the death of their infant son; the murder of Athaulf by his rivals; her return to Honorius and reluctant marriage to the general Constantius in 417; the birth of a daughter (Honoria) and a son (the future Valentinian III); the elevation of Constantius III as Honorius' co-Augustus (and Placidia as Augusta) in early 421; and the unexpected death of Constantius III 7 months later.[54]

In 423, she found herself in Ravenna with two children, a troop of Gothic guards, and a difficult imperial brother. The allegation that the childless Honorius became enamored of his half-sister suggests slander by hostile contemporaries, but there is no way to tell. However, Placidia had returned to Ravenna with Gothic bodyguards and there was street fighting in Ravenna between her Goths and soldiers loyal to Honorius.[55] Remembering Stilicho's fate, Placidia felt that she and her children were in physical danger. She decided to find safety in the one place where she knew they had to take her in. It would be interesting to know how she managed it, but in the spring of 423 she and the children suddenly arrived by ship at the court of her nephew, Theodosius II, in Constantinople.[56]

The surprise arrival of Aunt Placidia and her offspring was probably greeted with mixed feelings by the east Roman court. On the one hand, she was family, so proprieties had to be observed. Also, she still had her own palace in Constantinople, left to her by Theodosius I. On the other hand, it is doubtful that

---

[52] Zosimus 5.38–9.
[53] Oost 1968:85–6.
[54] See, generally, Olympiodorius, fr. 29–39; *PLRE* 2, Fl. Constantius 17, Aelia Galla Placidia 4; Salisbury 2015:69–131; Sivan 2011:67–72, 79–87; Oost 1968; *LRE*, vol. I:97–210; Gibbon, ch. XXXIII.
[55] *CAH XIII*:116; Salisbury 2015:115, 132–3; Sivan 2011.
[56] She arrived while the city was celebrating the "victory" in the Persian War. Salisbury 2015:133–4; McEvoy 2013:214–15; Sivan 2011:89.

Figure 7 Cameo of Galla Placidia and her children (Getty Images).

the pious and well-ordered court at Constantinople was eager to complicate its delicate relations with the court at Ravenna by getting involved in an unsavory squabble between Honorius and Placidia. In addition, there was the tricky fact that the eastern court had never recognized the elevation of either Constantius III or Placidia to the rank of Augustus/Augusta, an omission that had important implications for the status of young Valentinian.[57]

All this changed on August 27, 423 when Honorius died at Ravenna. The news probably reached Constantinople by the end of September.[58] Since Honorius was childless, it immediately opened the question of who would now rule in the west. From the Theodosian point of view, there were only two possible

[57] Philost. XII.12. Sivan suggests that Honorius had taken away her title of Augusta. Sivan 2011.
[58] Theophanes AM 5915.

options. One was that Theodosius II, as the only living and legitimate Augustus, would assume control over both halves of the empire, much as his grandfather and namesake had done. There are some indications that this was the initial impulse at Constantinople.[59] The other option, if Placidia really was a legitimate Augusta, was that her son would become the western emperor.

However, the course of events in Ravenna followed neither of these dynastic options. In November, 423 a civilian official of the western court named John was proclaimed emperor.[60] Although not a powerful figure himself, John had the support of several military figures at the western court. This probably included the senior western general, Castinus.[61] However, it has also been suggested that John relied on less prominent officers, such as Gaudentius and that general's son, a younger officer named Aetius.[62] There were apparently some initial attempts by the east Roman court to win the support of Castinus for the claim of Theodosius II.[63] However, Castinus was an enemy of Placidia, and he may have become convinced that he was better off supporting an emperor of his own making than one who might have dynastic support.[64] Although John sent an embassy to Constantinople seeking recognition as the western Augustus, the eastern court rejected the request and arrested the ambassadors. This made it clear that the eastern empire was not going to tolerate a usurper, and would instead seek a dynastic, Theodosian solution.

The question remained whether that solution would be to simply extend the authority of Theodosius II to the west or whether it would involve a role for Placidia and her son. Discussions went on in Constantinople during the winter of 423/424, and both Placidia and Pulcheria were heavily involved in the negotiations.[65] In the spring of 424, an agreement was reached—Theodosius

---

[59] Van Nuffelen in C. Kelly 2013:149–50.
[60] Soc. VII, 23; Philost. XII, 11; Olymp., frag. 46; *CAH XIII*:133–6; *LRE*, vol. 1:221–3.
[61] Castinus seems to have held this position under John. *PLRE* 2, *Fasti,* 1298–9.
[62] *PLRE* 2, Fl. Castinus 2, Gaudentius 5, Fl. Aetius 7. *Cf.* McEvoy 2013:227; Matthews 1975:379; and *LRE*, vol. I:22; with Wijnendaele 2017a and 2015a:57–61. Placidia had the support of some western officers, such as Boniface, the *comes Africae*, as well as Candidianus, who accompanied her and Aspar in the expeditionary force.
[63] Wijnendaele suggests that Theodosius II was initially willing to deal with Castinus, as evidenced by his recognition (probably in late 423) of Castinus as western consul for 424. However, this was revoked in April, 424 presumably because Theodosius had been persuaded to support Placidia. *PLRE* 2, Fl. Castinus; Wijnendaele 2015a:57–61; Klaasen 2012.
[64] *CAH XIII*:136; Salisbury:136–7; *LRE*:222; Van Nuffelen in C. Kelly 2013:149–50.
[65] Salisbury:138. Gibbon acidly said that the outcome represented an "agreement of the three females who governed the Roman world." By this, he meant Pulcheria, Placidia, and the emperor's new wife, Eudocia. Constantinople also issued three series of *solidi* honoring Pulcheria, Eudocia, and Placidia. Dynastic solidarity was expressed in this coinage by giving each of these women the *nomen*, Aelia, referring to the first wife of Theodosius I (even though Placidia was a descendant of his second wife, Galla). Sivan 2011:112; Kent 1984, *RIC*, vol. X:75–6.

would recognize Placidia as an Augusta, and he would give her son Valentinian some recognition with the title of "*nobilissimus.*" It was further agreed that this recognition of their status would eventually be reinforced by a marriage between Valentinian and his cousin, Theodosius' infant daughter, Eudoxia. In the meantime, Placidia would act as effective ruler for her son in the west until he became of age. Finally, it was agreed that disputed portions of Illyricum would be transferred to the eastern empire.[66] Since Constantinople had chosen to re-establish the western Theodosians in Italy, the east Romans would have significant influence in this new western regime.

The most immediate problem was that neither the east Romans nor Placidia controlled the west.[67] There was going to have to be a military effort by the east Romans—and this again brings us to Ardaburius and Aspar. Since Theodosius had neither the experience nor the inclination to be a general the task was going to have to be handled by those who did, which meant generals such as Ardaburius and Aspar.[68] The recent "victory" against Persia may have encouraged the eastern court to believe that it could successfully manage another military effort.

In the summer of 424, the east Roman expeditionary force left from Constantinople to capture Salona in Illyricum as a base for the invasion of Italy.[69] Originally, Theodosius planned to accompany the invasion force, but he only went as far as Thessalonica and returned to Constantinople.[70] However, in October, 424 there was a ceremony at Thessalonica in which the five-year-old Valentinian was elevated to the rank of Caesar by eastern officials.[71]

The campaign strategy involved a two-pronged invasion, with a force of infantry (under Ardaburius) sailing across the Adriatic to land near Ravenna, and a force of cavalry (under Aspar and Candidianus, a west Roman officer who supported Placidia) taking the overland route around the Adriatic.[72] The latter met with little resistance. Much of John's army had been sent to Africa in an

---

[66] On the negotiations in general, see Arnold 2014:50–1. On Illyricum, Bury believed that although the transfer was agreed at this time, it was not effected until the marriage of Valentinian III to Eudoxia in 437. *LRE*, vol I:221, n. 3. However, there is doubt whether this transfer ever occurred. A recent study of an inscription found in this area and dated to 452 acknowledges only the west Roman consul for the year. Basic & Zeman 2019:128; Croke 2001:54, 75.

[67] An exception was Africa, where the *comes* Boniface had declared his support for Placidia and had fought armies sent by John. See Wijnendaele 2015a:62–6.

[68] As Gibbon puts it, "The gentle mind of Theodosius was never inflamed by the ambition of conquest or military renown ..." Gibbon, ch. XXXII.

[69] Soc. VII, 23; Olympiodorus, fr. 46; and Philstorgius, XII. *See also*, McEvoy 2013:223–34; *LRE*, vol. 1:221. On Aspar's role in this campaign, see Salisbury 2015:139–45.

[70] Millar 2006:54–5.

[71] *PLRE* 2, Placidus Valentinianus 4, 1139.

[72] *CAH XIII*:136; *PLRE* 2, Candidianus 2 and 3; Sivan 2011:91 n. 11.

unsuccessful attempt to subdue the loyalist Boniface.⁷³ Aspar's force moved so quickly that it surprised and captured the key city of Aquileia in northern Italy.

It is significant that Placidia and Valentinian went with the forces under Aspar, not with the more senior Ardaburius. This may reflect Placidia's concerns about the hazards of another sea crossing. Her voyage from Ravenna to Constantinople had been very stormy, causing her to vow that she would build a church to St. John in Ravenna in exchange for safe passage, a promise she later fulfilled.⁷⁴ Her journey back to Italy gave Aspar a chance to become better acquainted with Placidia, which would be important to his future career.

Things did not get off to a good start. The concerns about a sea crossing were realized when a storm scattered the fleet carrying Ardaburius' troops. Although Ardaburius survived, he was taken prisoner by John's forces.

This had to be one of the most critical moments in the career of Aspar. Receiving news at Aquileia of his father's capture, Aspar might well have decided to halt the invasion or even to withdraw. However, the presence of Placidia may have helped to strengthen his resolve. The outcome speaks well as to Aspar's ability to work effectively with Placidia while under pressure to do something about his father.

It turned out that he did not need to be overly concerned, since it seems that the captured Ardaburius' skills were not limited to the military arts. Although a prisoner in Ravenna, Ardaburius was treated with uncommon courtesy by the usurper John, including freedom to roam about the city and to talk to officials, including John's military commanders. This was a huge mistake, since Ardaburius took advantage of the opportunity to win over these men, and to organize them in a conspiracy to overthrow John. Finally, and most significantly, Ardaburius was able to smuggle out a letter to Aspar telling him of the plot and directing him to advance rapidly on Ravenna.⁷⁵ In the meantime, Aspar and Candidianus had some military success in winning over several cities in northern Italy.

Ravenna had been chosen as an imperial capital and refuge in 402 by the emperor Honorius, who believed that its surrounding marshes would make it impregnable to capture by Alaric's Goths. However, arrangements were made for a shepherd to show Aspar a path through the marshes. This allowed his troops to surprise the garrison, capture the city and the usurper, and rescue Ardaburius. Although some of our sources piously claim that this guide was really an angel

---

⁷³ Prosper, s.a. 424; Wijnendaele 2015a:62–6; Jacobsen 2012:72.
⁷⁴ Salisbury 2015:214–15; Sivan 2011:89.
⁷⁵ Olympiodorus fr. 46; *PLRE* 2, Candidianus 3.

"in the guise of a shepherd," the result was that Ravenna and John were now in the hands of Ardaburius and Aspar.[76]

Despite his generous treatment of Ardaburius, the usurper John was not treated well. He was sent to Placidia, who was waiting in Aquileia. She had him publicly mutilated and beheaded. The war to re-establish the Theodosians in the western empire appeared to be at an end. Unlike the war with Persia, this was a true military success for the east Roman government.

It is surprising that we know almost nothing about the fate of Castinus, who supposedly had been the military power behind John. While some sources suggest he was "exiled," this seems lenient compared to what happened to John. However, other sources note letters between Augustine and Boniface indicating that Castinus sought refuge in Africa. This seems strange because Boniface and Castinus had earlier quarreled during an abortive Spanish campaign in 422, but it may have some basis in fact.[77]

However, there was one final matter to resolve, and although it may have seemed at the time like a postscript, it would have important consequences. Among the west Roman officers who had supported John was Flavius Aetius whose family came from the Danubian frontier. As a young man, Aetius had lived for a while as a Roman hostage among the Huns and had become familiar with that people. Anticipating the east Roman invasion of Italy, Castinus (or possibly Aetius' father, Gaudentius) sent Aetius off to the Huns to see if he could hire some Hunnic mercenaries as reinforcements for John's regime. Aetius successfully recruited a large force of Huns, which he then led back to Italy.[78] Unfortunately for John, this force arrived at Aquileia three days after John had been executed by Galla Placidia.

The abrupt arrival of the Huns created an awkward and dangerous situation for all concerned. The would-be emperor, John, was now dead and no longer able to fulfill whatever promises of payment Aetius had offered to the Huns. On the other hand, Placidia and her allies (including Ardaburius and Aspar) were now faced with a large and unhappy group of Huns, who they did not want to see running amok in Italy. Some sources suggest that there was fighting between these Huns and the east Roman forces. However, Placidia somehow found the

---

[76] Soc. VII, c. 23.
[77] Wijnendaele 2015a:61–5; Blockley, *CAH XIII*:136; *PLRE* 2, Fl. Castinus (citing Prosper s.a. 422).
[78] Gaudentius had meanwhile been killed in a military mutiny at Arles. *PLRE* 2, Gaudentius 5. On the size of the Hun force, Philost. XII:14, (*FCH*) says 60,000 Huns. However, Maenchen-Helfen 1973:77, n. 319, believes that the number was only about one-tenth of that. See also Renatus Frigeridus, in Gregory of Tours, II, 8; Wijnendaele 2017a:5 n. 23; A.H.M. Jones:176. However, given that the imperial expeditionary force may not have been large, even 6,000 Huns would have been a problem.

money to pay the Huns to go home, while also satisfying Aetius with a high rank in the west Roman army (although not the top job) and sent him off to pacify Gaul. It is likely that the east Romans provided some of the money, and that Aetius kept some of the Huns as personal retainers in the army he took to Gaul.[79]

There were two long-term problems with this solution. First, it probably showed the Huns the weakness of the west Roman empire, and perhaps gave them a taste of the plunder that it offered. Second, Placidia's grudging acceptance of Aetius may have been necessary at the time but created long-term tensions. Despite Aetius' military abilities, there were others in the west Roman military who Placidia may have preferred. One was Boniface, who commanded the Roman forces in Africa, and who had remained loyal to her during John's usurpation. Another was a general named Felix, who was chosen for the top western military command, possibly because his wife was a friend of Placidia or possibly because the east Romans wanted him. Aetius would never enjoy a high level of trust with either Placidia or her son.[80]

With the Huns riding off and Aetius en route to Gaul, the new regime headed to Rome in October, 425 for a coronation ceremony.[81] This event would demonstrate the legitimacy of the re-established western branch of the Theodosians, but the key role of eastern officials also subtly suggested the seniority and primacy of the eastern emperor at Constantinople.[82]

News of the victory over John was received with great joy and public celebration in Constantinople.[83] The news arrived while Theodosius II was presiding over the races in the Hippodrome. He immediately stopped the races and called on the people to march to the Great Church with him to give thanks to God, which they proceeded to do while singing psalms. The date became an annual holiday (with games) in the calendar of Constantinople.

Although Theodosius II decided not to travel to Italy for his cousin's coronation, an east Roman official named Helion acted on his behalf, formally investing young Valentinian III as an Augustus.[84] The Roman empire now had

---

[79] Wijnendaele 2017a. Maenchen-Helfen 1973:77 follows Philost. XII:14 in stating that the resolution was not reached until after a battle between the Huns and the Romans. See also Prosper, s.a. 425; Jordanes, *Romana*, 328; Cassiodorus, *Chronica* s.a. 425; Wijnendaele 2017a:5–7, esp. n. 23; Stewart 2014:8. Bury (*LRE*, vol. I:224), Gibbon (chap. XXXIII), and Jones 1964 (at 176) do not mention a battle, but this does not mean that it did not occur.
[80] *PLRE 2*, Aetius 7, Fl. Constantius Felix 13; *CAH XIII*:137 (Blockley).
[81] *PLRE 2*, Placidus Valentinianus 4; Matthews 1975:381; Sivan 2011:94–6.
[82] *CLRE*:387; Van Nuffelen 2013:148–9, in C. Kelly (ed.) 2013.
[83] Soc. *HE*, 7.23.11–12; Arnold 2014:67, n. 29; Van Nuffelen 2013:134; Millar 2006:54–5; Gibbon ch. XXXIII.
[84] We have an ivory casket illustrating the scene. Sivan 2011:117, n. 96.

Figure 8 *Solidus* of Theodosius II with a young Valentinian III, *c.* 425 (*RIC* X 234; (wildwinds.com)).

two men with the rank of Augustus (Theodosius and Valentinian) as well as three women with the rank of Augusta (Pulcheria, Eudocia, and Galla Placidia—soon to be joined by a fourth when her daughter was raised to this rank). However, both the symbolism of the investiture and the reality of the situation suggested that the senior member of this family firm was Theodosius II.[85] Not only was he the senior Augustus in age, but it was clear to everyone that Placidia and her son would never have succeeded in re-establishing themselves in the west without the military support provided by Constantinople.

Quite a few east Roman officials had travelled to the west with Pulcheria, and they stayed on to play influential roles in her new regime. One indication of their continuing influence can be seen from the consular lists for 425–35. It had become the custom for each half of the empire to nominate one of the two consuls for each year. However, in the years just after Placidia's restoration, there were several years when *both* courts nominated east Romans. The implication is that those nominated by Placidia's regime were east Romans who had served her in the west.

One of those who received this honor from the west was Ardaburius the Elder, who received a consulship in 427.[86] McEvoy suggests that where two easterners became consuls, one of them may have been serving in the west.[87] If

---

[85] *CAH XIII*:136 (Blockley); Matthews 1975:381–6; Van Nuffelen 2013:134; Gillett 1993:20.
[86] *CLRE*:388–9.
[87] McEvoy 2014:255.

so, then Ardaburius (and Aspar?) may have remained in the west for several years after John's overthrow. However, it is unknown what Ardaburius was doing there since Felix held the top command.

As we will see in the next chapter, Aspar also received this honor from the western court in 434, at which time he was campaigning in Africa. It has been suggested by one modern historian that Aspar was actually offered the western throne at this point, but this cannot be correct, and the story appropriately belongs in the east in 457.[88]

After being named consul for 427, Ardaburius the Elder disappears from our sources. It is possible that he may have lived on briefly after that, since there seems to be no record of a successor being appointed to his military position until Areobindus in 434. It has been suggested that because both he and Plintha are portrayed in a nimbus on the *missorium* (made c. 434) they might have died by that date. However, we know that Plintha was still active in his post until the late 430s.[89]

The obvious question was whether Placidia would be able to establish a stable government in the beleaguered western empire, or whether she would continue to need support from Constantinople. When the next crisis arose in the west, conflict among her generals left her unable to respond effectively. As in 423, she was again forced to seek military aid from the east. And not surprisingly, the eastern army sent to her aid was led by Aspar.

---

[88] Sivan claims that Aspar's famous remark declining the throne was "more likely" made in connection with an offer of the western throne at this time than in "467 [sic]." Sivan 2011:105, n. 45. First, her reference to *PLRE* 2, 168 refers to the interval between the death of Marcian and the accession of Leo *in the east*—in 457, not 467. The reference to the "senate of Rome" is really to the senate at Constantinople, of which Aspar was the *princeps* in 457. Further, who might have offered Aspar the western throne in 425? Not Placidia, whose sole objective was to see her son on that throne. Not Theodosius II or his court, who had launched the campaign precisely to restore a Theodosian to that throne. As most historians have concluded, the comment was more likely made in connection with events in the east in 457. Alan Cameron 2015:279; see also ch. VIII, *infra*.
[89] *PLRE* 2, Fl. Ardabur 3; Fl. Plintha; 1290.

5

Aspar in Africa: The War with the Vandals (431–5)

At the beginning of the fifth century, the Roman provinces in Africa (particularly the ones near Carthage) were among the most agriculturally productive and prosperous areas of the western Roman empire. As a main source of grain for the city of Rome, they were of critical strategic value, since a hostile regime there could easily cause starvation and rioting in Italy. The capital of Roman Africa was the great seaport of Carthage, with its extensive shipyards.

The African provinces had only a small military garrison, sufficient to ward off raiding desert nomads, but also needed to control the region's sectarian religious violence.[1] Around the turn of the fifth century, there were also several revolts by local military leaders, but each had been suppressed by the imperial government.[2] During the usurpation of John in the early 420s, the area had been under the control of a Roman officer named Boniface (Bonifatius), who had supported Placidia.[3] As the 420s ended, Roman Africa enjoyed relative peace and had been spared the "barbarian" invasions that had swept through the rest of the western empire.

In 429, all this changed.

The change arose from two problems in the western empire. The first was the rivalry among the military leaders of Placidia's regime. The second was the continuing conflict among the west Romans and the several barbarian groups that had settled in Spain, notably the Vandals.

Military Politics at the Court of Galla Placidia

While Placidia would have been concerned about anyone who might challenge her rule, her life had shown her that a strong military leader could be especially

---

[1] See Shaw 2011, on the violent Donatist controversy in North Africa; Gaddis 2005:103–50.
[2] *PLRE* 1, Firmus, Gildo; *PLRE* 2, Heraclianus 3; Wijnendaele 2017b, 2017c.
[3] *PLRE* 2, Bonifatius 3; Wijnendaele 2015a:57–64.

dangerous. With her son on the western throne, she did not want to see either of them dominated by yet another general.⁴

Placidia had two possible replacements for Castinus—one was Fl. Aetius, who had supported John but had arrived too late with his army of Huns; the other was his rival, Boniface, who had loyally held Africa for Placidia.⁵ However, they apparently were not the only choices. Placidia instead chose Fl. Constantine Felix as *magister utriusque militiae*, the senior military command in the west.⁶ He was also given the title of *patricius*.⁷ Aetius was confirmed as *magister militum* for Gaul, and Boniface (the *comes Africae*) was given the additional title of Count of the Domestics (the imperial guards).⁸ Whether this reflected Placidia's preference for a division of military power in the west, or whether Felix had some attribute that made him more suitable, it was a recipe for future trouble.⁹

Prosper, our primary source for what happened next, tells us that in 427 Felix had an order sent to Boniface ordering him to return to the imperial court in Italy to face accusations of disloyalty.¹⁰ Understanding the potentially fatal implications, Boniface refused. His enemies in Ravenna characterized this to Placidia as an act of rebellion. A military force was sent to dislodge Boniface, but it was defeated.¹¹ A second army was sent in 428, commanded by a Goth named Sigisvult.¹² This army had greater success, apparently regaining Carthage, but not definitively defeating Boniface.¹³ Since Boniface understood that he was in peril, he may well have looked around for allies with whom he could fight back. Like

---

⁴ Oost 1968:209.
⁵ *PLRE* 2, Bonifacius, citing Procopius, *Wars* I 3.14–15; John Ant. Fr.196; Theophanes AM 5931.
⁶ *PLRE* 2, Fl. Constantius Felix 14. She did not choose Candidianus, who disappears from our sources after 425, and may have died. Wijnendaele 2015a:68 suggests that Felix may have been the preferred choice of the east Romans. Another possibility is the influence of Felix's wife, Padusia. Salisbury 2015:162, 170.
⁷ Prosper, s.a. 429; *PLRE* 2, Fl. Constantius Felix 14, 461–2; Wijnendaele 2017:10–1; Mathisen 1999:176.
⁸ Augustine, *Ep.* 220, par. 4; *LRE*, vol 1, 244 n. 6.
⁹ Wijnendaele 2017a:10–13 and 2015a:65–72.
¹⁰ Procopius attributes this plot to Aetius, whereas Prosper names Felix as its instigator. Mathisen 1999:175 n. 7. However, Oost 1968:221 n. 46, 224, Sivan 2011:107 n. 51, and Wijnendaele 2015a:69–72 all follow Prosper who wrote closer in time to the events.
¹¹ *LRE*, vol. I:.245. Clover 1966:16–18, 29, reads Prosper s.a. 427 as suggesting that some of this force may have defected to Boniface, although this could be to explain its failure.
¹² *PLRE* 2, Fl. Sigisvultus, 1010; Wijnendaele 2015a:72 ff. Mathisen 1999:176–8 suggests that his real mission was to negotiate a peaceful resolution with Boniface. Hence, the inclusion of the Arian bishop Maximinus, who told Augustine that he had come from Carthage at Sigisvult's orders to discuss peace. Augustine, *Collatio* I, 179–80. He may also have tried to influence Boniface's Gothic wife, Pelagia, who may have been known to Placidia. Sivan 2011:107–8.
¹³ Prosper s.a. 427; *LRE*, vol. I:245; Jones 1964:190.

many fifth century Roman generals, he probably considered recruiting some barbarian auxiliaries for his army.[14]

Such troops were available nearby—among the Vandals in southern Spain. While some sources allege that Boniface invited the Vandals to migrate to Africa, any "invitation" by Boniface is more likely to have been a limited request to hire some Vandal mercenaries for a short term, much as Aetius had done with the Huns in 425.[15] An alternative explanation is that the Vandals, then under heavy pressure from other peoples in Spain, may have looked at the internal strife among the Romans in Africa and decided that it was an opportune moment to move from their threatened Spanish base to a prosperous new area.[16] The Vandals may have already had interests beyond Spain, as shown by Vandal raids in the late 420s on the Balearics and perhaps an exploratory raid into Mauretania.[17]

Whatever the cause, in May 429 most of the Vandal people, plus many non-Vandal fellow travelers, crossed the strait of Gibraltar to Africa.

Geiseric—The Vandals (and Alans) Come to Africa

As we have seen, in 409 several barbarian peoples had settled in Spain, including the Alans, the Sueves, and two groups of Vandals (the Asdings and the Silings).[18] Seeking to regain control of Spain in 418, the west Romans hired the Visigoths (then resident in northeastern Spain), who proceeded to destroy the Siling Vandals and inflict a serious defeat on the Alans, whose survivors took refuge with the Asding Vandals. I will use the term "Vandals" and (after 439) "Vandal

---

[14] Clover 1966:21–30 suggests that *both* Roman factions sought reinforcements from the Visigoths. Mathisen 1999, App. I, 189–91, note reports of Arians (Visigoths?) arriving in North Africa in 427, and Wijnendaele 2015a:77–8 reads Prosper as referring to the transfer of Visigothic auxiliaries to Sigisvult.

[15] Sivan 2011:106. Cf. for the idea that Boniface invited the Vandals to migrate, Procopius, *Wars*, III.323–4; John Ant., fr. 196; Theophanes AM 5931; Jordanes, *Getica*, 167–9; Gibbon ch. XXXIII; *LRE*, vol. I:145; Shaw 2011. However, contemporaries such as Possidius and Augustine do not make this charge. Jones 1964:190 and 1106 n. 40, citing Stein, *Bas-empire*, I, 575. Clover 1966:30–1 concludes that Boniface's complicity in the migration is "impossible to prove or disprove completely" but smacks of the "scapegoat" trope in which Roman failures are attributed to treachery by a Roman or "faithless barbarian."

[16] Others think the Vandals simply took advantage of Boniface's limited request due to their deteriorating situation in Spain. Collins in *CAH XIV*, 124; Wijnendaele 2015a:74 ff; Merrills & Miles 2010:53; Mathisen 1999, App. II. Several sources suggest pressure on the Vandals in Spain; Possidius, *Vita Aug.* 28; Hydatius, 90; see also Jacobsen 2012:80.

[17] Clover 1966:12–15, 30–1.

[18] See ch. III, *supra*. The Siling Vandals had settled in the rich province of Baetica in southern Spain, while the Asding Vandals initially settled in the less prosperous region of Gallaecia with the Sueves. Merrills & Miles 2010:42–4.

kingdom" to refer to this diverse group of Asding Vandals, Alans, and the various Goths, Sueves, and Hispano-Romans who joined them.[19]

Two subsequent attempts by the Romans to regain control of Spain had more dubious results. Around 420, the Roman general Asterius defeated the Asding Vandals. However, this caused them to move to the more attractive lands in southern Spain that had previously been occupied by the Silings. A second effort by Castinus in 422 ended in his defeat by the Asding Vandal leader, Guntharic.[20] Guntharic died in 428, and was succeeded by his (possibly illegitimate) relative, Geiseric.[21]

Geiseric was one of the most important figures in the life and career of Aspar, and perhaps in all of fifth century Mediterranean history.[22] He is believed to have been born in the early 390s, which would have made him slightly older than Aspar, and he lived until 477. He had a strategic approach to the situation of the Vandals in the western Mediterranean, with a shrewd sense of how and when to combine military force with negotiation and alliances. Jordanes describes him as "a man of deep thought and few words, holding luxury in disdain, furious in his anger, greedy for gain, shrewd in winning over the barbarians, and skilled in sowing the seeds of dissension to arouse enmity."[23]

As for his religious views, Geiseric had apparently converted to Arianism in 428.[24] As we have seen, the Alans in Spain (like the Alan family of Aspar) were mostly Arian. If, as in Visigothic Spain and Ostrogothic Italy, Arianism was "a badge of apartness within a certain accepted unity" might this have been a way to unify the Vandals and the Alan refugees?[25] Also, Boniface had an Arian wife, and was accused by Augustine of having Arian sympathies. Could Geiseric have seen some advantage in converting to Arianism in dealing with Boniface? Finally, conversion might also have been a way for the Vandals to avoid being drawn into the Catholic v. Donatist conflict in Africa.

Whatever the reason for his decision to lead his people to Africa, Geiseric deserves credit for his management of the crossing. Other groups had tried it

---

[19] Heather 2013; Clover 1966; Kaperski 2015:50. Whether the Alans retained a separate identity is debated. See ch. II, *supra*.
[20] Hydatius, 299.26; Greg. Tur., *LH*, II.2; Merrills & Miles 2010:45–7.
[21] Cf. Conant 2012:21, who suggests that Geiseric and Guntharic were half-brothers, who had both become kings prior to 411. Geiseric was sole ruler after 428. Merrills & Miles 2010:49–50, 74.
[22] Wijnendaele 2015:87; Gillett 2002b:110 n. 31; Jacobsen 2012:78; Merrills & Miles 2010:57; Clover 1966. My thanks to. J.W.P. Wijnendaele for bringing Clover's early work to my attention.
[23] Jordanes, *Getica*, ch. XXXIII, 168.
[24] Hydatius s.a. 428 79(89).
[25] Anderson 1974:118.

and failed.[26] The Vandal population that moved to Africa in 429 reputedly numbered 80,000 people, although the actual number has been debated.[27] Even if the true number was smaller, it was a very large number of people, animals, and supplies to transport.

The Vandals landed in the Roman province of Mauretania Tingitana (modern Morocco), where they may have already had a base. After plundering Mauretania, the Vandals moved eastward along the coast road towards the city of Hippo Regius.[28] The bishop of Hippo was Augustine, one of the most important figures of late antiquity.[29] Now about seventy-six years old, he sadly faced the loss of Africa to Arian conquerors. But when the Vandals approached Hippo, they were finally confronted by the main Roman army in Africa, commanded by Boniface.

Things had changed since 428, and Boniface now had the full support of the west Roman government. Would it be enough to stop the Vandals?

Aspar Comes to Africa

To understand what had happened, we need to recall Boniface's conflict with the government in Ravenna. While Sigisvult had been sent to Africa to oppose Boniface, his mission also included a peace effort. Friends of Boniface in Italy had persuaded Placidia to let them send an emissary to Africa to try to patch things up.[30] These efforts led to a rapprochement between Boniface and Placidia's court, perhaps because Felix appears to have been losing his influence with Placidia.[31]

However, as Felix's influence waned, Aetius' influence grew. Placidia probably would have preferred to bring Boniface to Italy as a military counterweight to Aetius, but the Vandal invasion made it difficult for her to do so. To provide troops for Africa she summoned Aetius and his army from Gaul, but Aetius

---

[26] *CAH XIII* (Blockley):127; Wijnendaele 2015a:77 n. 90.
[27] *LRE*, vol, I, 246, accepts the figure of 80,000 from Victor Vit., I, 2, over that of Procopius *B.V.* I, 5; Jacobsen 2012:80–1. If that was the total number of people, and about a quarter were fighters, that suggests a military strength of about 20,000.
[28] Possidius, *Vit. Aug.* 28; Victor Vit., I, 1–3, and Augustine, *Ep.* 228; *LRE*, vol., I, 257.
[29] On the last days of Augustine, Brown 1967 (rev.2000):419–33.
[30] The emissary was Darius, who corresponded with Augustine. He also seems to have secured a temporary truce with Geiseric. *PLRE* 2, Darius 2.; Augustine, *Ep.*229, 230, 231; *LRE*, vol. I:247–9.
[31] In 426 Felix had instigated the assassination of Patroclus, Bishop of Arles. Prosper 1292, a.426. Sivan 2011:110 makes the point that Patroclus had been appointed by Placidia's late husband, Constantius III. However, whether this was still important to Placidia is unclear. Wijnendaele 2017a:12.

apparently disobeyed her order.³² Then, on May 5, 430, Felix and his wife Padusia were killed in a struggle in Ravenna.³³

This left Placidia facing the prospect of domination by Aetius, with whom she had had strained relations since 425. Much as she wanted to bring Boniface to Ravenna, what would that do to the effort to save Africa from the Vandals? Even if Boniface could be spared from that war, who else could safely be trusted to command the Roman forces in Africa?³⁴ As in 423, Placidia sought a solution by appealing to Constantinople to send troops and to send Aspar, someone she knew and apparently felt she could trust. Aspar's relations with Boniface were probably good. They had both supported Galla Placidia during the usurpation of John. Boniface was not an Arian, but he had developed Arian connections through his Gothic wife, and his daughter had been baptized by Arian clerics.³⁵

Our sources for the course of the war with the Vandals in North Africa are sparse. Although a Vandal attempt to take Carthage by surprise in early 430 was foiled, Boniface was defeated in the battle near Hippo Regius in May, 430 and was then besieged in that city.³⁶ Staying with his flock, Augustine despaired, saying that he was prepared to suffer or even die at the hands of the Vandals.³⁷ In fact, he died (of natural causes) several months into the siege, on August 28, 430.

The Vandals were able to maintain the siege for fourteen months. It may be that it was the prospect of the fall of Hippo that caused Placidia to call for assistance in late 430. Although we know little about the discussions between Ravenna and Constantinople, sometime in the early summer of 431 eastern reinforcements led by Aspar arrived in Africa.³⁸ Placidia also sent some west Roman reinforcements.³⁹ With this additional strength, the combined forces of

---

³² Wijnendaele 2017a:11–18.
³³ John of Antioch, fr. 85, 201; Prosper s.a. 430; *LRE*, vol. I:243; Jones 1964:176. The murders were probably instigated by Aetius, who had the most to gain. Wijnendaele 2017a:111–13. It is less clear whether Placidia had any responsibility. Sivan 2011:109.
³⁴ *PLRE* 2, Fl. Sigisvultus. Mathisen 1999:184 suggests that Sigisvult was given the rank previously held by Felix, although it is unclear when. Sigisvult apparently led the west Roman reinforcements that were sent to Africa in 431 and may have remained there at least until the treaty of 435.
³⁵ Mathisen 1999:178–81; Wijnendaele 2015:79.
³⁶ Clover 1966:33–9.
³⁷ Brown 1967:425.
³⁸ Clover 1966:40. Aspar's exact title at this point is unclear. It has been suggested that he may have been designated as a *magister militum vacans*, which was a title used at times by the east Romans for generals commanding expeditionary forces who were neither regional commanders nor a *m.m. praesentalis*. Zuckerman 1994, nn. 41 and 42; also suggested by Wijnendaele to author. *PLRE* 2, 1292.
³⁹ For Aspar's arrival, Wijnendaele 2017a:13; 2015a:95–6; Clover 1966:40; Thompson 1950:58–75. The arrival of these reinforcements at Carthage may have caused the Vandals to lift the siege of Hippo. Procopius, *Wars*, 1.3.35–6 and Clover 1966:40 suggest that they arrived *after* the siege had been lifted, but it is possible that Geiseric knew of their impending arrival.

Boniface and Aspar took the offensive, but were again defeated by the Vandals somewhere near Carthage.[40] Although the Vandals did not follow up with an attack on Carthage, they then made a second attempt on Hippo, which they finally captured and sacked.

Despite this defeat, Placidia felt that she could no longer wait to recall Boniface to Ravenna. Apparently, she viewed the growing power of Aetius as a more immediate threat, and a threat to the throne usually outweighed threats by barbarians elsewhere. Also, with Aspar now in Africa, she may have felt that she had a commander there who she could trust.[41] Accordingly, Boniface went to Ravenna in 432, where he was given the top rank of *magister utriusque militiae* and made a patrician.[42]

Open warfare soon broke out between Boniface and Aetius, the west Romans' two leading generals. Late in 432, their armies clashed near Rimini. Boniface's army won the battle, and Aetius took refuge with the Huns. However, Boniface was mortally wounded and died soon thereafter. Placidia, who could not have been pleased, quickly appointed Boniface's son-in-law, Sebastianus, as her new *magister utriusque militiae*. However, once Aetius threatened to return to Italy with an army of Huns, Placidia replaced Sebastianus in favor of Aetius.[43] Aetius was now the undoubted military strongman in the western empire and would remain so until his death in 454.[44]

In the meantime, Aspar was continuing to fight the Vandals in Africa.[45] His main goal was to prevent them from capturing Carthage, and the important shipyards that the Romans wanted to keep out of the hands of the Vandals. In this, he succeeded.[46]

---

[40] Procopius, *Wars*, 1.4; also *Chron.Min*. I, 473–4 and II, 22; John of Antioch, 201; Prosper, s.a. 432; *Chron. Gall*, s.a. 433, Hydatius, 99, 103, 104; Marcell. *comes*, s.a. 432. See also *LRE*, vol, I, 248; Jones 1964:176; Jacobsen 2012:104–8. Salisbury 2015:168–9 notes that despite this defeat "Aspar remained in good standing with Placidia and [Theodosius II]."

[41] Wijnendaele 2015:95ff. While *PLRE* 2, Fl. Sigisvultus, suggests that Sigisvult went back to Italy in 429/430, he could have returned to Africa with reinforcements in 431 and shared the command with Aspar once Boniface left.

[42] Prosper s.a. 432; *Chron. Gall*. s.a. 432; Hydatius 99 (s.a. 432); Procopius *Wars*, I, 3.36; Theophanes AM 5931. *PLRE* 2, Bonifatius 3.

[43] Hydatius s.a. 432–89(99); *PLRE* 2, Sebastianus 3; Wijnendaele 2017a:18–19; C. Kelly 2009:109–10. Sigisvult apparently shared titles with him. He and Aetius were both consuls in 447. *PLRE* 2, Fl. Sigisvultus; *CLRE*, 405–6.

[44] *PLRE* 2, Aetius 7. Aetius married Boniface's widow, Pelagia. Salisbury 2015:170.

[45] Although some have suggested that Aspar left Africa after his initial defeat in 431, other evidence suggests that he remained there. For example, he was still in Carthage when he received his consulate for 434. *PLRE* 2, Fl. Ardabur Aspar; *CLRE*:402–3; Wijnendaele 2015a:96; Clover 1966:43–5.

[46] Salisbury 2015:168–9; Moderan 2014:118–19 also has a more positive view of Aspar's campaign, crediting his forces with checking Vandal attacks towards Carthage, and ultimately leading to the treaty of Hippo in 435. Lee *CAH XIV* 2000: 39 ("limited success").

Although there does not appear to be any detailed account of the course of the fighting between Geiseric and Aspar during the years 432–5, the treaty that was reached in 435 is perhaps our best evidence. It is clearly a compromise between the Vandals and the Romans. The most plausible explanation is that Aspar, having learned to avoid direct battles with the Vandals, had instead engaged in a war of attrition that ultimately caused Geiseric to negotiate. Geiseric's weakness was that, having brought his entire people with him, he needed to do more than just reward his warriors with plunder; he needed to reliably feed, supply, and settle the Vandal people. This was always the greatest source of leverage for the Romans when dealing with barbarian invaders, as opposed to raiders like the Huns, and it may well have been why Geiseric agreed to this treaty.[47] He may also have understood that the east Romans were anxious to bring their troops home because of concerns about the Huns (they made an expensive treaty with the Huns in 435).[48] The return of Aspar and his eastern troops to Constantinople would weaken the Roman forces in Africa.

On February 11, 435, the west Romans and the Vandals entered into a treaty dividing the North African provinces between them, but retaining the city of Carthage and its surrounding territories for the Romans.[49] We have limited knowledge of the negotiations, but we know that Placidia sent civilian negotiators and it is probable that both Geiseric and Aspar were involved.[50] Whether they actually met during these or earlier negotiations is unknown, although it is something that some sources assume as a basis for a hostile view of this and later events.

From both the east and west Roman point of view, the major gain of the treaty was that Carthage and much of its hinterland in the province of Africa Proconsularis was preserved for the empire. This assured the continuation of the vital grain shipments to Rome and kept the shipyards at Carthage in Roman hands.[51] From the Vandal point of view, the major gain was that they were given "federate" status and a place to live within the empire. Although the Vandals were required to pay an annual tribute to the Romans (probably in grain and

---

[47] Another example is west Roman strategy with the Visigoths in 415–18.
[48] Wijnendaele 2015a:98.
[49] Prosper, s.a. 435; Isidore, *HV*, 74; Procopius, *B.V.*, I, 4; *LRE*, vol. I:248–9; Jones 1963:190; Courtois 1955:170. The treaty was negotiated by the west Roman diplomat Trygetius. *PLRE* 2, Trygetius 1; *LRE*, vol. I:295.
[50] Blockley 1992:60; Zuckerman 1994:163; Sivan 2011:105; Jacobsen 2012:108; Clover 1973:108; Clover 1966:43–5.
[51] Even without Carthage, the Vandals had naval resources and were able to raid Sicily in 438. Jacobsen 2012:110; Clover 1966:59–64.

other produce), it is likely that the treaty also entitled them to receive financial and other benefits from the Romans. These terms alleviated or solved Geiseric's problem of security for his followers and their families.[52] The treaty is silent about other Roman territory in North Africa which suggests that those areas remained under Roman rule.[53]

In sum, while Aspar had failed to defeat or destroy the Vandals in battle, it is likely that his war of attrition led to a negotiated solution that preserved actual or nominal west Roman rule in the most critical strategic areas of North Africa.[54]

Aspar's efforts appear to have been appreciated by both Ravenna and Constantinople. As we have seen, he was given the honor of being named by the west Romans as one of the consuls for the year 434. This may have reflected Placidia's gratitude for his prior services in 425 as well as for his more recent services in Africa.[55] Since this honor was recognized in the east, it was presumably also endorsed by the government in Constantinople.

Aspar and Geiseric

Aspar's experience in Africa became the basis for an important, if fanciful, story in our sources that would shadow his later career. Indeed, Clover called it "one of the most bizarre incidents in Byzantine history."[56]

The story is from Procopius, an east Roman historian who wrote over a century later, although he may have derived much of his information from the fifth-century historian, Priscus.[57] It needs to be stressed that Procopius can sometimes be a biased narrator for events in Africa, since he is often eager to contrast the later success of Belisarius, his hero and patron, against the earlier failures of the east Romans against the Vandals.

According to Procopius, a senior officer on Aspar's staff named Marcian was captured by the Vandals and held with other prisoners in an open, unshaded

---

[52] Courtois emphasized that grain was both a necessity for the Vandals and a potential weapon against the Romans. Courtois 1955; cf. Clover 1966:125–8.
[53] Prosper 1327, s.a. 435; Jacobsen 2012:109–10; Merrills & Miles 2010:60–61; Barnwell 1992:115–16; Clover 1966:53–8.
[54] C. Kelly 2009:116. But at 122, he also suggests that Theodosius II thought Aspar had failed. See also Mathisen & Shanzer 2016:187 (Lenski, calling it a "rout"). But cf. Lacey 2022:348–9.
[55] *LRE*, vol. I:225. Prof. J.J. Arnold has suggested to author that this may also show gratitude for the assistance of the east Romans and perhaps a subtle acknowledgement of the seniority of Theodosius II.
[56] Clover 1966:41; Scott 2010:116–18.
[57] Procopius, *Wars*, III.4.2–11; Clover 1966:41–3.

area. Geiseric supposedly decided to view the prisoners and noticed that an eagle was keeping its position in such a way as to shade the sleeping Marcian. The Vandal leader is said to have seen this as a sign of divine favor, and a prophecy that Marcian would someday become emperor. Geiseric decided not to harm a man who enjoyed such divine favor, so he released Marcian—but only after first extracting an oath that Marcian would never in future fight against the Vandals.

This is a charming story, and it might even have some basis. It is possible that Marcian was captured by the Vandals but later released. Marcian was a high-ranking Roman officer, and thus a valuable captive.[58] Procopius says that Geiseric released Marcian given "how great a power Aspar exercised in Byzantium." However, Procopius may be projecting his knowledge of Aspar's later power back into the 430s.[59] While we know almost nothing about negotiations during the war, some scholars believe that "some form of friendly contact" was established between Aspar and Geiseric during this war.[60] It is conceivable that Aspar asked for Marcian's release, or else that Geiseric released him to gain some advantage.[61] There is some evidence that Aspar may also have had discussions with other leading Vandals. For example, a general known to us as John the Vandal subsequently became an east Roman *magister militum* in the Balkans in the late 430s. Clover attributes his appointment to the influence of Aspar and suggests that it may have been a reward for something John had done for the Romans while Aspar was in Africa.[62]

However, the fact that Procopius included this story points to a more basic issue that clearly bothered the east Romans, as it has bothered many later historians. In fact, it was probably intended by Procopius as a way of explaining later events. For Marcian did in fact become the east Roman emperor in 450. Although he was a popular emperor who took a strong stance against the Huns and other enemies of Rome, the one enemy he never fought was the Vandals, not even after they sacked the city of Rome in 455. This odd passivity required both contemporary and later historians to provide an explanation, and the eagle story may have been Procopius' attempt to do so.[63]

---

[58] Clover 1966:46–53. Procopius *Wars*, III.4.7, Theophanes AM 5931, 5943; *PLRE* 2, Marcianus 8.
[59] Procopius, *Wars*, III.4.8; Clover 1966:45 n. 2.
[60] Clover 1973:108. Gillett has suggested that the jester Zercon (see ch. VI, *infra*) was perhaps a gift from Geiseric to Aspar. Gillett 2003:257.
[61] Procopius, *Wars*, III.4.2; Theophanes AM 5931, 5943; Evagr. *HE*, II.1; Zon. XIII 24.12–16; Cedr. I.604.
[62] Clover 1966:46–53.
[63] Procopius, *Wars*, III:4; Merrills & Miles 2010:55. On a possible offensive by Marcian in 457, see ch. VII, *infra*. Theod. Lect. 1.7; Clover 1966:41–3.

There is also another way to look at this story. Marcian and Pulcheria later became the targets of fierce religious opposition arising from their role at the Council of Chalcedon in 451. Scott has suggested that this and other stories about Marcian originated as orthodox, pro-Chalcedonian stories seeking to demonstrate Marcian's legitimacy by signs of divine favor.[64] This may well be true, but the fact that this story focuses on the Vandal war in the 430s and on the specific promise about not fighting the Vandals seems to show that people were trying to explain Marcian's later inaction with the Vandals.

But the story may also point to a concern about Aspar. Marcian was a long-time associate of the Ardaburii. He had served under Ardaburius the Elder during and after the Persian War in 421 and later came to Africa with Aspar. In 450, Aspar played a crucial role in the choice of Marcian as emperor. Procopius' story should perhaps be seen as part of a theme about Aspar in our sources.[65]

We should remember two important things about Aspar—first, that he was of Alan descent, and second, that he was an Arian Christian. These two facts were enough to provide suspicious minds with a basis for reviving the "faithless barbarian" accusation. The fact that the Vandals included some Alans, and that Aspar was of the same religious confession as Geiseric, was probably too much of a coincidence for Aspar's enemies and "Romanist" historians to resist—did Aspar and Geiseric reach an understanding that not only Marcian, but Aspar himself, would never again fight against the Vandals and, perhaps, would keep the east Romans from doing so?[66]

There is, of course, no definitive evidence for such an understanding. However, as we will see, there are several facts about Aspar's subsequent career that might suggest a pattern:

a. In 441, another expeditionary force was sent by Constantinople to try to recapture Africa. We know the names of the east Roman generals who led this force—but they do not include Aspar, the east Roman general with the greatest experience in fighting the Vandals.[67] Perhaps other threats seemed more important, and some believe that Aspar opposed this expedition on the ground that more attention needed to be paid to the Huns.[68]

---

[64] Scott 2010:115–32; Scott 2009:31–57. See ch. VII, *infra*; Watts 2013:269–84.
[65] Roberto 2009.
[66] Gibbon, ch. XXXI, XXXIII. Clover 1966:32, 41–3 suggests that the story suggests possible direct contacts between Aspar and Geiseric.
[67] Blockley 1992:207, n. 1 says Aspar's absence is "*usually explained* by his pro-Vandal sympathies or his unwillingness to risk another defeat at their hands." (emphasis added); C. Kelly 2009:121–2.
[68] C. Kelly, ibid. See ch. VI, *infra*.

b. Throughout the reign of Marcian (450–7), a time when Aspar supposedly had great influence, no major action was taken against the Vandals, even after they sacked Rome and abducted the family of Valentinian III. Although some sources indicate that (over Aspar's opposition) Marcian may have been planning an expedition at the time of his death in 457, nothing was done for another decade, a period during which (at least until 465) Aspar had influence with the new emperor, Leo I.

c. After Aspar's influence was reduced in 465, Leo soon adopted an aggressive policy against the Vandals. In 468, (and again over Aspar's objections) Leo sent the greatest east Roman expeditionary force of the fifth century against the Vandals. Unlike the situation in 440, there was no longer any distracting threat from the Huns. Was Aspar's opposition based on military prudence or something else? When the attack ended in disaster, allegations were made that Aspar had suborned its commander to fail. As we will see, two sources claim that Basiliscus hesitated at the key moment because he wanted to win favor with Aspar, who had asked him to "spare" the Vandals.[69]

d. After the death of Aspar, the Thracian Goth leader Theoderic Strabo claimed to be Aspar's heir. In a treaty with Leo I, Strabo agreed to lead his Goths against any foe of Leo "except only the Vandals."[70] Blockley comments that Strabo "[i]n this respect, declared himself the successor of Aspar."[71]

We have already noted that the Romans had a long history of suspecting and slandering anyone who could be portrayed as a "faithless barbarian," no matter how assimilated they had become. As Conant points out, the rise of the Vandals to a major Mediterranean power in a single generation "seemed inexplicable," and the repeated failures to defeat them caused the Romans to provide an explanation in the form of "treachery" by corrupt Romans (such as Boniface) or by "faithless barbarians" (such as Aspar).[72]

---

[69] In the controversial final entry of his chronicle for 468, the contemporary chronicler Hydatius records that Aspar had been disgraced and Ardaburius executed because they "had been discovered plotting with the Vandals against the Roman Empire." Hydatius s.a. 468, 241 (267). See ch. XI, *infra*.

[70] Malchus, 2 (in Blockley 1983, vol. II, 409). Why did it single out the Vandals, but no other people that Leo might have fought? The proviso is similar to the oath alleged to have been sworn by Marcian.

[71] Blockley 1983:457 n. 9; Clover 1966:40ff.

[72] Conant 2012:183, especially n. 259. See also the story of Berichus in ch. VI, *infra*.

Moreover, the split between orthodoxy and Arianism added a religious dimension to this accusation, which made Aspar doubly vulnerable.[73] Clover suggests that any affinity between Aspar and Geiseric was probably not based on ethnicity, but on their common religion.[74] If so, it is ironic that the relief force that Constantinople sent to Africa in 431 was led by Aspar, an Arian general, and likely included many Arian soldiers.

If Aspar in fact agreed to use his influence to discourage future attacks on the Vandals, why would he do so? Religious affinity alone does not seem sufficient. If anything, given the bias against Arians in Constantinople, Aspar might have wanted to play down his religious affinity with Geiseric.

The timing of the accusation may also be important. While our sources show that an accusation of "treachery" and a secret collaboration with the Vandals was made against Aspar after the failure of the Roman expedition in 468, it is less clear whether an overt accusation was spread in 435. Later sources (such as Procopius) may have written with knowledge of the disaster in 468 as well as the later fall of Aspar. If so, they may have tried to explain things with a story about Aspar/Marcian and Geiseric set in Africa in the 430s.

With the conclusion of the treaty with the Vandals, Aspar was able to return to Constantinople in 435. He may have felt that the greater strategic threat to the eastern empire was now the Huns. He had encountered the Huns in Italy in 424, and he may have had a healthy respect for their fighting abilities. He may also have been updated by his father-in-law, Plintha, who had been the main east Roman negotiator with the Huns, a job to which Aspar may have succeeded. Aspar's career over the next fifteen years would largely be determined by relations between the east Romans and Huns, and by the rising power of their new leader, Attila. However, there would be continuing issues with the Vandals long after Attila's death in 453. Attila was a huge problem for Aspar while he lived, but Geiseric would cast a longer shadow over Aspar's career.

---

[73] C. Kelly notes that part of the "trope" used to slander heretics, including Arians, was that they were prone to bribery and corruption. C. Kelly 2004:169. On the persecution of Catholics by the Vandals: Merrills & Miles 2010, 54–5, 177–203; Conant 2012:159–86.
[74] Clover 1966:43, n. 2. Traina 2009:35, 91; Millar 2006:149–57 on Theodosius and heresy; Matthews 1975:121–4 on Theodosian legislation against Arians.

6

Aspar and Attila: The Wars with the Huns (440–50)

We have little information on Aspar for the period between his return to Constantinople in 435 and the accession of the emperor Marcian in 450. It is necessary to piece together a coherent story from scattered references and our general knowledge of the eastern Roman empire during that time. Yet this is clearly a critical transition period, since Aspar went from being a general to playing a critical role as a political power broker in resolving the succession crisis caused by the unexpected death of Theodosius II. Paradoxically, it was a difficult decade for his military career and reputation. This chapter will focus on both his military role in the wars with the Huns, and his civilian role in the court politics of Theodosius II's final decade.

The treaty of 435 with the Vandals did not last. As early as 438 Vandal ships were raiding Sicily, but Carthage was still denied to them. Then, in 439, Gaiseric made a surprise attack in which he finally captured that city.[1] With its shipyards and resources now in the hands of the Vandals, the Mediterranean world shuddered. In addition to their naval threat, the Arian Vandals expanded their persecution of non-Arians (especially the orthodox clergy).[2] The loss of the area around Carthage was most keenly felt in the western empire, since it was both a key agricultural supplier for Rome itself and a major source of income for many members of the western senatorial class. Both the east and west Roman governments felt that something had to be done.

Geiseric knew that the Romans would come against him soon. But in the year 440 the Romans (and particularly the east Romans) had several enemies to worry about—and generals like Aspar had to advise on how best to deploy their forces.

---

[1] Hydatius, s.a. 439; Marcell. *comes*, s.a. 439. Arnold notes that Geiseric made a surprise attack during a "false peace" (*dolo pacis*) Arnold 2014:44, n. 27. See also Prosper 1339; Cassiodorius, *Chron.* s.a. 439; Moderan 2014:119. However, Clover 1966:65–8, attributes allegations of treachery to the "scapegoat" trope used to explain Roman defeats.
[2] Prosper s.a. 437; Merrills & Miles 2010:54–5, 177–2013; Conant 2012:159–86.

The Persian Front

The peace negotiated between east Rome and Persia in 422 lasted for almost twenty years. However, in 438 a new monarch named Yezdegerd II succeeded to the Persian throne. Like Theodosius II in 421, the new ruler seemed eager to establish himself with a military victory. This threat may have become apparent to the Romans as early as 439 or 440, and in 441 the Persians attacked in both Armenia and Mesopotamia. Even if not directly encouraged by Geiseric, the invasion may have been precipitated by knowledge that the east Romans were planning to commit troops against the Vandals.[3]

The east Roman military commander on the Persian frontier was a general named Anatolius.[4] He was in this post no later than 433, perhaps earlier, and held it until 447. Possibly in recognition of his efforts to strengthen the frontier, Anatolius was named a consul for 440. He defended the empire against the Persian attacks in 441 and was apparently successful enough that the Persians agreed to a one-year truce. In fact, this truce would last much longer as the Persians became occupied with other enemies.[5]

The Vandal Threat

The Vandal capture of Carthage created a general fear of Vandal seaborne raids throughout the Mediterranean.[6] In the spring of 440, the Romans learned that a Vandal fleet was preparing to sail from Carthage. Defensive measures were undertaken throughout both empires, even at Constantinople, where Theodosius II ordered a strengthening of the city's sea wall.[7] In the west, Sigisvult was sent to prepare coastal defenses in southern Italy.[8]

The Vandal fleet ultimately made its main assault on Sicily, but attacks were also made against the west coast of Italy, Sardinia, and possibly (and ominously) Rhodes in the eastern Mediterranean. It has been suggested that these targets indicate an attempt to disrupt, or at least threaten, the grain supplies of both Rome and Constantinople. If intended by Geiseric to discourage the Romans

---

[3] Theodoret, *HE*, v. 1; *Nov. Theodos*, V.1 (June 26, 441).
[4] *PLRE* 2, Fl. Anatolius 10:84–6.
[5] Crawford 2019:146.
[6] Roberto 2009 (the prospect of a "vandalic thalassocracy").
[7] Croke 2021:255 n. 14; C. Kelly 2009:120.
[8] *Nov. Val.* 9; *LRE*, vol. I:25. In the east, Clark 2021:176; Millar 2006:58. In the west, Priscus fr. 9(4); Maenchen-Helfen 1973:108; MacGeorge 2002:170; *PLRE* 2, Fl. Sigisvultus; Mathisen 1999:184–6.

from attempting to retake Carthage, it had just the opposite effect.[9] An agreement was quickly reached between Ravenna and Constantinople for a new military offensive against the Vandals. Faced with the arrival of east Roman forces in Sicily in 441 under Areobindus, a senior east Roman general, the Vandals withdrew to defend Carthage. However, the east Roman troops stayed in Sicily, alternately skirmishing and negotiating with the Vandals. It has been suggested that the leaders of the east Roman force were not aggressive because of Aspar's opposition to the expedition, and because they expected to soon be recalled to the Balkans.[10]

This expectation soon became a reality. The Hun invasion of the Balkans in 441 created a serious new crisis, necessitating a quick settlement with the Vandals in 442 to facilitate the return of the army from Sicily to the Balkans.[11] Unlike the treaty of 435, this new treaty recognized a more equal status between the parties. This was not a traditional *foedus*, but a division of Africa between equals. It allowed the Vandals to keep Carthage in return for a commitment to continue to supply food to Italy. A particularly fateful provision was that Geiseric's eldest son would go to Ravenna, with the prospect of a marriage into the western imperial family.[12] This clause had consequences that would color Vandal/Roman relations into the 460s and beyond.

The Huns and Attila

The third major threat to the east Romans in 440 came from the Huns.

Whatever their origin, the Huns were a nomadic group or confederation that erupted into eastern Europe from the Eurasian steppes in the late fourth and

---

[9] Clover 1966:68–78.
[10] Priscus, fr. 9 (4); Theophanes AM 5942. Because they were mostly "German," Clover 1966:82–7 suggests that all of the leaders of the Sicilian expedition were "under the control of Aspar." However, Aspar's rank at this time was not senior to Areobindus, nor did Aspar have the influence he would attain later.
[11] Priscus, fr. 9 (4); Theophanes, AM 5942, 5948. An interesting question is whether Geiseric may have instigated attacks by the Huns, and possibly even the Persians, to distract the Romans. See ch. VII, *infra*. On Vandal diplomacy, see Gillett 2003:67–70; 160; 232–5; Clover 1973:104–17. On the resolution of the Vandal war, see Cassiodorus, *Chron.* s.a. 442; Prosper s.a. 432; Linn 2012:299–302; Merrills & Miles 2010:112–13; Clover 1966;88–95. Clover has noted the connection between Africa and the Balkans in east Roman strategic thinking in the 430s and 440. Clover 1973:108.
[12] Prosper, s.a. 442; Clover 1966:68–78, 125–6. Merrills & Miles 2010:61–4. The treaty initiated 13 years of general peace between the west Romans and the Vandals. See Linn 2012:298–321 on the grain supply; Conant 2012:22–7 on the provisions re Huneric. Clover even suggests that the west Roman court may have seen the Vandals as a useful counterweight to Aetius. Clover 1966:102.

early fifth centuries.[13] After a successful attack on the Alans, they moved westward around 375 against the aged Gothic king, Ermanaric, who ruled a large area north of the lower Danube and into the Ukraine. It was this attack that led many Goths (and some refugee Alans) to cross the lower Danube into Roman territory in 376, and eventually to the Roman disaster at Adrianople in 378.[14] Goffart believes that in the early fifth century, the Huns made a further move into the Hungarian plain which dislodged several other peoples, including the Vandals.[15] Although many Alans became part of the Hun confederacy, they appear to have had an inferior status.[16] The Huns were generally pagan so, unlike the Vandals, there is no reason to think that Aspar's religious heritage gave him any affinity with these opponents.

The Huns were organized into many bands, some of which were apparently available for hire by the Romans.[17] Even under Attila, it would be wrong to think of the Huns as a unified military force, but more as multiple war bands consisting of Huns (and other peoples) who followed a Hun leader while acknowledging his authority to varying degrees.[18] With regard to the Huns, "empire" does not signify an organized, city-based polity like that of the Romans.[19]

The first Hun leader identified in our sources is Uldin.[20] In the year 400 he and his people resided north of the Danube. When the fleeing Gainas tried to cross the Danube, Uldin killed Gainas and sent his head to Constantinople, where it was displayed by the government of Arcadius for the enjoyment and instruction of the people.[21] However, Uldin's relations with the east Romans were mixed. Despite his helpful defeat of Gainas, he led major raids into the eastern

---

[13] On origins, see H Kulikowski 2019:75–80, 325. For general histories of the Huns see Maenchen-Helfen 1973; Gordon 1960; and Thompson 1996. Also, M. Maas (ed.) 2015; C. Kelly 2009; Wolfram 1997:123–44; *CAH XIV*, 704–12; Blockley 1992:59–71. On climatic issues, see Harper 2017:163, 190–7; Kulikowski 2019:73–4, 320.
[14] Others may have taken advantage of the chaos after Adrianople. The east Roman general Fravitta later defeated a group of slaves and bandits who were "calling themselves Huns." Maenchen-Helfen 1973:29, 59 n. 215.
[15] Goffart 2006:75–8.
[16] Maenchen-Helfen 1973:443.
[17] Maenchen-Helfen 1973:26–59. There were several mixed Alan/Hun units in Roman service around 400, one of which split around 405, with the Alans (but not the Huns) joining in the crossing of the Rhine in 406. Goffart 2006:91–3.
[18] Meier 2017:47–9; Maenchen-Helfen 1973:12–13.
[19] Kulikowski 2019:76–7; Maenchen-Helfen 1973:51, 193–7.
[20] John of Antioch, fr.187 says that the Huns who joined Theodosius I's army in 395 arrived under their *phylarchoi*. Maenchen-Helfen views this as the leader of a war band, but not a king. Maenchen-Helfen 1973:49–51. Other than the "shadowy" figure who Jordanes calls Balamber, Maenchen-Helfen says that "Uldin is the first Hun mentioned by name" but not a "king." Ibid.:63.
[21] Zosimus, V 21:9 and 22:1–3; Maenchen-Helfen 1973:59.

empire's Balkan provinces in 404/405 and again in 408, although the latter ended badly for him. After this, his power seems to have declined and fragmented.[22]

Around 412, we hear of a Hun "king" named Charaton, but we have few details nor do we know how many Hun bands he controlled.[23] We also do not know whether Charaton's rule extended to the Huns who raided the east Roman empire in 422.[24] However, some Hun leader was able to negotiate and carry out the deal with Aetius in 424 whereby a large force of Huns was "rented" to the western usurper John.[25] In the later 420s the Hun confederacy apparently "lost much of its cohesion."[26] This may have been the result of the death of Charaton, and possibly a struggle among the Huns over the succession. However, by 430 a new family had emerged as "kings" of the Huns—the family of Attila.

Jordanes tells us that Attila was the son of a man called Mundzuc. Two of Mundzuc's brothers, Octar and Ruga (or Rua), were kings of the Huns, but not Mundzuc.[27] The two "kings" ruled various Hun groups in different (presumably adjacent) territories.[28] When Octar died around 430, Ruga became the sole ruler. In 434, he took advantage of the dispatch of Aspar's army to Africa to launch an invasion of Thrace.[29] Initially successful, and badly frightening the court at Constantinople, the invasion ended in an abrupt Hun withdrawal and negotiation of a treaty between the east Romans and the Huns. One of the negotiators of this treaty, and of its extension in 438, was Plintha, the *m.m. praesentalis* and father-in-law of Aspar. The 438 treaty is also his last appearance in our sources. Aspar may have been viewed as his replacement in matters relating to the Huns.[30]

The date of Ruga's death appears to have been in the later 430s, and probably not before 435.[31] By 439 Ruga had been succeeded by two of his nephews, the brothers Bleda and Attila. Like Ruga and Octar, each initially ruled over different groups in different territories, with Bleda ruling the eastern group and Attila the western Huns.[32]

[22] Maenchen-Helfen 1973:63–9.
[23] Olympiodorus fr. 19 (Blockley 1983). Olympiodorius calls Charaton "the first of the kings." See also Maenchen-Helfen 1973:73–4.
[24] Marcell. *comes*, s.a. 422. This may have been the reason why the east Romans ended their war with Persia.
[25] See ch. IV, *supra*.
[26] Maenchen-Helfen 1973:80.
[27] Jordanes, *Getica*, 180; Maenchen-Helfen 1973:81. There was apparently a fourth brother, Oebarsius, who was still alive in 448 but does not appear to have been a "king."
[28] Jordanes, *Getica*, 181; Prosper, 480; Maenchen-Helfen:85–6.
[29] Zuckerman 1994:161 The deployment of any significant part of the east Roman army outside the Balkans in the mid-fifth century repeatedly served as an invitation to the Huns to raid imperial territory.
[30] Maenchen-Helfen, 1973:92–3; Kelly 2009:90–2, 109–10.
[31] Maenchen-Helfen:91–4; Zuckerman 1994:160–1.
[32] Maenchen-Helfen:85–6.

There are two points to notice here. First, Attila was from a family that was regarded as "royal," or at least very high status, among the Huns. He and his brother were nephews (not sons) of the previous kings. Although we do not know how the Huns determined the succession, there may have been other claimants.[33] Second, if there was a territorial division, it may have been Bleda (and not Attila) who was Aspar's initial opponent in the war that broke out on the Danube in 441, although both Hun leaders soon became involved.[34]

The Strategic Debate of 440

In 440, these threats on three fronts presented a strategic problem for the east Roman empire.[35] It is believed that Aspar argued that the greatest threat was from the Huns and that the Vandal problem should be addressed by diplomacy.[36] However, given the appeals for help from the west Romans, and the dynastic investment that had been made there, the east Roman government decided that the priority should be a military effort in Africa. The hope was that the army would have a quick success, so that it could soon return to the Balkans to deal with any trouble with the Huns.

For most of the fifth century, the east Romans had five senior military commands. The top rank was that of a *magister militum in praesentalis*, i.e., the commander of an army "in the presence" of the emperor. There were two of these praesental armies, both based near Constantinople. There were also three regional commands, one for the east (the *m.m. per Orientem*, based in Antioch); one for Thrace (the *m.m. per Thracias*, i.e., the eastern Balkans, based in Marcianople); and one for Illyricum (the *m.m. per Illyricum*, i.e., the western Balkans, based in Sirmium). However, a number of other "special" *magistri militum* are known and there are several gaps and uncertainties in our lists.[37]

---

[33] Maenchen-Helfen:86. Priscus, fr. 2 (*FCH*:227) says the 439 treaty required the Romans to return Hun fugitives, naming "Mama and Atakam, children of the royal house." They were duly returned and promptly executed.

[34] Some of our sources conflate events in 447 (when Attila was the sole ruler) with events in 441–2 (when Bleda was still alive). Others refer to events that took place in 441 as done by "the Huns" or "the kings of the Huns" or "Attila and Bleda." This could mean that the two brothers campaigned together in 441, or that Bleda's Huns started the war, but Attila joined in at some point. Bleeker 1980. I am not aware of any source that *only* mentions Bleda. Maenchen-Helfen:116; Kelly 2009:122. See the *Suda* entry on Zercon, Z 29, which says that he was captured and sent to the Hun "kings" but only Bleda liked him (*FCH*:287–9).

[35] Cf. Roberto 2009, C. Kelly 2009:120–2; Rubin 1968:13–62.

[36] C. Kelly 2009:121.

[37] *PLRE* 2, 1290–3. But now see Kaldellis & Kruse, 2023.

In 440, the east Romans had to decide which of their generals would be responsible for dealing with each of the three threats. It appears that Anatolius was given the assignment of dealing with the Persians; Areobindus the Vandals; and Aspar the Huns.[38]

The surprising thing is that Aspar did not get the Vandal assignment. It is surprising because Aspar was clearly the east Romans' most experienced general in warfare with the Vandals. He was also well-regarded by Galla Placidia, whose cooperation would be essential. The most likely explanation is that Aspar was not sent against the Vandals because it was felt that his presence was more urgently required in the Balkans.[39] As McEvoy comments, the fact that "the experienced Aspar had not been sent with the fleet to Sicily but remained at Constantinople reinforces the picture of eastern anxiety [with regard to the Huns] at this time."[40]

Admittedly, there could be another explanation. As we have seen, some sources allege that Aspar and Geiseric had an "understanding" between them that was contrary to Roman interests.[41] While these charges against Aspar were certainly made after the failure of the great east Roman offensive in 468, they could have been made earlier if doubts had arisen about Aspar's "reliability" in a Vandal war. However, it is unlikely that both the east and west Romans would have approved the choice of Aspar as consul in 434 if they felt such accusations were credible. This suggests that the allegation of collusion between Aspar and Geiseric in our sources may have been written later with knowledge of the events of 468. Blockley says that while Aspar's absence is "usually explained" by other concerns (i.e., loyalty), he believes that a disagreement over the priority to be given to the Balkans might have been as significant as any other factor.[42]

However, one should never overlook the possible influence of east Roman politics. For example, Aspar's exact military title in 440 is unclear. It is interesting that Aspar did not succeed his father as a *m.m. praesentalis* in 434, when that position went to Areobindus.[43] It is possible that Aspar did not get the job

---

[38] Marcell. *comes*, s.a. 441; *PLRE* 2, Fl. Ardabur Aspar, Fl. Anatolius 10.
[39] Maenchen-Helfen 1973:111, ("evidently because the situation, in spite of the truce [with the Huns], was too precarious to be handled by anyone else."); Kelly 2009:120-2, suggests that this was a calculated gamble by Theodosius II based on the assumption that the campaign against the Vandals would be short and successful, a strategy Aspar opposed.
[40] McEvoy 2013:262-5.
[41] Roberto 2009.
[42] Blockley 1992:67.
[43] *PLRE* 2, *Fasti*, 1290.

because he was still in Carthage at that time with the rank of *m.m. vacans*.[44] But he does not seem to have received the other *m.m. praesentalis* position when his father-in-law, Plintha, left the scene around 438. It may be that Aspar briefly held a praesental position in 441–3, or that he had a position as a special type of *magister militum*.[45] There is a gap in our lists, but by 443 the second praesental post seems to have gone to an officer named Apollonius.[46] The timing of Apollonius' appointment is interesting. As we will see, the period around 440 saw the rise of the eunuch chamberlain, Chrysaphius, who gained great influence with Theodosius II and became an enemy of Pulcheria. Given Aspar's ties to Pulcheria, Chrysaphius might not have supported the promotion of Aspar. The hostility of Chrysaphius may also be inferred from an intrigue in 441 against Aspar's alleged ally, John the Vandal, that was instigated by Chrysaphius. When Chrysaphius finally fell from power in 450, Pulcheria (Aspar's ally) had Chrysaphius executed by John's son, Jordanes (at that time another Aspar ally).[47]

Another possible opponent was the empress Eudocia, who was at the height of her power in 439/440. She too might have had reason not to support the promotion of a general who was close to Pulcheria. Finally, Arnold has suggested that Theodosius II might have been concerned that Aspar would be *too* successful (much as Justinian would worry about Belisarius). Or perhaps, Chrysaphius may have played on the emperor's concern by raising rumors about Aspar's collaboration with Geiseric.[48]

If Aspar did not have praesental rank before the outbreak of the Hun war in 441, and was not a *m.m. vacans*, then he may instead have held a regional command in the Balkans to deal with the Huns. An edict dated March 6, 441 was sent by Theodosius II to Areobindus, with a copy to Aspar, each of whom are identified simply as *magister militum*.[49] But *magister militum* of what? We do not know who held the post of *m.m. per Illyricum* between 423 and 449.[50] My belief is that may have been Aspar.[51] For one thing, this was the region where trouble

---

[44] PLRE 2, 1290, 1293.
[45] PLRE 2, 1293.
[46] PLRE 2, Apollonius 3, *Fasti* 1290.
[47] PLRE 2, Ioannes 13 agrees that this was a "political murder" but also suggests that it could relate to concerns about John's loyalty in light of the renewed war with the Vandals.
[48] Communication from Prof. J.J. Arnold to author.
[49] *Nov.Th.* 7.4 (March 6, 441); Millar 2006:47. However, I do not agree with Millar that it is shows Aspar was "apparently in *Oriens*" at the time. One might speculate that he was writing to them as his two praesental generals, which might mean that Aspar had the title at that time.
[50] PLRE 2, 1291.
[51] Zuckerman 1994:171–2 is in agreement with this; however, Wijnendaele has suggested to author that Aspar might have been a *magister militum vacans*, which may have been his title in Africa, or held some other special title. In *Nov.Th.* 7.4 (441), Aspar is addressed as a "*comes illustris*" and "*magister militum*." See PLRE 2, 1292–3.

with the Huns was likely to occur. The initial Hun attack in 441 was directed against Margus, a city for which the *m.m. per Illyricum* was responsible, and it was Aspar who negotiated a truce with the Huns afterwards.

There is another piece of evidence which also suggests that Aspar was active in the Balkans around 441. In support of his statement that the Roman forces in the Hun war of 441–2 were "led by Aspar," Maenchen-Helfen simply cites the entry for "Zercon" in the *Suda*, a tenth-century Byzantine encyclopedia entry whose source is likely Priscus.[52] Zercon was a Moorish jester who had been given to Aspar during the African campaign.[53] According to Priscus, who met him, Zercon was "captured [from the Romans] when the barbarians [the Huns] invaded Thrace and was brought to the Scythian kings [Attila and Bleda]."[54] As Aspar's jester, Zercon would not have been far from Aspar. If Zercon was captured "when the barbarians invaded Thrace," then it is likely that Aspar was in the Balkans at the time. The date of Zercon's capture can be tied to the war of 441–2 because of Priscus' reference to Bleda, who was not killed until 444/445.[55] Zercon's story is further evidence that Aspar was commanding east Roman forces in the Balkans during the Hun war of 441–2.

In sum, in 441 Aspar was possibly the *m.m. per Illyricum*. Whatever his exact title, he was the Roman commander most likely to deal with the Huns.

The Hun Wars of the 440s

The rise of the Huns under Attila presented a major threat to east Rome in the 440s, and "a very powerful sense of danger" is present in contemporary sources and later accounts of this period.[56] This concern would escalate to panic at the end of the decade and would not really abate until after Attila's death in 453. While some sources treat the whole period 441–7 as one war, other sources and most modern authors see two separate conflicts.[57]

---

[52] Maenchen-Helfen, 1973:116, n. 545; Mathisen & Shanzer 2016:191–2 (Lenski). On Priscus fr.13.2 as source, *FCH*:287–8.
[53] Bleeker 1980:25.
[54] Priscus, fr. 13.2 (*FCH*). I do not believe this reference to "Thrace" takes away from the argument that Aspar was initially *m.m. per Illyricum*. The initial fighting was clearly in Illyricum. Although the war expanded into Thrace in its second year, Aspar may have retained the title as his forces retreated. Moreover, he may have had to assume overall responsibility since the *m.m. per Thracias*, John the Vandal, is attested only for 441 and was apparently killed. *PLRE* 2, Ionnes 13, 1292.
[55] Maenchen-Helfen 1973:104–5, 113.
[56] Millar 2006:41, citing Soz. IX.6.1, Priscus fr. 10 (*FCH*:241–3), Theodoret, *HR*, XXVI.19 and Callinicus, *Vita Hypatii*, 52.
[57] Cf. Theophanes AM 5942 with Marcell. *comes*; Priscus, fr. 6 and 9 (*FCH*:231, 235); Zuckerman 1994:164–5; Bleeker 1980.

i. The First War (441–2)

Across the Danube from the Roman city of Margus was a Roman outpost called Constantia that had been designated in the treaty of 439 as a "safe" market town for both Huns and Romans. However, in 440 the Huns made a surprise attack and captured the Roman fort at Constantia.

This occurred shortly before the east Roman expeditionary force left to fight the Vandals, and it is possible that the Huns knew that the east Romans were taking troops from the Danube frontier.[58] Since Constantinople was not anxious to have a Hun war in the Balkans while much of its army was committed against the Vandals, it was important to buy time by negotiating with the Huns to discuss their breach of the treaty. Kelly believes that the Roman negotiator was Aspar, which would be appropriate if he was the *m.m. per Illyricum*.[59]

When Aspar arrived at Margus, he offered to arbitrate the dispute. The Huns rejected this proposal, claiming that the treaty had been breached first by the Romans. They claimed that the bishop of Margus had crossed the Danube to rob Hun tombs near Constantia. And not just anyone's tombs, but the tombs of high-status relatives of Bleda and Attila.[60]

Modern historians disagree as to whether the Huns' claims were justified. Kelly, noting the Huns' "open hostility to Christianity," finds it "just too suspiciously neat that they should accuse a bishop of violating their dead."[61] However, Maenchen-Helfen says that "the Huns were undoubtedly right."[62] He notes that grave-robbing by Christian clergymen (even of Christian tombs) was apparently a serious problem in late antiquity. An imperial *novella* of 447 is aimed at this behavior, and there are references to it in the early fifth-century sermons of John Chrysostom at Constantinople.[63] Nor does the subsequent conduct of the bishop of Margus inspire faith in his innocence.

Once the negotiations collapsed, Aspar had a military problem on his hands. The Huns crossed the Danube and captured a number of important cities, including Sirmium (which was Aspar's headquarters if he was *m.m. per Illyricum*). This apparently led some among the Romans to take a long look at the bishop of Margus:

---

[58] Meier 2017:46; Zuckerman 1994:163.
[59] C. Kelly 2009:121–3.
[60] Priscus, fr. 6 (*FCH*); Zuckerman 1994:165; C. Kelly:97–101.
[61] C. Kelly 2009:123.
[62] Maenchen-Helfen 1973:110.
[63] Ibid., 110, n. 508 (but date should be 447, N.Val. 23.1 in Pharr 2011).

[S]ome were arguing that the bishop of Margus should be handed over, so that the whole Roman people should not be endangered by the war for the sake of one man. He, suspecting that he would be surrendered, slipped away from those in the city, and promised that he would betray the city [of Margus] to [the Huns] if the [Hun] kings made him any reasonable offer.[64]

Having received appropriate guarantees for his safety from Bleda and Attila, the bishop re-crossed the river and opened the city to the Huns. Priscus dryly concludes that "[w]hen Margus had been laid waste in this way, the position of the barbarians was greatly improved."[65] It is hard to find much good to say about the bishop of Margus.

It is also difficult to reconstruct the course of military events in 441 and 442. However, it appears that the fighting in 441 was concentrated mainly in the western Balkans and did not favor the Romans. At some point in 441, Aspar was able to negotiate a one-year truce, which would allow the troops sent to Sicily to return.[66] Prosper makes the link explicit: "Because the Huns ravaged Thrace and Illyricum with wild devastation, the fleet, which had been stationed in Sicily, returned to defend the eastern provinces."[67]

We do not we know whether the Huns tried to strike again before these reinforcements were in place, or whether the east Romans (emboldened by the reinforcements) took the offensive in 442. What we know is that the war resumed, and the result was a disaster for the east Romans. Having overrun much of Illyricum, the Huns were successfully invading Thrace when some unknown event caused them to withdraw. This could have been an outbreak of plague, or an uprising by some of the tribes in central Europe that the Huns had previously subdued.[68] A new treaty was then negotiated between the east Romans (probably including Aspar) and Bleda/Attila.[69] The war apparently ended in late 442 or early 443.[70]

The war of 441/442 did not enhance Aspar's reputation in either the military or the political sphere. While he may have been correct in advising against the diversion of troops against the Vandals, he was unable to stop the Huns. We do

---

[64] Priscus, fr. 6 (*FCH*:231).
[65] Ibid.
[66] Theophanes AM 5942; Maenchen-Helfen:116; Zuckerman 1994:165; Croke 2001:57–8; Barnwell 1992:115–16.
[67] Prosper, s.a. 442; Maenchen-Helfen:111, n. 518; Salisbury 2015:182.
[68] Maenchen-Helfen:117; Zuckerman 1994:166–7. Similar abrupt Hun withdrawals ended Ruga's invasion in 434 and Attila's invasions of Thrace in 447 and Italy in 452.
[69] Zuckerman 1994:167 believes that the Huns withdrew without a treaty. However, given Attila's later reference to specific amounts promised, a treaty was eventually made.
[70] Maenchen-Helfen 1973:117.

not know whether this was due to lack of troops, the effective tactics used by the Huns, or in-fighting among the east Romans.[71] Nonetheless, whereas one could debate whether Aspar's African campaign had been a "success," there was no doubt that in the Hun war of 441/442 the east Roman army had failed.

However, worse was to come.

ii. The Second War (447–8)

There is a major difference between the first and second wars between the east Romans and the Huns in the 440s. In the first war, the Huns were led by *both* Bleda and Attila. In the second war, the Huns were led *only* by Attila.[72] In the interval, Attila had murdered his brother and become the sole leader of the Huns. We do not know why—perhaps because of a difference in personalities, or perhaps because of Attila's lust for power.[73] The probable date for Bleda's death is most likely 445.[74]

The first war had ended with a renewal of the treaty that had been made in 439 by Plintha. If that treaty fixed the annual payment to the Huns at 700 pounds of gold, then the 442 treaty doubled it to 1,400 pounds. It is likely that at least one such payment was made.[75] Although these treaties had other important provisions (particularly the obligation to return Hun fugitives), the payments were the most important to Attila because they enabled him to reward his followers. As Maenchen-Helfen says of an east Roman embassy: "Roman rhetorics never prevailed with Attila unless they were accompanied by the sound of Roman *solidi*."[76]

However, by late 442 there are indications that the government at Constantinople had regained its confidence and begun to harden its policy towards the Huns.[77] A law of August 21, 442 indicates that normal judicial proceedings had resumed in Illyricum, the scene of the original Hun incursion. In the fall of 443 there is evidence that the Danube flotilla and the forts along the

---

[71] Ibid.:111. Several sources note that "John, *magister militum* [of Thrace?], a Vandal by race, was killed in Thrace by the treachery of Arnegisclus." *PLRE* 2, Ionnes 13. Clover 1966:46–53 suggests that John owed his position to Aspar.
[72] Maenchen-Helfin:115, 117, 124–5. Evagrius mentions *only* this second war as "the famous war of Attila." Evagrius, *HE*, I, 17. This is also true of Jordanes and Callinicus.
[73] C. Kelly 2009:102–5. The Zercon story shows their different personalities. Priscus fr. 132 (*FCH*: 287–9); *Suda* Z 29.
[74] Maenchen-Helfen 1973:104–5; Zuckerman 1994:167.
[75] Maenchen-Helfen:117–18 suggests that the payments were couched as "subsidies" to an "ally" to avoid calling them "tribute."
[76] Maenchen-Helfen 1973:106. See also Meier 2017:49.
[77] Zuckerman 1994:164. This may reflect the growing influence of Chrysaphius.

Danube were being strengthened by the east Romans. Finally, an edict of November 29, 444 forgave delinquent taxes (which had perhaps been raised for the payments to the Huns). All of this (plus Attila's later demand for payment of arrears) suggests that the annual payments may have stopped as early as 443.[78]

Surprisingly, given the importance of the flow of gold, Attila did not immediately take any major military action against the east Romans until 447, although he apparently began to complain about non-compliance as early as 445 or 446.[79] He demanded that the Romans hand over fugitives and make up the omitted payments. If not, "he would not willingly restrain his Scythian forces," (which may either suggest that the Huns were anxious for war or that Attila's control of them was less than absolute at that time).[80] The reaction of the east Roman court shows a much tougher attitude than in 441; this time they refused Attila's demands outright but again offered to negotiate.[81]

It did not really matter—Attila was not interested in negotiations. While some fighting between Hun war bands and the east Romans appears to have begun earlier, Attila's first move in late 446 was aggressive but limited in scope. He invaded Roman territory and captured the important city of Ratiaria.[82] This city was also the headquarters for the Romans' Danube flotilla, which had been strengthened since the 442 war, and its potential for blocking the Danube may have been of concern to Attila.[83] The fall of Ratiaria may have given Theodosius' government pause as to their harder stance with the Huns, but in January, 447, something unexpected happened that shook their confidence even more.

A fundamental tenet of east Roman strategy was that Constantinople itself was impregnable. Its walls had only recently been rebuilt and strengthened. However, on the morning of January 26, 447, a strong earthquake struck Constantinople. The most alarming result was the collapse of long stretches of the Theodosian Walls.[84]

The shock and terror caused by the earthquake are perhaps best demonstrated by the remarkable response from the emperor himself. Later that day, the

---

[78] Maenchen-Helfen 1973:114, 117; *Cod. Just.*, II, 7.9; *Nov.Th.*, 24 and 26. 1; Zuckerman 1994:168; C. Kelly 2009:132. Priscus, fr. 9.3 (*FCH*:237–41) emphasizes the hardships caused by the payments to the Huns, but this appears to refer to the greater payment made after the end of the second war in 447.
[79] Maenchen-Helfen 1973:117–18.
[80] Ibid., 119.
[81] Priscus, fr. 9.1, (*FCH*:235).
[82] Ibid.
[83] C. Kelly 2009:132.
[84] Marcell. *comes* 447.1; Malalas 363.20–364.2; *Chron. Pasch.* s.a. 447, 450; C. Kelly 2009:130–6; Croke 1981:122–47.

scholarly and pious Theodosius II, barefoot and wearing only a simple tunic, walked the seven miles from his palace to the Hebdomon military parade ground outside the city, where he led his people in prayers that God "have mercy upon us."[85] There was little doubt by the emperor or his frightened people that news of this disaster would soon reach the Huns.

Despite this display of piety, the practical response of the east Romans to this disaster was equally astonishing. "Although never doubting the power of prayer, the praetorian prefect of the East, Flavius Constantinus, had no intention of waiting for God to come to Constantinople's rescue."[86] Not only did he rapidly organize skilled workers to make repairs, but he also provided them with a most unusual labor force—Constantinople's notorious "circus factions," the rival Blues and Greens. He cleverly assigned each faction to different sections of the walls so that they could compete in making the repairs. Working through the night, the city's people completed the repairs in under two months.[87] This meant that the walls were repaired by the end of March, 447 just before the campaigning season began.[88] The east Romans again had a base that would be extremely difficult for the Huns to capture.

If Aspar was in the city during this time, he may have personally participated in some of this work. Not only would it have pleased the emperor and enhanced his popularity with the citizens of Constantinople, but it would have been consistent with Aspar's reputation for public-spirited behavior. We will see this during the great fire of 464. However, it is possible that Aspar was not in the city but with the army preparing for the coming war.

Given the sparse nature of our sources, it is difficult to reconstruct the course of the fighting between the Huns and the east Romans in 447, although the outcome is clear enough. Kelly has constructed a narrative that seems plausible.[89] He believes that the east Roman army was divided between three commanders. One was Areobindus, the *m.m. praesentalis* who had commanded the expedition to Sicily in 441; the second was a general named Arnegisclus, who was the *m.m.* for Thrace;[90] and the third was Aspar, who may have been the *m.m. per Illyricum*.

---

[85] Van Nuffelen 2012:189–90. This ritual was annually re-enacted by the emperor through at least the reign of Marcian. Croke 1978:5–9, 1981:122–47.
[86] C. Kelly 2009:133.
[87] A marble inscription survives in Istanbul at a gate in the walls, proudly noting that "By Theodosius' command, Constantinus triumphantly built these strong walls in less than two months." C. Kelly 2009:134–5.
[88] Kelly describes the rebuilding of the walls as a "deadly serious race" between the Huns and the Romans C. Kelly 2009:134.
[89] C. Kelly 2009:137–8.
[90] Marcell. *comes*, s.a. 447. Although he is called *magister militum Mysiae* in one source. Jordanes, *Rom.* 331; *PLRE* 2, Arnegisclus.

These forces were deployed to cover the approaches that might be used by the Huns to attack Constantinople.[91] While they were ultimately unable to stop the Hun raid, it seems that they did affect its course and speed.[92]

The Roman strategy was essentially defensive, perhaps reflecting a reluctance by the Romans to chance everything on a pitched battle. This may have been influenced by memories of the Roman disaster at Adrianople in 378. However, it could also have been the result of Aspar's more recent experiences in Africa and in the Hun war of 441.

As it happened, Attila did not make a direct dash for Constantinople in 447. His object was not to conquer the eastern empire, but to obtain plunder for his troops and then extort a large "subsidy."[93] To this end, he first besieged and captured the major city of Philippopolis (modern Plovdiv). Although the siege took time, Kelly believes that the city was too strong to leave in the rear of the Hun advance.

However, some Huns (whether or not under the control of Attila) did come very close to Constantinople. The Huns apparently reached "the Pontus and the Propontis," which means the Black Sea north of Constantinople and the Sea of Marmara to its south. While they did not capture Heraclea, on the Propontis, they did get there, as well as to the fortress of Athyra, only twenty miles from Constantinople.[94]

It is interesting that the Huns are reported to have captured two cities, Callippus and Sestus in the Chersonese (the modern Gallipoli peninsula). This suggests at least some Huns swerved away from Constantinople into an area which does not seem to have offered them a major reward—indeed, it would appear to detract from any serious attempt against Constantinople. It also forced them to fight on a narrow peninsula where the terrain was broken and the sea on either side would prevent sweeping cavalry movements.[95] Why would the Huns do this?

One possibility is that they were chasing someone, perhaps a Roman army on their flank. Put differently, perhaps they were purposely drawn after that force to pull them away from Constantinople. This army may have been led by Aspar, who eventually withdrew his forces from the peninsula by sea. Although the outcome was viewed as yet another defeat for the Romans, the battle may have

---

[91] C. Kelly 2009:137.
[92] Ibid. See also Zuckerman 1994:166.
[93] Kulikowski 2019:209 calls this "the protection racket he ran against the eastern empire."
[94] Theophanes AM 5942; C. Kelly 2009:137, 311; Maenchen-Helfen 1973:113.
[95] C. Kelly 2009:137.

been equally costly to the Huns. According to Priscus, "[a]fter the battle between the Romans and the Huns in the Chersonese, a treaty was negotiated by Anatolius."[96] This does not necessarily mean that the battle was so adverse to the Romans that they immediately sought to end the war—it might mean that heavy losses on both sides led both parties to enter into negotiations.

By this point, the war had reached its final phase. Attila began to withdraw his forces towards the Danube. Perhaps he felt he had gathered enough booty and could now make another favorable treaty with Theodosius II at his leisure. Perhaps he was running out of supplies. Perhaps disease had again broken out among the Huns, or an uprising had occurred among the Huns' subjects. Any of these causes might have been a reason for the Huns to withdraw, since Attila's objective was not conquest.

The Hun withdrawal took them through as yet unravaged territory in Thrace, and towards the large city of Marcianopolis (the headquarters of the *m.m. per Thracius,* Arnegisclus). Arnegisclus decided to attack the Huns as they were crossing the river Utus. Attacking barbarian raiders returning home encumbered with plunder and captives was an old Roman strategy. However, Arnegisclus is said to have died fighting heroically and the city of Marcianopolis was then taken and sacked by the Huns.[97]

For modern and ancient historians alike, the Hun war of 447 was a great disaster for the east Romans.[98] Marcellinus calls it "a mighty war, greater than the previous one."[99] Even Nestorius, the former patriarch of Constantinople, in exile in the Egyptian desert, heard enough to say that the Huns had become "the masters, and the Romans slaves."[100] The modern scholar, Otto Maenchen-Helfen, calls it "the greatest victory the Huns ever won."[101]

By the end of 447 the east Romans were anxious for a new treaty with Attila.[102] It took some time to conclude, but it increased the annual amount of gold to be paid to the Huns to 2,100 pounds.[103] In addition, there was a one-time payment of gold owed under the treaty of 442. The Romans were also required to withdraw from a large swath of land along the south bank of the Danube. This would make it easier for the Huns to again raid the eastern empire and make it harder for the Romans to launch a pre-emptive attack.

---

[96] Priscus, fr. 9.3 (*FCH*:237–41).
[97] *PLRE* 2, Arnegisclus; C. Kelly 2009:138, 144.
[98] Evagrius, HE, 1.17; Meier 2017; Kelly:138; Zuckerman 1994:164.
[99] Marcell. comes, s.a. 447.
[100] Nestorius 366; Maenchen-Helfen 1973:94.
[101] Maenchen-Helfen 1973:125.
[102] Zuckerman 1994:167–8.
[103] Priscus, fr. 9 (*FCH*:237–41); Kulikowski 2019:126, 137.

Unlike the treaty of 442, this time Aspar was not among the negotiators. The Roman side was represented by Anatolius, who had been brought from Antioch and promoted to the rank of *m.m. praesentalis*, plus a civilian official (and ally of Chrysaphius) named Nomus.[104] The fact that the treaty was not negotiated by Aspar, or Areobindus, or any other of the "barbarian" generals of the eastern empire is significant. Both Aspar and Areobindus had been dismissed from their military posts because of their failure to stop the Huns.[105] This may also reflect political changes at Constantinople, especially the growing influence of Chrysaphius, which we will consider in the next section. However, the bottom line was that Aspar, and his military allies were blamed for the Roman defeat.[106]

The second Hun war also saw the rise of a new figure in the east Roman military, an Isaurian officer called Zeno.[107] In 447, Zeno's troops were successful in defeating some of the Huns near Constantinople. He was then rapidly advanced, being named consul for 448 and Anatolius' successor as *m.m. per Orientem*.[108] Zeno took a strong position against appeasement of the Huns and later became Chrysaphius' greatest opponent.[109]

Zeno's career also reflects the developing role of the Isaurians as an important element in the east Roman military aristocracy.[110] The Roman army's failure against the Huns seems to have caused a revival of anti-"barbarian" sentiment at Constantinople and the Isaurians (even though they may have been viewed as "internal barbarians") were perhaps seen as more "Roman" and more reliable.[111]

The post-447 atmosphere at Constantinople is shown by Priscus' recollections of an east Roman embassy to Attila in 449. He tells us that a Hun named Berichus suddenly took offense because the Roman ambassador, Maximinus, had allegedly said "that the generals Areobindus and Aspar carried no weight with the Emperor and of pouring contempt upon their achievements by arguing that

---

[104] On Anatolius and Nomus, *PLRE* 2, Anatolius 10, Nomus 1. Both had been on a list of "acceptable" negotiators provided by Attila. Anatolius replaced Areobindus, who (like Aspar) had been dismissed in 449.
[105] Zuckerman 2014:171.
[106] C. Kelly 2009:144–5. Beers 2013 believes that Priscus is critical of the Roman negotiators' fear of Attila. This may reflect the state of mind of Chrysaphius and possibly Theodosius II in the negotiations, especially after Chrysaphius' assassination plot went awry.
[107] This Zeno should not be confused with his later namesake, who became emperor in 474. *PLRE* 2, Fl. Zenon 6; Thompson 1946:18–31.
[108] *PLRE* 2, Fl. Zenon 6; *FCH*, Priscus fr. 14, n. 88. Holum 1982:206 dates his appointment as *magister militum* to 449 but cf. *PLRE* 2 which says 447–51.
[109] *FCH*, Priscus, n. 95; Meier 2017:52.
[110] The shadowy Apollonius, who became a *m.m. praesentalis* in 443, was an ally of Zeno and may also have been an Isaurian. *PLRE* 2, Apollonius 3.
[111] Arnold 2014:159–60 on Isaurians as "internal barbarians"; Malalas on a raid by Isaurians into Roman Syria, Jo. Malalas:14:2; John Chrysostom's fear of Isaurian bandits during his exile, Gaddis 2005:.213.

they were unreliable barbarians."[112] Zuckerman explains Berichus' outburst as a belief that Maximinus had insulted the Huns and made light of Attila's victory by attributing it to poor leadership by the empire's generals.[113] This may be another example of the "scapegoat" trope that sought to explain Roman failures by blaming Roman "traitors" (such as Boniface) or "unreliable barbarians" (such as Aspar and Areobindus). But it may reflect what was being said in Constantinople.

The Hun war of 447 marked the nadir of Aspar's reputation as a military leader. However, Aspar always lived at the intersection of two worlds in Constantinople—the world of the east Roman military and that of the east Roman civil government. It is therefore necessary to shift our focus to court politics in Constantinople in the late 440s to understand why Aspar's position had become so weak and why things changed so suddenly afterwards.

East Roman Politics in the 440s

The early part of the reign of Theodosius II had seen the emperor guided in both religious and secular affairs by his older sister, the empress Pulcheria. She continued to play a large role in secular matters (including military decisions that involved Aspar) but starting in the 420s Pulcheria seems to become more focused on religious issues. And other people come into the picture.

One person we need to consider is the emperor's wife, the empress Eudocia. Initially, Eudocia and Pulcheria seem to have worked well enough together.[114] However, this initial amity may never have run very deep. Pulcheria, born and raised in Constantinople as an imperial princess, had two main concerns—her deep commitment to orthodoxy and the protection of the Theodosian dynasty. In contrast, Eudocia (originally Athenais) was raised in Athens as the daughter of a pagan professor of rhetoric.[115] It would not be surprising if there was tension.[116]

Their relationship seems to have grown worse in the 430s, as did relations between Theodosius II and Eudocia. This was perhaps due to the failure of

---

[112] Priscus, fr.14 (*FCH*:295); Zuckerman 1994:169-70. Rather than "unreliable," an anonymous reviewer has suggested that Priscus' word "*kouphoteta*" meant that their influence was diminished or weak. Note that Maximinus had been an associate of Ardaburius the Elder. See ch. IV, *supra*.
[113] Zuckerman 1994:170.
[114] Although several sources contain stories that Pulcheria helped choose Eudocia as the emperor's bride, Holum calls them "singularly ill-founded." Jo. Malalas 14; Chron. Pasch. s.a. 420-1; Jo. Nikiu, 84.25-37; Theophanes AM 5911. Holum 198:112-16. Even if true, others likely played a role in this choice as in other major decisions. Harries 2013; cf. Herrin 2013 on her role in religious matters.
[115] *PLRE* 2, Aelia Eudocia 2; Holum 1982:112-16.
[116] Holum 1982:131. *LRE*, vol. I:239; Herrin 2013:220-1,

Figure 9 *Solidus* of Valentinian III showing his marriage to Licinia Eudoxia, with Theodosius II as *pronubis*, *c.* 437 (wildwinds.com).

Eudocia to produce a male heir to the east Roman throne.[117] She apparently did give birth to a son named Arcadius II, but his story is murky. He was never recognized by Theodosius II as a Caesar or a co-Augustus, and he seems to have died around 440.[118] The anti-Chalcedonian John of Nikiu has a story that Theodosius and Eudocia stopped having conjugal relations because they had been advised by Egyptian monks that they did not want to see a heretic as their heir.[119]

For whatever reason, things changed for Eudocia in 437. For one thing, her daughter was married to the western emperor Valentinian III and left for Italy. Although Eudocia (unlike Pulcheria) had not previously shown an interest in religious matters, she now did. Perhaps this was the result of a genuine religious experience from a meeting with the holy ascetic, Melania the Younger (who had come to Constantinople at this time to see her senatorial uncle, a guest at the wedding); perhaps it arose from a sense of isolation after her daughter left to live in the west, and the death of her son; or perhaps she decided to more directly assert her role in the palace as her relationship with Theodosius II deteriorated.[120] Whatever the cause, Eudocia began to develop her own identity as a woman of

---

[117] Agnellus 42, CIL XI 276; *PLRE* 2, Arcadius 1, Aelia Eudoxia 2; *LRE*, vol. I:220 n. 3. On the dynastic strategy, see McEvoy 2019a:118–21.

[118] Kulikowski 2019:183–4; see *infra* re Paulinus.

[119] Watts 2013:277, 281–3; Scott 2009:44. To anti-Chalcedonians, Marcian would have been a heretic. Religious views on monogamy apparently precluded a divorce. Herrin 2013:2, 27, 174.

[120] On "female ascetism" and Melania the Younger, see Clark 2021; Testa 2016:488–9; Herrin 2013:25, 27.

piety.¹²¹ This inevitably created conflict with Pulcheria because it challenged Pulcheria's public image as the chief female imperial champion of orthodoxy.¹²²

In 438-9, Eudocia made a religious pilgrimage to Jerusalem, from which she returned to great acclaim with a number of important relics, thereby re-enacting the role of St. Helena. This moment was the apex of Eudocia's public power at Constantinople.¹²³ Emboldened by this success, Eudocia began to openly challenge Pulcheria in ways that would eventually lead to the eclipse of both empresses and the emergence of Chrysaphius as a new power broker at the east Roman court.¹²⁴

The rise of Chrysaphius may have begun with a quarrel between the empresses that arose shortly after Eudocia's return from Jerusalem. The issue was that an official normally assigned to the reigning Augusta was serving Pulcheria, whereas Eudocia argued that he should be assigned to her. The real issue was that there were two women with the title of Augusta in Constantinople, and Eudocia wanted to assert her precedence. The emperor rejected her request, but Eudocia then tried another approach—since Pulcheria had dedicated herself as a "holy virgin," why not have her formally ordained as a deaconess? This was a nice trap, since it would have required Pulcheria to withdraw from involvement in secular affairs. Pulcheria, deciding on a discrete retreat, simply sent the official to Eudocia and withdrew from the palace.¹²⁵

Several modern historians attribute the instigation of this dispute to Chrysaphius.¹²⁶ But if it had removed Pulcheria from the palace, Eudocia was still there.

That soon began to change. It is possible that the young Arcadius II had recently died, which would have weakened Eudocia's importance and influence.¹²⁷ However, several people who were associated with her suddenly fell from power in 443. One was Cyrus of Panopolis, a poet from Alexandria who had a meteoric

---

¹²¹ Holum 1982:178, 184-5; *LRE*, vol. I:239. Several fifth century imperial women were acclaimed as a "new Helena" including Pulcheria, Eudocia, and Verina. Angelova, 2015; Herrin 2013.
¹²² Angelova 2015:230, 243-5; Holum 1982:145-6.
¹²³ Gibbon, ch. XXXII; *LRE*, vol. I:239.
¹²⁴ Relics of St. Stephen, a martyr of particular interest to Pulcheria, were brought by Eudocia to Pulcheria's church of St. Lawrence. Angelova 2015:156; Holum 1977:153-72; 1982:103-10. Whether this was a gift of friendship, or a demonstration of Eudocia's religious superiority, is an interesting question.
¹²⁵ However, this did not mean that she was totally absent. Pulcheria owned two palaces outside the Great Palace. Angelova 2015:152-7; Matthews in Grig & Kelly 2012:88, 94.
¹²⁶ Holum:131, n. 85 and 191-2; Kulikowski 2019:182-4. Holum:191 states that Chysaphius received the title of *spatharius* (swordbearer for the emperor) around 440, although *PLRE* 2 dates this to 443, Chrysaphius may well have had enough power in 440 to instigate the dispute between the empresses, since he seems to have instigated the death of John the Vandal in 441.
¹²⁷ *PLRE* 2, Arcadius 1.

rise that began in 439 when he was named as Urban Prefect of Constantinople in March and then, in December of the same year, was also appointed to the even more exalted post of praetorian prefect of the east. Although it was unusual, if not unprecedented, for anyone (let alone a former poet) to do so, Cyrus held both of these senior posts simultaneously from the end of 439 until early in 443.[128] His extensive program of civic improvements made him popular with the people of Constantinople, eventually perhaps too popular for the emperor.[129] In 443, Cyrus was suddenly dismissed from both of his positions and forced to become a bishop. A source claims that his sudden fall was the work of Chrysaphius, who had advanced to the post of *praepositus sacri cubiculi*.[130] Alan Cameron has suggested that Cyrus was an ally of Eudocia and that removing him suggests a purge of her supporters by Chrysaphius.[131]

Another victim was the *comes* Paulinus, a childhood friend of the emperor and supposedly one of the people who helped him choose Eudocia as his bride.[132] In 443 Paulinus was suddenly exiled and later executed at the emperor's command, apparently because of something involving Eudocia.[133] Although the charge was supposedly denied by Eudocia even on her death bed, it appears that Chrysaphius had been able to convince the Emperor that there had been adultery between his wife and Paulinus.[134] Eudocia thereupon withdrew from the court and retired to Jerusalem, where she did religious work until her death in 460. Although he removed Eudocia from his coinage, Theodosius never deprived her of the title of Augusta. He may have felt unable to do so because of the idea of

---

[128] John Lydus, *De mag.* ii.12; Jo. Malalas, xiv.361; *PLRE* 2, Cyrus; Kulikowsi 2019:182–3.

[129] At one point, in the presence of the emperor, the crowd in the Hippodrome was heard to shout, "Constantine built the city, but Cyrus renewed it." *LRE*, vol. I:228; *PLRE* 2, Fl. Taurus Seleucus Cyrus 7, 336–9.

[130] *V. Dan. Styl.*, 31; *PLRE* 2, Cyrus 7, 338 says that he later left the priesthood and returned to a comfortable secular life in Constantinople. Holum suggests that he was pardoned by Marcian, which suggests that his return was part of the rehabilitation that occurred after the downfall of Chrysaphius. Holum 1982:193, n. 74.

[131] Alan Cameron 1982:217–89; *LRE*, vol. I:228–9.

[132] *PLRE* 2, Paulinus 8; Jo. Malalas, 353, 355–57; *Chron Pasch.*, s.a. 421, 444; Jo. Nikiu, 87.3–13; Zonaras XIII 23.28–35; Theophanes AM 5940; Holum 1982:112–31.

[133] It has been suggested that the accusation may have involved the true paternity of the recently deceased heir, Arcadius II. *PLRE* 2, Arcadius 1; Kulikowski 2019:183–4. Marcell. *comes* suggests the date of the fall of Paulinus may have been in 440, but cf. Holum 1982:194. On adultery as a common charge against an empress, see Holum 1982:193, n. 81.

[134] Our sources have a fable about an apple that was given by Theodosius II to Eudocia but is then given by her to Paulinus. Malalas 14.8 and Chron. Pasch. 1.584–1.85.23. As Scott and Burgess have shown, this story originated after 451 as an anti-Chalcedonian propaganda piece slandering Pulcheria and Marcian; a popular orthodox response then changed the characters to Eudocia and Paulinus; and the anti-Chalcedonian response was a new version that put the blame mainly on Paulinus. The death bed "denial" is thus open to question. Scott 2010:115–31; Scott 2009:42–5; Burgess 1994:50–1; Holum 1982:176–8, 192–3. See also *PLRE* 2, Aelia Eudocia, Chrysaphius, Paulinus 8; John of Nikiu, 87.1–13.

Christian monogamy, or else that the title of Augusta was held for life.[135] By the end of 444, Chrysaphius had become the dominant advisor to Theodosius II and the greatest power in the government.[136] While it may be surprising to some that a court eunuch achieved this role, one might recall the earlier career of Eutropius in the time of the emperor Arcadius.[137]

There is an interesting postscript to Eudocia's story that would eventually involve Aspar. Eudocia retired to Jerusalem with a large religious entourage and was so lavish in her charitable donations that Theodosius sent a general named Saturninus to get control of the situation. Saturninus became involved in a quarrel that ended with the deaths of two of Eudocia's priests. Allegedly, Eudocia is then said to have had Saturninus killed. The death of Saturninus would have unexpected consequences during the peace negotiations with Attila in 449/50 and may have been a factor in Aspar's return to favor.

Although Chrysaphius now dominated the east Roman government, Aspar had retained his military command until his defeat by the Huns in 447. Moreover, his family had continued its string of honors, since Aspar's eldest son, Ardaburius the Younger, was named as eastern consul for 447. The fact that the eastern court gave Aspar's family this honor (something which was probably decided in late 446, i.e., before the disastrous 447 campaign) shows that the Ardaburii were still in good standing at that time. Nor was the honor taken away, as the *Fasti* show that the younger Ardaburius took office and served as the eastern consul for 447.[138] Things changed *after* the army's poor showing against the Huns in 447, but there is no indication that Theodosius (or Chrysaphius) attempted to change the senior military commands of the east Roman army before then.[139]

A second question is whether the ascendancy of Chrysaphius led to any change in the east Roman government's foreign policy, particularly with the Huns. We know that after the first war with the Huns the east Roman government strengthened its defenses and felt confident enough to stop the annual payments to Attila. We do not know how Aspar felt about this strategy, only that both Plintha and Aspar had previously negotiated treaties with the Huns that provided for such payments. It is possible that Aspar may have preferred a negotiated

---

[135] Holum 1982:192–4; Herrin 2013:2, 27, 174. See also the attempt of Honorius to deprive Placidia of her title in 423 and the same with Valentinian III and Honoria around 451.

[136] Priscus fr. 15 (5) (*FCH*:301); Jo. Ant. fr. 198; Jo. Malalas, 14:16 and 19; Holum 1982:192. Chrysaphius may also have used the "circus factions" to extend his power. Malalas 14:19 and 14:32; Alan Cameron 1976:21–2, 127.

[137] Ch. III, *supra*.

[138] *PLRE* 2, *Fasti Consulares*, 1243; *CLRE*:428–9; McEvoy 2016:487.

[139] Although there remains the puzzling appointment of Apollonius, rather than Aspar, as a *m.m. praesentalis* in the early 440s and Chrysaphius' role in the death of John the Vandal in 441.

solution with Attila to avoid a renewal of the Balkan war, whereas Theodosius (and Chrysaphius) may have favored a more aggressive policy.

However, the military debacle in 447 had a profound and negative effect on the career of Aspar. Several of the senior generals who had led the east Roman army at the start of 447, including Aspar and Areobindus, were gone from their posts by 449.[140] They were replaced by new men from outside the old military aristocracy, such as Anatolius, Apollonius, and Zeno. This may reflect the greater influence of Chrysaphius and would seem to confirm Berichus' allegation that Aspar and Areobindus had lost influence with the emperor.

Moreover, the military failures in 447 caused the east Roman court to change its tactics with the Huns. Having been unsuccessful in military operations, Chrysaphius tried covert means. This included the use of Priscus' embassy in 449 as the cover for a plot to assassinate Attila.[141] It represents a change in east Roman strategy from trying to beat the Huns in battle to disrupting their confederacy by striking down its leader.[142] The plot failed when the intended assassin revealed the plot to Attila, who sent the man back to Chrysaphius with a bag of gold around his neck and a demand that Theodosius II hand Chrysaphius over for execution. Theodosius did not comply, but the incident seems to have badly rattled him and may explain his willingness to accede to many of Attila's demands in the peace negotiations. For example, when it was learned in 450 that the Augusta Honoria, the unmarried sister of the western emperor Valentinian III, had made an offer of marriage to (of all people) Attila, Theodosius advised Valentinian that he should hand her over rather than risk war with Attila.[143] Conceivably, the failed plot may also have weakened Chrysaphius' influence with the emperor, and perhaps allowed other voices (such as those of Pulcheria and Aspar?) to be heard again.

The negotiations with Attila for a new treaty were both protracted and extremely fragile. There was no guarantee that they would not break down or that the volatile Attila might not decide to suddenly return with his army. In this atmosphere, the east Romans were anxious to avoid anything that might upset the Hun leader. However, in 449, Zeno (the newly appointed *m.m. per Orientem*) created an incident that threatened to do exactly that.

---

[140] Beers 2013.
[141] Priscus, fr. 11, 15 (*FCH,*).
[142] Meier 2017:49–52.
[143] Priscus, fr. 15 (*FCH*); Priscus, fr. 17 (*FCH*); Meier 2017; Croke 2014 (rev. Croke 2021:43–4).

Attila had become adept at finding ways to extract lucrative benefits for his followers from the Romans.[144] This included his secretary, a Roman named Constantius, who handled correspondence with both the east and west Romans. During the post-447 negotiations, Attila's representative (possibly Constantius himself) informed the east Roman government that Constantius would like a bride, preferably a "high-ranking" (i.e., wealthy) woman. Since Chrysaphius was anxious to meet this demand, "the Emperor agreed to this proposal."[145]

The intended bride was the daughter of Saturninus, the man who had been killed in the dispute with the empress Eudocia's priests in Jerusalem, and "a man of considerable wealth."[146] However, at some point in 449, this woman was carried off by Zeno's soldiers, and married to a man named Rufus, one of Zeno's "associates" and the brother of the *m.m. praesentalis* Apollonius.[147] Constantius complained to Attila that he wanted either the original woman or "another with a comparable dowry" (which shows what this was really all about), and the issue was raised with the east Roman ambassador, Maximinus.[148] When Theodosius II (or Chrysaphius) learned that the intended bride was no longer available, he confiscated the woman's estates.[149] Zeno, correctly seeing this as a move by Chrysaphius to punish him (and Rufus) for interfering in the negotiations with the Huns, sent a letter to the emperor blaming Chrysaphius and demanding that Theodosius hand Chrysaphius over to Zeno for punishment. Theodosius refused to give up Chrysaphius; Zeno "prepared to revolt"; and the east Roman government was about to order Maximinus to move against Zeno, its own *m.m. per Orientem*.[150] As Priscus dryly puts it, "Being sought by both Attila and Zeno, Chrysaphius was in dire straits."[151]

As if this was not enough for Chrysaphius, he had also become involved in the theological battles that so obsessed the east Romans. He had supported the heterodox monk Eutyches in a struggle with Patriarch Flavian of Constantinople, which put him at odds with Pulcheria (as well as the Pope in Rome and

---

[144] Attila himself could sometimes directly profit from these "gifts." For example, Constantius had promised that he would pay Attila if Attila could help him get a rich Roman wife. Priscus, fr.15 (*FCH*:295,).
[145] Ibid.
[146] Priscus fr.14 (*FCH*:291).
[147] *PLRE* 2, Rufus 1, Apollonius 3; Priscus fr. 23 (*FCH*:315 n. 114), Zuckerman 1994:172–5 (suggesting that Zeno and Chrysaphius had become "sworn enemies" over what Zeno regarded as the appeasement of Attila); Burgess 1992:876.
[148] Priscus, fr. 14 (*FCH*:291). Priscus was now serving on Maximinus' staff. The demand for the bride was conveyed back to Constantinople at the same time that Chrysaphius learned of the failure of his plot and Attila's demand for his execution.
[149] Holum 1982:206; Priscus (*FCH*:389 n. 95).
[150] Priscus, fr. 16 (*FCH*:301); Zuckerman 1994:172–3; Holum 1982:206–7; Meier 2017:52.
[151] Priscus fr. 15 (*FCH*:295).

Valentinian III).¹⁵² However, Chrysaphius' hold over the emperor at this time was too great for even Pulcheria to overcome. In August, 449, an ecumenical council known as Second Ephesus reversed Pulcheria's theological victory at First Ephesus. Flavian was deposed and so mistreated that he died, a result that greatly upset the sensitive Emperor.¹⁵³ Nonetheless, as late as March, 450, Chrysaphius apparently was able to dictate letters from Theodosius to Valentinian III and the Pope rejecting their support of Flavian.

At this point, something changed in east Roman politics. Holum believes "although no source suggests it" that Pulcheria finally was able to persuade her brother that Chrysaphius was in the wrong in the Eutychean controversy.¹⁵⁴ Theodosius' support for the heterodox views of Chrysaphius must have infuriated Pulcheria, and she is likely to have used the full force of her personality to persuade her brother that Chrysaphius had led him to make a serious error of faith. The religious issue was Pulcheria's top concern—she was horrified by the results of Second Ephesus and was anxious for a new council that would restore the religious formula that had been reached with her support at First Ephesus in 431.

Theodosius also may have finally had some doubts as to the military position in which he found himself. Theodosius now had to face a potential revolt by Zeno, one of his own generals, while the peace treaty with Attila remained unsigned. It happened that one of the major remaining issues in these negotiations was Attila's continuing demand about a bride for Constantius.

All of these issues centered on Chrysaphius. And so Chrysaphius finally fell from power sometime between March and June, 450.¹⁵⁵ Theodosius ordered the confiscation of his property and had Chrysaphius exiled to an island.¹⁵⁶ Priscus sheds no tears for Chrysaphius: "During the reign of Theodosius, Chrysaphius controlled everything, seizing the possessions of all and being hated by all."¹⁵⁷

---

[152] Eutyches was both the godfather of Chrysaphius and a "spiritual adviser" to the emperor. Gaddis 2005:292.
[153] Holum 1982:200–5. The religious views of Theodosius II were equivocal—he had been slow to endorse First Ephesus but (under the influence of Chrysaphius) accepted the results of Second Ephesus. Watts describes him as "one of the last Roman emperors embraced as orthodox by both Chalcedonian and anti-Chalcedonian Christians." Watts 2013:269 in C. Kelly 2013. In general, Gaddis 2005; Frend 1972; Alan Cameron 1976:143–4.
[154] Holum 1982:205. Kulikowski 2019:187 confesses that we do not know how Pulcheria was able to replace Chrysaphius at this time. However, a religious argument would be a good bet given the personalities involved. The failure of Chrysaphius to deal with Attila may also have helped her.
[155] Holum 1982:207. Beers 2013 places the fall of Chrysaphius *after* the death of Theodosius II. I disagree, since that would have left the palace under the control of Chrysaphius and required a coup by Pulcheria and Aspar. Nothing like that appears in the sources.
[156] Cf. Beers 2013, who does not believe that this exile occurred.
[157] Priscus fr. 15 (295).

Holum believes that the key development was the re-emergence of Pulcheria in early 450, who had personal, dynastic, and religious reasons for seeking the downfall of Chrysaphius. However, as a woman, she still needed to buttress her personal power with military power and for that she apparently relied on Aspar.[158]

There are two important points about Aspar here. The first is that Chrysaphius had refused to recall Aspar when Zeno threatened to revolt in early 450. This is consistent with what we know of the policies of Chrysaphius since he presumably was the person responsible for Aspar's dismissal from his military position in the first place. However, the interesting point is that someone (Pulcheria?) had suggested Aspar's recall to lead the expedition against Zeno in the early months of 450. It is important to remember that Aspar did not entirely leave the scene when he was dismissed in 447. He remained a leading member of the Constantinopolitan senate and is likely to have had a continuing and significant presence in the city and perhaps the court. In addition, as we will see, some modern historians believe that Aspar and Zeno may have acted in unison against Chrysaphius.[159]

The second point is that Aspar soon returned to favor. It has been suggested that this may have been because he was able to help the emperor in resolving the problem about the promised bride.[160] The woman who was eventually provided was either a daughter or daughter-in-law of the general Plintha, Aspar's father-in-law.[161] Since her husband had recently died in a campaign, she was an available and wealthy widow. Since Plintha and Ardaburius the Elder both disappear from our sources around 440, it is likely that Aspar had become the effective "head" of their combined families. If so, this would support Holum's suggestion that "her availability thus depended on [Aspar] and reflected his strong position at court." Or, perhaps, a way for him to return to that position.

The timing here is important—did these events happen before or after the fall of Chrysaphius? Priscus puts it "about the early summer of 450," which would mean very near or just after the fall of Chrysaphius. But since he places the story after the return of the ambassadors Anatolius and Nomus from their latest negotiation with Attila, it might have been a little earlier in 450, i.e., possibly just *before* the fall of Chrysaphius.[162] Since the Roman ambassadors reported that the

---

[158] Holum 1982:207; *LRE*, vol. I:235.
[159] Zuckerman 1994:175–6.
[160] Holum 1982:207; Zuckerman 1994:171–2.
[161] Cf. Holum 1982:207 ("daughter") and Zuckerman 1994:171–2 ("daughter-in-law").
[162] Priscus, fr. 15 (*FCH*:295).

bride issue had become one of the final stumbling blocks in concluding this much-desired treaty, Aspar's offer of assistance would have come at an opportune time, and reminded the emperor of his usefulness.[163] One might even speculate that it was Aspar who suggested Plinthas' daughter to the emperor or perhaps to Pulcheria.[164]

The important point is that by July, 450 both Pulcheria and Aspar had re-emerged as leading figures in the government at Constantinople. The treaty between Attila and the east Romans was finally concluded (probably because Attila now had his eyes fixed on the western empire). The fall of Chrysaphius satisfied the primary demand of Zeno, as well as Pulcheria and Aspar. By mid-July, 450 a new regime had formed around the emperor in which Pulcheria and her allies (including Aspar) again played a major role.[165]

We will never know how this regime might have developed under Theodosius II. On July 26, 450, the emperor fell from his horse while hunting. He died on July 28 at age 49. Ironically, considering the many efforts by the emperor and his sisters to protect the Theodosian dynasty, he left no male Theodosian heir at Constantinople.[166]

---

[163] Zuckerman 2014:172 ("by delivering his sister-in-law to the Huns, Aspar's defeat was forgiven by the emperor"). How the poor woman felt about this is unknown.
[164] Priscus, fr. 15 (*FCH*:295) says that "the Emperor persuaded" the woman to marry Constantius. This may suggest that Theodosius himself was directly involved.
[165] Holum:207; *LRE*, vol. 1:235; cf. Beers 2013.
[166] McEvoy 2019:115–17, 126; C. Kelly 2013:53–4.

7

Aspar and the Choice of Marcian (450–7)

The Accession of Marcian

The unexpected death of Theodosius II left a political vacuum at Constantinople. This could easily have been a turning point in east Roman history, resulting in the kind of chaos that erupted in the west Roman empire just a few years later after the death of Valentinian III. However, a new emperor, Marcian, was acclaimed by the senate of Constantinople and the eastern military leadership on August 25, 450, about a month after the death of Theodosius II. The hiatus tells us that the choice was not easy, and that high politics were at play in the eventual, and surprising, choice.

It is with the accession of Marcian that Aspar went from being an east Roman general to being a "kingmaker." The sources note Aspar's presence at the bedside of the dying Theodosius II.[1] However, this was because Aspar was the *princeps* of the senate, not because of any military rank. He is described as being there with "the other senators," but he is the only one named. The fact that Marcian was relatively obscure, except for his long career in the service of the Ardaburii, points directly to the influence of Aspar in his selection.[2] However, it would be a mistake to equate Aspar's role in the selection of Marcian in 450 with the more commanding role that he would play later in the selection of Leo as emperor in 457. In 450, Aspar was still recovering from his dismal record in the Hun wars. He also had to contend with several other major players interested in choosing Theodosius' successor. In 457 Aspar could more readily impose his choice on a simpler field with fewer players.

Several scenarios have been proposed to explain what happened in 450. Our ancient sources divide over the role of Pulcheria, reflecting their attitude towards her later role at the Council of Chalcedon. Among modern scholars, Holum saw

---

[1] Jo. Malalas, 14.27; *Chron. Pasch.* s.a. 450; Cedr. I 603; *PLRE* 2, Fl Ardabur Aspar.
[2] Theophanes, AM 5931, 5943; Procopius, *Wars,* I :7; *PLRE* 2, Marcianus 8.

Pulcheria as the moving force who had recently replaced Chrysaphius as the emperor's chief advisor and was intent on reversing the results of the Second Council of Ephesus.[3] In contrast, Burgess emphasized the role of Aspar, while Zuckerman took a more nuanced view in which Aspar needed to negotiate matters with a rival group of generals led by the Isaurian general, Zeno.[4] Beers attempted to harmonize these models as "a careful compromise" among the two groups of generals, the Orthodox Church, and Pulcheria.[5]

It is significant that all of these models agree that Pulcheria played an important role in the choice of Marcian. This view is supported by the way in which both our Chalcedonian and anti-Chalcedonian sources portray her. Given the complex attitudes towards "powerful women" in the late Roman and Byzantine empires, orthodox sources sought to minimize the role of Pulcheria whereas the anti-Chalcedonians emphasized it and attacked her on multiple grounds, including a lurid story of forbidden love between Marcian and the "holy virgin."[6] As usual, the truth lies in between—one should discount the salacious stories, but it is likely that Pulcheria did play an important role in the negotiations, mainly because she was anxious for an emperor who would reverse the results of Second Ephesus, but also because she could offer dynastic legitimacy to the eventual choice. While she may not have been the person who suggested Marcian (that was probably Aspar) she almost certainly had to approve the choice and especially his religious views. She presumably had support from the orthodox clergy and the military power of Aspar, but both Zuckerman and Beers are probably right that there were other parties who had to be accommodated.

Stories that Theodosius had, on his death bed, named Marcian as his successor can be discounted as a likely fable to support and legitimize Marcian's rule.[7] If that had happened, there probably would not have been a month-long hiatus.

In making their choice, the east Romans had several options. First, the death of Theodosius II left the west Roman emperor Valentinian III, his son-in-law

---

[3] Holum 1982:208–11,
[4] Burgess 1994:62–6; Zuckerman 1994:176. *CAH XIV* (Lee), 42–3 also points to Aspar as the "kingmaker."
[5] Beers 2013 differs from other scholars in assuming that both Pulcheria and Aspar were still out of favor at the time of Theodosius' death, so that the fall of Chrysaphius was later and essentially a coup by Pulcheria with the support of Aspar. I have instead followed the sequence of events set out by Holum and others, in which Pulcheria re-emerges *before* the death of Theodosius II.
[6] Scott 2010:116–28; Burgess 1994:50–61.
[7] A.D. Lee in *CAH, XIV*, 42; *LRE*, vol. I:236–8; Beers 2013; C. Kelly 2009:233. Burgess 1994:55 discusses a story that Marcian was revealed to Theodosius II in a dream, which he later disclosed to "Aspar and all the other senators." He rightly views this as a later invention to strengthen Marcian's "extremely weak political position" (59). However, he regards the mention of Aspar as significant (62).

and cousin, as the empire's sole surviving male Augustus and male Theodosian. Valentinian was now in the same position that Theodosius II had been when the western emperor Honorius had died without an heir in 423. At that time Theodosius II initially considered ousting the usurper John and taking control of both halves of the empire himself, just as his grandfather had done in 394.[8] However, whether influenced by the unexpected arrival of Galla Placidia in Constantinople, or perhaps becoming persuaded of the limits of his own resources, Theodosius had instead decided to send an expedition to Italy to restore Placidia's family to the western throne.

In 450, Valentinian was already recognized by the east Romans as an Augustus. He could have been recognized as emperor in the east as well as in the west.[9] Moreover, it was frequently the case that in the event of the death of an Augustus, his successor was chosen by the senior surviving Augustus. The Theodosian dynasty itself had supposedly been established in this way in 379, when Gratian appointed Theodosius I to replace his late brother, Valens.[10]

Much of the later Monophysite criticism of Marcian focuses on this failure to obtain approval from Valentinian III, mainly as an attempt to undermine Marcian's legitimacy and hence the Council of Chalcedon. Burgess even suggests that this "snub" in 450 led to the "final split" between the two halves of the empire and the east losing all interest in the west. However, I think this overstates matters for several reasons. For one thing, Valentinian did eventually recognize Marcian in 452, in grudging acknowledgment of eastern military assistance during the Hun invasion of Italy. Similarly, in 457 the east Romans recognized the legitimacy of the western emperor Majorian. Finally, in the period from 467–73, the eastern emperor Leo I provided two emperors for the west, one of whom (Anthemius) cooperated in the joint east/west expedition against the Vandals in 468. I would suggest that it is the failure of the Vandal expedition in 468 that marks the "final break" between east and west in the fifth century.[11]

Tradition aside, acceptance of Valentinian as emperor in the east was always unlikely, since it had become clear since the death of Theodosius I in 395 that the eastern court intended to protect its separate status and go its own way.[12] For this

---

[8] See ch. IV, *supra*.
[9] Greatrex 2015:27.
[10] However, recent scholarship suggests that Theodosius may actually have forced his appointment on Gratian. Kulikowski 2019:91–2; Omissi 2018:255–63; Sivan 1996:198–211.
[11] Burgess 1994:49, 63–4. Not the break was ever "final," as shown by the brief emergence of a Gothic/Roman regime in Italy, and the reconquests of Jusinian. Procopius, *Wars*; Heather 2018:154–6, 287–302; Arnold 2014.
[12] While Marcian would recognize Valentinian III as the senior Augustus in his initial imperial announcements, Valentinian III did not recognize Marcian until March, 452. Burgess 1994:63.

reason, it would have required a major military campaign by the west Romans to assert their authority in the east.[13] However, Valentinian did not have the military resources to conquer the stronger eastern empire, particularly with both the Huns and the Vandals threatening Italy at the time.[14] Even though the impulsive Valentinian may have considered it, Aetius knew better. Therefore, the Roman empire was not going to be reunified under Valentinian III.

Despite this, the dynastic principle remained strong in Roman thinking about imperial succession.[15] Wickham has observed that the fifth century saw "a trend towards a view that imperial legitimacy was allied to genealogy."[16] Indeed, there would be only one occasion in the fifth century (in 457) when the eastern succession did not involve a biological or marital connection to the previous dynasty.

If the goal was to maintain the Theodosian dynasty, there might still have been a way for Valentinian III to have a role in the eastern succession. One possibility is that Valentinian III might have been permitted to choose who the next east Roman emperor would be, just as Gratian had picked Theodosius I in 379 and Leo I would later pick emperors for the west. Anicius Olybrius might have been a likely candidate, as he "may already have been betrothed" to the daughter of Valentinian III in 450. However, the date of the betrothal is unclear. Moreover, as a member of an old Roman family, Olybrius may have been too much of a westerner to be accepted in Constantinople. Indeed, this was likely why Leo I (and Geiseric) later thought that Olybrius would find support as a *western* emperor.[17] Another problem with this idea is that Valentinian III might have picked someone who was not acceptable to Pulcheria or to other powerful interests in Constantinople.[18] Finally, he was far away, and there was some urgency in resolving the succession crisis.

Once the idea of any involvement by Valentinian III was rejected, it was clear that the next best choice would be someone who had a dynastic connection to the Theodosians and was acceptable in Constantinople. McEvoy has pointed out how imperial women could be used as "living emblems" to convey legitimacy, as

---

[13] Burgess 1994:63–4.
[14] Priscus, fr. 30 (*FCH*:327–9). Valentinian later alleged that "Aetius wished to deprive him of power in the West, *as he had done in the East, insinuating that only because of Aetius did he not go to remove Marcian from the throne.*" (emphasis added).
[15] McEvoy, 2019:115–16; Börm 2015:240, 250, 259–604; Croke 2015:98–9; Hekster 2023:31, 243.
[16] Wickham 2009:96–9.
[17] Burgess 1994:64. See also the difficulties faced by the easterner Anthemius in being accepted in the west. Arnold 2014:16–20, 125.
[18] Burgess 1994:64 suggests that it was Aspar's desire to have his own candidate selected that was the reason that Valentinian III was not consulted.

in the unsuccessful case of the fourth century usurper Procopius.[19] For this reason, the best answer in 450 was Pulcheria, a crowned, "born in the purple" Augusta of east Rome, the child and grandchild of Theodosian emperors, and a person who was admired for her great piety and many acts of charity in Constantinople.[20] However, there were two obvious problems with this solution—first, no woman had ever ruled the Roman empire alone as an Augusta; and second, Pulcheria had taken a vow of virginity.

There are several interesting points about the "Pulcheria alone" argument. It is true that no Augusta had ever ruled all or part of the Roman empire alone. There had been women with the title of Augusta who had effectively "ruled" through their children, e.g., the Severan empresses, the Palmyrene usurper Zenobia, or the more recent example of Galla Placidia.[21] But they did not rule alone in their own name.

How strong was this feeling against female rulership in the fifth century empire? As it happens, at about this time, the west Romans were dealing with the "Honoria affair," in which Valentinian's sister (a crowned but unmarried Augusta) had apparently sent an offer of marriage to, of all people, Attila.[22] Attila demanded his new bride and threatened that "if she did not receive the scepter of sovereignty, he would avenge her."[23] The west Romans rejected this, and said that "she had no right to the scepter since the rule of the Roman state belonged not to females but to males."[24] Whether or not this was correct, and as respected and powerful as Pulcheria was in Constantinople, it was unrealistic to consider that she would ever be secure ruling alone.

And yet, Pulcheria *did* rule alone in Constantinople for at least one month. Everyone probably viewed this as a temporary situation while negotiations went on behind the scenes. And yet she was in charge. If nothing else shows this, consider that one of her first acts was to order the execution of her old enemy,

---

[19] McEvoy 2016b:154–79.
[20] There was also the estranged widow of Theodosius II, the Augusta Eudocia. However, she was not a Theodosian except by marriage, and she had retired to a religious life in Jerusalem. Burgess 1994:64. One can only speculate about her possible role in 450 had she remained in Constantinople. Cf. Ariadne in 491.
[21] Beard 2021:238. In general, Langford 2013 on Julia Domna; on Zenobia, see Andrade 2018; Millar 1993; Stoneman 1992. See also Herrin 2013; James 2001 Angelova 2015. On "child-emperor" rule, McEvoy 2013. Placidia was not given the title of Augusta until the general Constantius III became a co-emperor. However, her unmarried daughter received the title. McEvoy 2021; Salisbury 2015; Sivan 2011.
[22] Meier 2017:42–61. McEvoy suggests that Honoria's unmarried state may have resulted from concerns that her marriage might create a rival to her brother. McEvoy 2016b.
[23] Priscus fr. 17, 20 (*FCH*).
[24] Priscus fr. 20 (*FCH*). One can only imagine how Galla Placidia, who had recently died, would have felt about that point of view. Meier 2017 questions whether it is even accurate.

Chrysaphius, which was duly carried out by Jordanes, one of Aspar's associates.[25] Not only did this show an alignment between Aspar's interests and those of Pulcheria, but this rough justice allowed Aspar to gratify his ally, Jordanes.[26]

While there must have been considerable pressure to quickly choose a new emperor, Pulcheria could not be ignored. She was a strong personality, with considerable support from the Orthodox Church and the populace. The solution was a compromise between the competing principles of dynasty and selection—the new emperor would be married to Pulcheria, and they would reign together. A precedent existed in the marriage of the Theodosian princess Galla Placidia to the general Constantius in 416, which had preserved the western branch of the Theodosians for another generation.[27]

But Pulcheria presented a special problem—her vow of virginity.[28] If the solution to the first issue was dictated by political and military factors, then the solution to this second issue was found in theology. The result was that Pulcheria would be married to the new emperor in name only. Such spiritual marriages were not unknown in the developing asceticism of the late fourth and early fifth centuries. In balancing between the church's need for Christian procreation and the ascetic desire to renounce worldly passions, it had come to accept marriages in which the partners had children but then lived separately in celibacy while remaining married. An example of this was Melania the Younger, who is of particular interest because she met with the imperial family (including Pulcheria) during her visit to Constantinople in 437.[29]

While it is impossible today to say who came up with this solution, it may have been Pulcheria herself. It is more likely to have come from someone like Pulcheria, who was familiar with orthodox doctrine, than from a general like Aspar or Zeno. And it was critical to Pulcheria that any solution be reconciled with her vow of virginity.[30] A spiritual or celibate marriage might be a way to do this that would be consistent with her orthodox beliefs. It is probable that

---

[25] *PLRE* 2, Chrysaphius; Marcell. comes, s.a. 450, n. 3; Chron. Pasch, s.a. 450, 80 n. 264); Holum 1982:208; Hekster 2023:232, 253.
[26] *PLRE* 2, Fl. Iordanes 3; Holum 1982:208.
[27] See ch. IV, *supra*. Cf. Cassiodorus (sixth century) blaming the decline of the western empire on Placidia's "soft" rule. Arnold 2014:48–9.
[28] Along with the failure to consult Valentinian III, this became one of the main points in the subsequent monophysite attacks on the legitimacy of Pulcheria and Marcian. Burgess 1994:60, 63.
[29] See ch. VI, *supra*. On Melania, Clark 2021. See also John of Nikiu, discussed by Watts 2013:77, on Egyptian monks who told Theodosius and Eudocia they would not produce a male heir, after which "they abandoned all conjugal intercourse, and lived, *by mutual consent, in befitting chastity.*" (emphasis added).
[30] Burgess 1994:64–5.

Pulcheria had to approve her consort, someone of solidly orthodox religious views who would commit to reversing the decrees of Second Ephesus.[31]

Aspar himself might have been a candidate, but there were several obstacles. For one thing, he may have been married at the time, and divorce was unlikely under views about "Christian monogamy."[32] More significantly, unless Aspar was willing to change his religious views (and, as we shall see in 457, he was not) he was an Arian, and therefore unlikely to be accepted by the Orthodox Church.[33] He might also have been unacceptable to Aspar's military rivals, such as Zeno or Apollonius (although Marcian, the final choice, was closely connected to Aspar, he was neither a "barbarian" nor an Arian). Finally, there may have been candidates from the aristocratic east Roman families (such as the Anthemii).[34]

In the end, the choice was Marcian. He was said to be Pulcheria's choice, which may well be true since he had many qualities which were important to her. He was a "Roman" from the Balkans with orthodox religious views, which was crucial to Pulcheria.[35] He had military experience, having served under both Ardaburius the Elder and Aspar. Since he apparently was a senator, he may have already been known to Pulcheria.[36]

However, the decisive reason Marcian was chosen was undoubtedly that he was the candidate of Aspar.[37] Choosing a trusted subordinate for the throne fits into a pattern that Aspar would employ again in 457 and is consistent with the "partnership" model of imperial rule.[38]

Yet while some refer to Aspar as a "kingmaker" in this succession crisis,[39] he may not have acted alone. Kelly suggests that Marcian may have been a

---

[31] This is why Pulcheria and Marcian are so vilified in the anti-Chalcedonian literature. Burgess 1994. Watts 2013:275–6 cites the *History of Dioscorus* as a text that compares Pulcheria's abandonment of her virginity to the sin of Eve. On Pulcheria's role in the Marian movement and the *Theotokos* controversy, see Angelova 2015:234–59; Holum 198:130–74.
[32] Herrin 2013:2, 27, 174.
[33] See ch. VIII, *infra*.
[34] McEvoy 2019a:122. However, no member of this family seems to have been prominent c. 450.
[35] *PLRE* 2, Marcianus 8; Beers 2013.
[36] Both *LRE* vol. I:236, and Gibbon, ch. XXXIV refer to him as a senator, but *PLRE* 2 does not. Starting in the mid- fourth century senior military officers were granted senatorial status in Constantinople. Davenport 2019:20. While it is possible that Marcian became a senator as a result of his military services, he had not been a *magister militum*. Marcian is sometimes said to have been a former tribune. Theod. Lect., *Epit.*, 354; Jo. Malalas, 14.27; *Chron. Pasch* s.a. 450. If so, he was appointed by the emperor, Kulikowski 2019:13, and may have been known to the imperial family.
[37] Burgess 1994:62.
[38] See ch. I, *supra*.
[39] A.D. Lee in *CAH XIV*:43; Kelly 2009:232–3; Blockley 1992:67.

compromise candidate because of his relative anonymity.[40] But if Marcian was a "compromise candidate" and Aspar had to contend with other players in 450, who were they?

Zuckerman has argued that in the summer of 450 the most powerful military figure in the east was not Aspar, but the Isaurian general, Zeno.[41] As he points out, Aspar no longer held any of the top eastern military commands and commanded no troops, while Zeno commanded the regional army in the east and his ally, Apollonius, held one of the two praesental commands. Moreover, after his accession, Marcian adopted policies which Zeno was known to favor, including the cessation of payments to Attila and a generally more aggressive strategy towards the Huns. In addition, Marcian granted the title of "patrician" to Zeno in 451 (as he apparently also did with Aspar), which Zuckerman characterizes as a reward for supporting Marcian's accession.[42] Nor was there any more talk of a military expedition against Zeno, and he remained in his post as *m.m. per Orientem* until his death, likely in 453.[43] On the other hand, Zeno did not have the long-standing connection to the Theodosians (particularly Pulcheria) and to the senatorial and civil officials in Constantinople that Aspar and his family had cultivated over decades.

Aspar and Zeno each had reasons to compromise, and so Marcian may have been their joint candidate.[44] A negotiated settlement would have been consistent with what we know of Aspar's approach. A compromise might also have been attractive to Zeno. As Kelly says, "In agreeing to Marcian's elevation, Zeno seized the opportunity to dominate imperial policymaking without having to fight."[45] Since the legitimacy of the new regime would be shaky, a civil war might have been fatal to the eastern empire. If the choice of Marcian was a compromise by Aspar and Zeno, then the result is truly ironic. As Zuckerman remarks, "the pious emperor Marcian, remembered for centuries to

---

[40] Kelly 2009:232. The choice of a junior officer as emperor recalls the military politics that led to the selection of Jovian after the sudden death of the emperor Julian in the fourth century. Kulikowski 2019:32–3.
[41] Zuckerman 1994:172–5. Any reference to "Zeno" should also include his allies, such as Apollonius. Elton notes the emergence of several high-ranking Isaurian officers in the 440s and observes that "Aspar and his supporters were important, but they were not the only important figures at court." Elton 2000:396.
[42] Ibid.; *CAH XIV*:43 n. 62. *PLRE* 2, Zenon 6 dates this honor to "late 451." Aspar seems to have received this title in "early 451," *PLRE* 2, Fl. Ardabur Aspar; Roberto 2009.
[43] Zuckerman 1994:174–5 places the death of Zeno in 451, but I prefer 453. That seems to be when Ardaburius the Younger succeeded Zeno as *m.m. per Orientem*.
[44] A.D. Lee in *CAH XIV*:43, citing Zuckerman 1994.
[45] C. Kelly 2009:233.

come for his orthodoxy, was the creature of an Arian, Fl. Aspar, and a pagan, Fl. Zeno."[46]

There may have been another factor which made Marcian a good choice. Not only was Marcian of mature age—in 450, he was 58 and Pulcheria was 51—but he was a widower with one daughter.[47] For this reason, it may well be that Marcian was chosen in part *because* he did not have a suitable male heir. A new emperor who already had an adult male son (as Aspar did) would mean a new dynasty. Marcian did not present this problem. Moreover, a man of his age would not be expected to have a lengthy reign, so it was likely that there would be another scramble for the throne sooner rather than later.[48] And when that scramble occurred, the best link to the Theodosians might be Marcian's unmarried daughter, which opened up opportunities for potential husbands. Indeed, this was exactly what happened.

If Marcian was a good choice, he was also a surprising choice because his background was respectable but not particularly distinguished. Coming from humble beginnings, Marcian had risen in the army to command a unit under Aspar's father during the Persian War of 421–2. Afterwards, he served as a *domesticus*, a senior officer under Aspar.[49] We have seen that Marcian accompanied Aspar on the African expedition of 431–5 where he supposedly was captured by the Vandals but later released.[50] We do not know anything about his later career, although it is possible that he either retired from the army or perhaps continued to serve under Aspar in a different capacity.[51] In 450, he seems to have had some status as a member of the Constantinopolitan senate.

That the choice of Marcian was surprising to his contemporaries can be seen from the several "miracle" stories about him.[52] The common theme is how unexpected (one can imply "divine") events repeatedly seemed to preserve his life, and to prefigure his future role as emperor. One such story describes how he

---

[46] Zuckerman 1994:176 refers to an "equilibrium" between a "German" faction and an "Isaurian" faction, a position questioned by others. Cf. Croke 2021:102–5. On the paganism of Zeno, Burgess 1992:876–7.
[47] Beers 2013.
[48] This may also have been a consideration in Ariadne's choice of Anastasius in 491. However, unlike Marcian, Anastasius lived for another 27 years.
[49] *PLRE* 2, Marcianus 8.
[50] See ch. V, *supra*.
[51] The sources claim that he served as *domesticus* for "fifteen years." If this began during or just after the Persian War, then he might have retired around 437, after he and Aspar had returned from Africa. He would only have been about 45 at the time, so conceivably he could still have had a military role. John Malalas, 14.28; C. Kelly 2009:232.
[52] Burgess 1994:58–9, 62; Angelova 2015:157, on his obscurity. Cf. Croke 1978:5–9, who describes him as "a vigorous Thracian general." However, his service as a long-time aide of the Ardaburii was the key to his selection.

was falsely accused of murder during his journey to join the east Roman army but was freed when the actual murderer unexpectedly confessed.[53] We have already seen another example, in which the Vandal king Geiseric allegedly foresaw Marcian's future as emperor and freed him from captivity.[54]

Such stories appealed to ancient audiences and appear throughout classical and Christian literature.[55] However, the stories about Marcian seem to be trying to make the point that his eventual accession was divinely favored. As with Pulcheria, this may reflect orthodox attempts to counter lingering concerns about his legitimacy, which later became a major argument of those who opposed his role in the Council of Chalcedon.[56] An official attempt to bolster his legitimacy can also be seen in the issuance of a gold *solidus* in 450 that showed Christ conducting (and thereby blessing) the marriage of Marcian and Pulcheria.[57] Similarly, an impressive Column of Marcian was erected in the early 450s in a part of Constantinople that was close to a palace of Pulcheria's, perhaps to remind people of how her lineage buttressed his legitimacy.[58] Finally, the coronation ceremonies may also have been designed to address this issue. In a separate ceremony, Marcian received the diadem and purple robe of an Augustus from Pulcheria.[59] One source indicates that the Patriarch Anatolius may have lent his religious aura to the coronation, although this is debated.[60]

By December, 450, Marcian was married to Pulcheria and had been crowned as the new Augustus of the eastern Roman empire.[61] With Zeno pacified and Attila focusing his attentions on the western Roman empire, Marcian had time to establish his rule.

---

[53] Evagrius, *HE*, book II, ch. 1; Priscus, fr. 18 (*FCH*). Burgess 1994:60 notes that Evagrius starts his life of Marcian "with a collection of prodigies and signs which foretold his future greatness," possibly a rebuttal to monophysite stories of contrary signs.

[54] See ch. V, *supra*.

[55] There are similarities to the origin stories for Justin I and for Leo I. Kaldellis 2018:10–1. Marcian's origin story is yet another, which suggests a trope in our sources used to explain the rise of unlikely emperors.

[56] Scott 2010:115–32; Scott 2009:81–57; Watts 2013:269–84.

[57] Kent 1984:.95; Holum 1982:209. This coin was based on the "marriage coin" issued for the wedding of Valentinian III in 437, which showed Theodosius II as the *pronubis*. In 450, there was no eastern Augustus who could act as *pronubis*, so Christ is shown as *pronubis*. Arnold has suggested to author that this may have been to show it would be a spiritual marriage. A similar coin was issued in 491 for the marriage of Ariadne to Anastasius, see chap. XIII, *infra*.

[58] Angelova 2015:157.

[59] Cf. C. Kelly:233–4; Burgess 1994:67; Holum 1982:208.

[60] Burgess 1994:56–7, 67 n. 82, cites the *Epitome* of Symeon the Logothete; on the role of the patriarch in 457, see Const. Porphyr., *De ceremoniis*. In the absence of either an Augustus or Augusta, this role could be taken by the Patriarch of Constantinople.

[61] In a letter to Pope Leo dated Nov. 22, 450, Pulcheria referred to Marcian as "my consort." Holum 1982:211–12.

Foreign and Military Policies of Marcian

The major foreign policy problem that confronted Marcian in 450 was how to deal with the Huns. In the final months of Theodosius II's reign, the east Romans had finally reached a treaty with Attila. A key provision was that they would pay arrears from the prior treaty, and then make increased annual payments to Attila.

Shortly after Marcian became emperor, Attila sent envoys to Constantinople to collect "the appointed tribute."[62] Perhaps influenced more by Zeno than by Aspar, Marcian said he would no longer make the annual payments, but might give "gifts" if they kept the peace.[63] Giving "gifts" to an allied king maintained the superior status of the Roman emperor while paying "tribute" did not. These "gifts" could also be disguised as salary associated with honorary ranks in the Roman army, although there is debate over whether Attila ever accepted such a title.[64] However, Marcian was taking a different stance from the policy of conciliation that had prevailed during the last years of Theodosius II.

Attila ultimately decided not to press matters with the east Romans at this time, but to instead launch two campaigns against the west Romans (Gaul in 451 and Italy in 452). In part, this may relate to the "Honoria affair." However, Jordanes suggests that this decision was also encouraged by Geiseric, and Priscus says that in 451 Attila acted "to lay up a store of favor with Geiseric" by attacking the Visigoths. However, Clover concludes that the Vandals remained neutral during the two Hun campaigns and that Priscus' comment may reflect Attila's strategy to keep the Vandals from using their navy to assist the west Romans. As to Bachrach's suggestion that Aspar (now back in power) may have wanted to avoid another round with the Huns and encouraged Geiseric to persuade Attila to march west, Clover finds the suggestion unsupported and contrary to the fact that Ardaburius the Younger fought the Huns in the Balkans in 451.

There is some evidence that Marcian sent an envoy to the west Romans to discuss a joint strategy against the Huns as early as 450. There are even reports that Marcian personally campaigned against the Huns in 451, perhaps to create a diversion from the Hun attack on Gaul. If so, this was the first time an east Roman emperor had taken the field since 394. Hydatius tells us that in 452 Marcian sent "auxiliaries" to the west to assist Aetius and that the east Romans

---

[62] Priscus, fr. 20 (*FCH*).
[63] Ibid.; McEvoy 2014:249–50.
[64] C. Kelly 2009:235; Meier 2017:53 n. 49.

also attacked the Huns in their "settlements" (a diversionary attack on the Hun homeland?). Perhaps with reluctance, Valentinian III finally granted recognition to Marcian on March 30, 452.[65]

Although Attila was preoccupied with the "Honoria affair" and his raids into the western empire, he did not forget his quarrel with Marcian.[66] After leading the Huns into Gaul in 451 and Italy in 452 with mixed results, Attila resumed his demand for the east Roman payments, while simultaneously threatening war.[67] The east Romans sent an ambassador to negotiate, but Attila refused to see him.[68] The ambassador was the *m.m. praesentalis* Apollonius, "an associate of Zeno." This may show the influence of Zeno's faction. Since he did not bring the tribute, this was perceived by Attila as an insult. He compared Apollonius unfavorably to the "better and more kingly men" that he had negotiated with in 449 (i.e., Anatolius and Nomus). Attila may also have recalled that Apollonius' brother had been involved with Zeno in the matter of the intended bride for Constantius. So, matters stood in late 452, and Blockley is right to conclude "that war would undoubtedly have broken out in 453 had not Attila died before the campaign could begin."[69]

The unexpected death of Attila in 453 was a vast stroke of luck for the east Roman empire.[70] Without Attila, the short-lived Hun empire rapidly broke up, as his sons quarreled over the succession and subject peoples rebelled. The east Romans became adept at manipulating the new political situation that emerged in the Balkans. The great Hun threat was over.[71]

A related development was the gradual improvement of relations between the east and west Roman governments.[72] While this may have been the result of eastern assistance against the Huns, it may also reflect the realism of Aetius and Valentinian III, who still considered himself the senior Augustus. This improvement would end with Valentinian's murder in 455 but would briefly revive in 457 with the accession of Majorian in the west.

---

[65] Blockley 1992:68; McEvoy 2014:250 n. 29; Maenchen-Helfen 1973:131; LRE, vol. I:295; Hydatius 146 (154); Meier 2017, n. 61.
[66] Priscus, fr. 15, 20, 98 (*FCH*); Kelly 2009:235.
[67] Priscus fr. 23 (*FCH*); Blockley 1992:68; C. Kelly 2009:264.
[68] *PLRE* 2, Apollonius 3; Priscus fr. 23 (*FCH*).
[69] Blockley 1992:68.
[70] It has been suggested that Attila's death was the result of a second (and more successful) assassination attempt, perhaps assisted by the west Romans. C. Kelly 2009:264–6; Babcock 2005:248–54. However, it is impossible to know this from our sources.
[71] Blockley 1992:67; Maenchen-Helfen 1973:143.
[72] Klaasen 2012:152.

Up to this point, we have not seen much evidence of Aspar's role in Marcian's administration. With regard to the Huns, the evidence points more to the influence of Zeno. However, this seems to change in 453.

For one thing, Zeno disappears from our sources around this time, suggesting that he may have died.[73] Zeno's successor as *m.m. per Orientem* was Aspar's eldest son, Ardaburius the Younger.[74] Ardaburius had recently distinguished himself in fighting the Huns in the Balkans.[75] Replacing Zeno with Ardaburius in the important military command at Antioch was a major step in Aspar's consolidation of power in the east Roman state. Aspar himself seems to have finally succeeded Apollonius as a *m.m. praesentalis* at some point during the 450s.[76]

Another development which relates to Aspar's growing power was the re-settlement of groups of Goths as imperial "federates" in the depopulated Balkan provinces. After the formerly-Hun subjects defeated Attila's sons at the Battle of the Nedao in 454, several groups of Goths sought permission from Marcian to settle south of the Danube. Such settlement was viewed favorably by the east Romans "in order to assist in the protection and repopulation of the Balkans."[77] Two of these Gothic groups deserve our attention because their conflicting interests would dominate Balkan affairs into the 480s. One group settled in Thrace and was led by Triarius. The other settled in Pannonia, in the northwestern Balkans, and was led by Valamir and his brothers Theodemir and Vidimer.[78] Their royal house was known as the Amals.

The Thracian Goths became an opportunity for Aspar to develop a new source of military power outside the structure of the east Roman army. While Aspar was involved in the re-settlement of these Goths as a Roman officer, he may also have drawn on his ethnic heritage to form personal relations with their leadership. Whether the Goths understood the difference is unclear. It has been suggested that Aspar concluded a treaty (*foedus*) with the Thracian Goths on behalf of the eastern empire, but the Goths may have regarded it as creating a

---

[73] Zeno was still alive in late 451 *PLRE* 2, Fl. Zenon 6, but was replaced by Ardaburius as *m.m. per Orientem* by 453. *PLRE* 2, Ardabur iunior 1. Jordanes merely says that Zeno died during the reign of Marcian. Jordanes, *Rom.*, 333; Priscus fr. 29 (*FCH*).
[74] *PLRE* 2, Ardabur iunior 1. He was also honored with the rank of *patricius*.
[75] *Suda* A 3803; *PLRE* 2, Ardabur iunior 1.
[76] *PLRE* 2, Aspar. Aspar was in this post by 457, so the appointment could have happened around the time Zeno seems to have died or perhaps not until the accession of Leo I.
[77] Blockley 1992:71.
[78] Wolfram 1998:257–61. This group of Goths may have already been settled in Pannonia by Attila, so that Marcian was merely recognizing an existing situation. Arnold 2014:144.

personal loyalty to him.[79] Aspar's third wife, who he may have married at this time, was a high-status Gothic woman who was closely related to their leader, Triarius. The sources are confusing, but it appears that she was either a sister or a daughter of Triarius.[80] Triarius also had a son, Theoderic, who later succeeded him, and was known as Theoderic Strabo ("the squinter"). After Aspar's death, Strabo claimed to be Aspar's heir and demanded his titles and status from the east Roman government.[81]

It is also worth recalling that Aspar's third and youngest son (perhaps the child of this third wife) was named Ermanaric.[82] The name is that of a Gothic king from the fourth century and may suggest that Aspar's wife was a member of the Gothic royal family. Just as Aspar's first marriage to Plintha's daughter had advanced the Ardaburii *within* the east Roman military aristocracy, these connections helped to augment Aspar's status *outside* the regular Roman army by giving him access to a valuable source of troops.[83]

As for the Goths who settled in Pannonia, their leadership would eventually pass to the son of one of their kings. Historians helpfully refer to him as Theoderic the Amal, as opposed to his rival, Theoderic Strabo. In accord with a provision of the treaty made with the east Romans, he spent almost a decade of his youth as an honored hostage in Constantinople.[84] During this time, he came to know many of the leading figures in the east Roman government, including Aspar.[85]

In short, in the 450s we see Aspar consolidating his military power in two ways—first, by increasing his control over the military structure of the east Roman army, and second, by creating a separate base of support among the Thracian Gothic federates. This highlights the duality in Aspar's identity as an east Roman general who was also capable of attracting important "barbarian" support. However, there is no evidence of Aspar leading military campaigns under Marcian.[86]

---

[79] Laniado 2015:16–24.
[80] *PLRE* 2, Fl. Ardabur Aspar. The confusion arises from Theophanes, who at AM 4964 refers to Strabo as Aspar's "brother-in-law" whereas at AM 5970 as the nephew of Aspar's wife. *LRE*, vol. I:316 n. 3, followed Brooks 1893 in relying on AM 5970. But Wolfram 1998:32 and Maenchen-Helfen 1973:166, rely on AM 4964. At the time of Aspar's death, he was reported to have had a Gothic "concubine" who may or may not have been this third wife. See ch. XII, *infra*.
[81] See ch. XIII, *infra*.
[82] See ch. III, *supra*. Wolfram 1998:32.
[83] See Arnold 2014 on the value of marriage into barbarian "royalty."
[84] Jordanes, *Getica*, 271; Croke 2021:54; Arnold 2014:144; Wolfram 1988:262–3.
[85] Croke 2021:54; Crawford 2019:44–5
[86] Beers 2013 suggests that the combination of Marcian and the formidable Pulcheria, at least until her death in 453, was "more than capable of preventing their generals from taking a larger role than their offices required."

This may be because during Marcian's reign military campaigns were generally limited and defensive in nature.[87] Both Anthemius and Ardaburius the Younger were successful against raiders in the Balkans, and Ardaburius later fought off some nomad attacks in Syria. Similarly, Priscus reports the repulse of some tribes who had been raiding southern Egypt.[88] The Persian front generally remained quiet, other than some Roman activity in Armenia and Lazica to prevent the expansion of Persian influence in those areas.[89] None of these efforts seem to have directly involved Aspar. However, it is likely that he spent time in the Balkans, dealing with the aftermath of the death of Attila and the re-settlement of the Thracian Goths.

The one area where there appears to have been no military activity at all was Africa.[90] This is particularly surprising since in 455 the Vandals, taking advantage of the confusion following the assassination of Valentinian III, sacked Rome and carried off female members of the Theodosian family, including the widow and daughters of Valentinian III.[91] Although this was seen as a great affront by the east Romans, it appears that Marcian did little more than dispatch an ambassador with a futile demand to return the Theodosian women. This inaction required an explanation from historians, and it may be the source of the story about Marcian's supposed pledge never to fight against the Vandals.[92] However, there is some indication that public outrage in Constantinople may have finally led Marcian to begin preparations for an expedition against the Vandals in late 456.[93] If so, Marcian's death in January, 457 put an end to this initiative. The story may also suggest some weakening of Aspar's influence, since an attack on the Vandals would have gone against Aspar's preferred policy of non-intervention.

In fact, there are other indications that Marcian was beginning to adopt a more independent streak in the later years of his reign. He advanced his son-in-law, the general Anthemius, in ways that seemed to make him a favorite to become Marcian's successor. In addition, Marcian appointed the official Tatianus to several high civil positions, and we know that Aspar would later oppose the choice of Tatianus as consul by the emperor Leo. Had Marcian lived longer, might his relationship with Aspar have developed along confrontational lines

---

[87] An exception being Marcian's activity in 451/452 to distract Attila during his attacks on the west.
[88] Priscus, fr. 26, 27 (*FCH*); Zuckerman 1994:176.
[89] Blockley 1992:169–70
[90] Gibbon finds it difficult to explain the "indifference" of Marcian towards the Vandals and falls back on Procopius' story. Gibbon, ch. XXX; Blockley 1992:68, citing Jordanes, *Romana*, 333; Clover 1966:170–3 (blames the influence of Aspar).
[91] Clover 1966:156–63.
[92] See ch. V, *supra*.
[93] See Theodor Lector, *HE* 367 and the articles cited in McEvoy 2014:250 n. 31.

similar to those that later developed between Aspar and Leo? Perhaps it was this show of increasing independence that led Aspar to conclude that the next emperor needed to be bound to him by marital arrangements that would guarantee an eventual succession by the Ardaburii.

Religious Policies of Marcian

With Pulcheria as Augusta, it was clear that a high priority would be to reverse the decrees of Second Ephesus.[94] In 451, Marcian called yet another ecumenical council to re-consider the doctrinal controversies. Unlike Second Ephesus, this council would be at Chalcedon, conveniently close to the imperial court and to the Balkans, the latter bring significant since Marcian might need to campaign against the Huns.[95] Not surprisingly, the Council of Chalcedon quickly condemned Eutyches and his allies, rehabilitated the prelates who had been expelled at Second Ephesus, and adopted a doctrinal formulation that would become a cornerstone of Nicene orthodoxy. However, anti-Chalcedonian views such as monophysitism would remain strong in the east for some time, and they would produce a literature in which Pulcheria and Marcian would be demonized.[96]

The irony is that Chalcedon continued a Theodosian trend in which the east Roman government and the Orthodox Church took an increasingly hard line against Arians. Although this would seem contrary to the role of Aspar in Marcian's regime, there appears to have been "grudging acceptance" of the religious difference, and (until the early 460s) a willingness to employ Arian generals.[97] Nonetheless, popular religious sentiment against Arians remained very strong in Constantinople in the mid-fifth century. Aspar undoubtedly was aware of this, which may have been a key consideration for him in 457 when the succession question arose again.

Dynastic Issues of Marcian

Marcian would be remembered as a popular and successful emperor.[98] During his reign, the empire managed to avoid any major wars on its frontiers. Not only

---

[94] See ch. VI, *supra*.
[95] Maenchen-Helfen 1973:131.
[96] Burgess 1994; Scott 2010; Watts 2013:269–84 in C. Kelly 2013.
[97] See ch. IV, *supra*; Gaddis 2005; Cohen in Arnold 2016:518.
[98] *ODB*, vol. 2, Marcian, 1297.

did Marcian stop the payments to the Huns, but he also repealed some of the special taxes that had been imposed in the later years of Theodosius II to fund these payments, a decision that was particularly popular with the senatorial class. Even with this remission of taxes, he was said to have left a very large surplus in the imperial treasury. Moreover, in contrast to the violent religious conflicts that had dominated the later years of Theodosius II, the Council of Chalcedon formulated a position that was widely accepted in Constantinople and much of the Roman east, although certainly not by everyone and particularly not in Egypt and Syria.[99] The lasting image of Marcian as an orthodox hero and a "good emperor" is shown by the fact that when Anastasius became emperor in 491, the crowd in Constantinople is said to have chanted "Reign like Marcian!"[100]

When Marcian died in 457, many of the key figures from the succession crisis of 450 were no longer on the stage. The empress Pulcheria had died in 453. Her sister-in-law, the empress Eudocia, lived on in Jerusalem until her death in 460 but she played no further role in imperial politics. Among the generals, Zeno had apparently died around 453 and Apollonius no longer held office and may also have died.

Important changes had also occurred in the west Roman branch of the imperial family. The aged empress Galla Placidia had died in 450. Lacking her restraint, and no longer having to fear Attila (who had died in 453), in 454 her son Valentinian III unwisely murdered Aetius, the veteran west Roman military commander. Valentinian himself was then murdered in 455 by vengeful soldiers who had served Aetius. In the resulting chaos, the Vandals sacked Rome and abducted Valentinian's widowed empress and her two daughters. Power in the west eventually came to rest in the hands of a "barbarian" general named Ricimer.[101]

When Marcian died on January 27, 457, there was only one person in Constantinople who had a strong claim to the throne as a Theodosian by marriage.[102] That person was Marcian's son-in-law, the general and patrician, Anthemius.

---

[99] Watts in C. Kelly (ed.) 2013; Burgess 1994.
[100] Const. Porphyr., *De Ceremonis*, I.92 (425); *LRE*, vol. I:432; Croke 2001:96.
[101] Ricimer was entirely of barbarian descent. His mother was the daughter of the Visigothic king, Wallia, who had defeated the Siling Vandals and the Alans in 418. His father was of royal Suevic blood, and his sister married a king of the Burgundians. *PLRE* 2, Fl. Ricimer 2.
[102] As we will see, there were two other Theodosians-by-marriage, but neither had as strong a claim. Valentinian III had two daughters, who in 457 were both captives of the Vandals in Carthage. One had been married to Geiseric's son, Huneric, but a Vandal candidate was unthinkable. The other had either been married or betrothed to the western aristocrat Olybrius, who had escaped the Vandal raid. However, even if they had married, he was a west Roman with fewer connections in the east.

Marcian's only surviving child was a daughter named Aelia Marcia Euphemia. In 453, she had married Anthemius, the grandson and namesake of a man who had been praetorian prefect of the east in 405–14.[103] This is the same family that was supposedly so threatening to Pulcheria that it led to her vow of virginity. An interesting question is whether Pulcheria approved this marriage, but since Pulcheria died in 453 it is unclear whether she was still alive at the time of the wedding. Anthemius' father had ancestral connections to the Constantinians. After the marriage, Anthemius was given military responsibilities in the Balkans. He apparently performed well enough to be named by Marcian as consul for 455 and received the title of *patricius*.[104] It is not unreasonable to suspect that Marcian was grooming Anthemius as his potential successor.[105] However, Marcian never made him an Augustus or even a Caesar, the title which was often used for the heir apparent.

What Aspar may have thought of this is unknown. Anthemius would yet come to wear the purple, but not in the way that Marcian may have intended. For when Marcian died in January, 457, the situation was the same as that which had occurred when Theodosius II had died in 450—there was no clear successor and the east Roman throne was again available.[106]

---

[103] Kulikowski 2019:216–26; MacGeorge 2002:178–26.
[104] McEvoy 2014:258, citing Mathisen 1991:195, suggests that Anthemius was the *only* patrician created by Marcian. Both Aspar and Zeno were given the title of *patricius* c.451 and Ardaburius apparently received it around 453 (perhaps after the death of Zeno). While giving the title to Anthemius in 455 perhaps took something away from the Ardaburii, the title was rare but not limited. Cf. McEvoy 2014:258; Mathisen 1991:195.
[105] Beers 2013.
[106] *PLRE* 2, Anthemius 3, Marcianus 8, Aelia Marcia Euphemia 6.

8

Aspar and the Choice of Leo (457)

Choosing an Emperor

At first glance, the situation that existed in Constantinople in January, 457 seems similar to the crisis that had occurred in July, 450 on the death of Theodosius II. In both cases, the reigning emperor died without a direct male descendant.[1]

However, the situations were different in several ways. One key difference was that in 450 the death was unexpected, whereas that was probably not the case in 457. For one thing, Theodosius was only forty-nine when he died in an accident whereas Marcian was sixty-five and in poor health, so serious thought about Marcian's successor was likely to have occurred.

On January 26, 457 Marcian took part in a religious procession that required him to walk seven miles from the palace to the Hebdomon. On a previous occasion, the patriarch Anatolius was so embarrassed by the aged emperor's display of piety that he left his carriage and followed the emperor on foot. It is possible that Marcian had been present at the time of the original procession in 447, which might have included Pulcheria. Perhaps his observance was a tribute to Pulcheria and her family, and a public reminder of his connection to them. Although Marcian had made the full march in previous years, this time he had to return early to the palace, where he died the next day. Croke identified this procession as the annual commemoration of Theodosius II's dramatic response to the destructive earthquake of 447.[2] Marcian had continued to perform this act of penance annually, but this time a barefoot walk of seven miles on a January day was too much for him.[3]

---

[1] Croke 1978:5–9; *CAH XIV*:45 n. 78.
[2] Croke 1978:6–9, citing Theodore Lector. On the earthquake of 447, see ch. VI, *supra*.
[3] Croke 1978:9, citing John of Nikiu *c*. 87; Van Nuffelen 2012 in Grig and Kelly 2012:189–90.

Concerns about Marcian's health may have arisen even earlier. Malalas comments that Marcian suffered from "swollen" or "inflamed" feet.[4] He also says that this condition had been aggravated by Marcian's reaction to an incident in the Hippodrome in August, 456 when the Greens had rioted over his alleged favoritism towards the rival Blues.[5] The riot was serious enough that the enraged Marcian issued a decree prohibiting any Green from holding military or civil office for three years. If this matter had seriously affected Marcian's health, the succession may well have been on people's minds for several months.

Another difference is that the transition in 457 happened much more quickly than it had in 450. In 450, Theodosius II died on July 28, but Marcian was not proclaimed emperor until August 25 (and was not actually crowned until December).[6] In contrast, Marcian died on January 27, 457 and Leo was acclaimed on February 7, only two weeks later.[7] This suggests that someone had moved swiftly to nominate and gain the necessary support for Leo. The most likely person to have done so was Aspar.

Aspar's leading role was easier this time because the politics of the situation in 457 were simpler that those in 450. For one thing, there was no other military leader in the east Roman government who might have challenged a candidate supported by Aspar.[8] By 457 Aspar had finally succeeded Apollonius as a *magister militum praesentalis*, and his son held the post of *m.m. per Orientem*. Aspar's military position had also become stronger through his association with the Thracian Goths.

Nor was there a potential claim from a west Roman emperor, as there was with Valentinian III in 450. Marcian's death occurred between the overthrow of the western emperor Avitus and the accession of Majorian in late 457. There was no legitimate western emperor whose interests had to be considered.

Nor was there an eastern Augusta who might have played a role. Pulcheria had died in 453. Theodosius II's widow, the empress Eudocia, was still alive but in religious retreat in Jerusalem. Theodosius' daughter, the Augusta Licinia Eudoxia, was a captive of the Vandals in Carthage. While this simplified things for Aspar, it also gave him a greater problem with "legitimacy" since there was

---

[4] Jo. Malalas, 14.28. Croke identifies this as gout, but it might suggest cardiovascular problems. Croke 1978:9.
[5] Jo. Malalas, 14.34; Croke 1978:9; Alan Cameron 1976:95, 188–9.
[6] *PLRE* 2, Theodosius 6, Marcianus 8. Pulcheria wrote to Pope Leo in November, 450 referring to Marcian as her "lord" and "consort." Holum 1982:211, n. 172.
[7] *PLRE* 2, Marcianus 8, Leo 6. Croke suggests that the 11-day hiatus "suggests a power struggle," Croke 2005:149–50. If so, it was most likely between Aspar and supporters of Anthemius in the senate.
[8] Other than possibly Anthemius, see *infra*.

no "born in the purple" Theodosian Augusta available to provide a link to the prior dynasty, as there had been in 450.⁹

However, there was one person in the east who did have a strong claim in 457. That was Anthemius, the son-in-law of Marcian.¹⁰ Anthemius had married Marcian's daughter in 453, and was then rapidly promoted, becoming a consul and a patrician in 455 as well as a *magister militum*. It looks like Marcian was positioning Anthemius to be his successor, although Anthemius never received the title of Caesar. If Marcian had become a Theodosian by his marriage to Pulcheria, then Anthemius' marriage to Marcian's daughter also made Anthemius a Theodosian-by-marriage, and the dynastic choice. In addition, Anthemius came from a distinguished east Roman family that had served the Theodosians in important posts since the beginning of the fifth century.¹¹ Finally, Anthemius was orthodox and a Roman. In short, he had excellent credentials. It is not surprising that he is believed to have been the first choice of the senate in 457.¹² Despite this, he lost out to Leo, a relatively unknown military officer who lacked any dynastic claim, whether by descent or by marriage.

The question would linger. A panegyric for Anthemius by Sidonius Apollinaris in 468 contains a suggestion that Anthemius had not wanted the eastern throne when it was offered to him in 457. This may be a trope intended to extol the expected virtue of modesty, but it may also have been an effort to explain away Anthemius' failure to be chosen in 457.¹³ Even after Leo was chosen as emperor, Anthemius apparently remained a viable alternative. When Leo later sent Anthemius off to be the western emperor in 467, his choice "might in part be explained by a concern to mollify an aggrieved party, while also conveniently removing him from the eastern scene."¹⁴ The failure of Anthemius to secure the succession in 457 is perhaps the ultimate testament to the power held by Aspar in the east Roman government and army at that time.

---

⁹ A.D. Lee in *CAH XIV*, 46. Marcian's daughter had never become an Augusta and thus could not crown her husband as a new Augustus, as Pulcheria and Ariadne did.
¹⁰ *PLRE* 2, Anthemius 3; Croke 2005:150.
¹¹ *PLRE* 2, Anthemius 1 and Procopius 2. His ancestors went back to the time of Constantine, including one who had attempted to claim the throne. Kulikowski 2019:38–40; McEvoy 2016b:154–79.
¹² Sidonius, *Carm.*, ii.210–2, 214; *PLRE* 2, Anthemius 3; Kulikowski 2019:190–1; Crawford, 2019:41–2; *LRE*, vol. I:314; Hekster 2023:268, n.26.
¹³ Omissi 2018:291, 297; Stewart 2014:7.
¹⁴ A.D. Lee in *CAH XIV*, 46, n.79. See Leo's alleged later efforts to encourage Anthemius to murder Ricimer, "as he had murdered Aspar." Even after the death of Anthemius in 474, his family continued to be of concern to emperors in the east into the sixth century. See ch. XIII, *infra*.

Though Anthemius may have been the first choice of the senate, he was not the first choice of Aspar.[15] As both ancient sources and modern historians suggest, this was Aspar's moment, and he had the power to make his choice stick. Procopius describes the emperor Leo as one "who had been set in this position by Aspar."[16] Modern historians agree that "the sources are explicit that the succession in 457 was determined by Aspar."[17]

In the years since his defeat by Attila in 447, Aspar had recovered and even enhanced his power and influence through a well-developed network of military and civil connections.[18] In addition to his military power, his non-military influence in Constantinople had grown. He was the *princeps* of the Constantinopolitan senate, and engaged in notable civic projects such as the construction of a major cistern for the city.[19] Like any senior Roman official, and despite his Arian religious beliefs, he regularly corresponded with leading bishops in both east and west, including Pope Leo at Rome, who recognized his powerful position in the east.[20] Despite his religion, he was generous and apparently popular with many people in Constantinople.[21]

In fact, we have suggestions that the throne may have been offered to Aspar at this time. According to a later comment by Theoderic the Amal, the offer was made by the senate of Constantinople but refused by Aspar.[22] When asked why he declined, Aspar is reputed to have enigmatically replied, "I am afraid lest a precedent be created for the empire by me."

This quote deserves closer analysis, since its meaning can be interpreted in several different ways. What was the "precedent" that Aspar thought disqualified him? Was it the fact that he was still viewed as a "barbarian" even though he had

---

[15] *LRE*, vol. I:314 ff. Kulikowski 2019:119, 190–1, 222, suggests that a junior officer like Leo might have been preferred over Anthemius, who might have been seen as too powerful, much like Valentinian I in the fourth century.
[16] Procopius, *Wars*, 3.5.7; Candidus, fr. 1 (*FCH*).
[17] A.D. Lee in *CAH XIV*, 46, n. 80. See also Blockley 1992:71; Heather 2013:21–2; Gibbon ch. XXXVI.
[18] On his military strength, Jones 1964:1:221.
[19] *Chron. Pasch* s.a. 459; Wickham 2005:158.
[20] For example, Theodoret, *Ep.*140; Theophanes AM 5952; Zach. *HE*, IV.7.
[21] Candidus fr. 1 (*FCH*:465–6) ("the fire which damaged the city, and the measures which Aspar took for the public good"); *Chron. Pasch* s.a. 459 ("Aspar the magister militum began to build the very large cistern"); also discussion of Malchus, fr. 1 (Blockely, *FCH*:405) in ch. XII, *infra*: McEvoy 2016:498; Gibbon XXXVI.
[22] *Acta Synchrodorum Habitarum Romae*, 5.23–6 (*MGH AA* XII, p. 425) in which Theoderic quotes Aspar as saying "timeo, ne per me consuetudo in regno nascatur." *PLRE* 2, Fl. Ardabur Aspar; McEvoy 2016:499–500; Laniado 2015:22; Croke 2005:150 n.10. Cf. Roberto 2009. The remark was supposedly repeated by Theoderic around 501 to a group of western bishops. Theoderic had known Aspar, and it is possible that he may have heard this from him directly. Arnold 2014:159–60; Moorhead 1992:8. Cf. Stewart 2014:15–16 (who seems to misunderstand the offer as coming from the senate at Rome with regard to the western throne). Theoderic may have had his own reasons to tell that story in view of his position as an Arian ruler in Italy.

spent his life as a member of the east Roman elite?²³ Or was it that his continued adherence to the Arian faith made him too controversial in the charged religious atmosphere of Constantinople?

McEvoy dismisses the "barbarian" issue, although it was undoubtedly one of the charges used against Aspar by his political opponents. She points to earlier generals "of barbarian descent" whose ancestry did not seem to disqualify them from becoming serious aspirants to the imperial throne.²⁴ It should be recalled that even Theodosius II and his siblings were partly of "barbarian descent" since they had a "barbarian" grandfather, the general Bauto.²⁵

The issue of Aspar's religion seems to have been more serious. Procopius writes that Aspar was an Arian "and since he had no intention of changing this, he was not able to assume the position of emperor, although he had the influence to advance someone else to it without difficulty."²⁶ Gibbon also saw this as a religious issue: "The patrician Aspar might have placed the diadem on his own head, if he would have subscribed the Nicene creed."²⁷ Laniado emphasizes the risk to Aspar's relations with his Gothic supporters, who "in the eyes of the authors of the literary sources, were neither Romans nor orthodox."²⁸

Given the anti-Arian sentiment in Constantinople, it is remarkable that Aspar achieved the status and influence that he did. However, there may have been some pragmatism as well. It has been observed that the Ardaburii were "at least grudgingly accepted in Constantinople" even when they intervened in matters involving the Orthodox Church.²⁹ As discussed, it has been suggested that the regime of Theodosius II may have tolerated heterodox views among its senior military commanders because it made them less likely to become successful usurpers.³⁰ Aspar may have realized that this toleration had its limits.

Does Aspar's alleged refusal of the throne show sincere religious beliefs or political calculation?³¹ We cannot know about his personal religious beliefs, but we can make some guesses about possible political motivations.

---

²³ Cf. Heather 2013:21–2 with McEvoy 2016:498–505; Croke 2021:102–7.
²⁴ McEvoy 2016:498 n. 87 and 2013:14; Croke 2005:153. Roberto 2009 interprets Aspar's remark as referring to ethnicity but recognizes the Arian issue.
²⁵ Wickham 2009:96–9.
²⁶ Procopius, *Wars*, 1.6.3; Lee, in Kelly (ed.) 2013:107.
²⁷ Gibbon, ch. XXXVI. He then observes that "[f]rom this disability of Aspar to ascend the throne, it may be inferred that the stain of *Heresy* was perpetual and indelible while that of *Barbarism* disappeared in the second generation." Marcell. *comes*, s.a. 471; Wood 2011:307; Croke 2001:96.
²⁸ Laniado 2015:22; Wood 2011:308.
²⁹ S. Cohen, in Arnold et al. 2016:518. He also suggests that Aspar may have been "light" in his Arianism, but while he may have been pragmatic his actions suggest a basic adherence to his religion.
³⁰ Lee, in Kelly 2013:107.
³¹ Crawford 2019:90.

The arrangement with Marcian seemed to have generally worked well for Aspar—he became a power behind the throne, while Marcian and Pulcheria satisfied the public need for imperial legitimacy and orthodoxy.[32] Admittedly, there are hints that Marcian developed a more independent streak later in his reign, particularly after the death of Pulcheria. But why should this type of arrangement not work well again with another of Aspar's Roman and orthodox subordinates? It also avoided any religious strain in relations with his Gothic supporters.[33] And perhaps the future could be secured for Aspar's family by the marriage of one of Aspar's sons to an imperial daughter.[34]

Aspar had dynastic plans of his own, but they did not include a Theodosian claimant such as Anthemius.[35] Aspar might have nominated his son, Ardaburius, as emperor.[36] At this point, Ardaburius had had a distinguished military career, and had also been a Roman consul. However, he also seems to have been a confirmed Arian, and may not have been willing (as his brother Patricius later was) to gain a crown by conversion. One wonders whether Ardaburius may have felt aggrieved at being passed over, and whether this might explain his subsequent involvement in conspiracies against Leo. The approach taken by Aspar was in keeping with that of some other barbarian "generalissimos" of the late fourth and early fifth century (notably Stilicho)—not to become the emperor themselves, but to marry their children into the imperial dynasty.[37]

This is the strategy that Aspar seems to have followed in 457. It appears likely that one of the conditions he imposed on Leo was that Leo's daughter would eventually marry Aspar's second son, Patricius.[38] Why Patricius and not the elder son, Ardaburius the Younger? For one thing, Ardaburius was already married. For another, Ardaburius (born c. 420) was probably too old for the very young Ariadne. Patricius may also have been somehow more "Roman" than Aspar's other sons. Unless a birth name was changed c. 451, his full name (Iulius Patricius) is suggestive of Roman ancestry. All this could be viewed as an extension of the strategy of *adfinitas*, marriage alliances, that had worked so well

---

[32] Which may reflect the idea of a "partnership" with a "ceremonial emperor," although Marcian and Majorian were active in military affairs and Leo would go his own way. McEvoy 2010:168–9.

[33] Which would include his family. An interesting speculation is whether he also considered the possible effect on his relations with the Vandals. See also McEvoy 2016a:504; Stewart 2014:17 ("Aspar wanted to be able to travel swiftly between Roman and non-Roman worlds."); Croke 2005:157.

[34] *LRE*, vol. 1–314 ff; Croke 2005:157 (rev. Croke 2021:60).

[35] Croke 2005:150.

[36] Croke 2021:54.

[37] MacGeorge 2002:13; O'Flynn 1983:59–61. See also the marriage of Anthemius' daughter, Alypia, to Ricimer.

[38] McEvoy 2016a:490 n. 39; Croke 2005:157; Arnold 2014:146, 159.

for the Ardaburii in their rise to power.³⁹ With his other sons taking military roles, it also fit the model of "ceremonial rulership" that had emerged in the late fourth century.⁴⁰

Leo had two daughters, Ariadne (who was born shortly before Leo became emperor) and Leontia (who was born shortly thereafter). It is somewhat unclear which daughter was the subject of the promise. If the promise was extracted before Leo became emperor (which makes more sense given Aspar's dynastic plan) then it could only have been Ariadne, and most historians assume this was the case.⁴¹ In addition, if Aspar had recently seen an unexpected show of independence from Marcian, he may have wanted the first available choice.

This promise would become a major point of contention between Aspar and Leo in the 460s. If we are right about Aspar's dynastic strategy, it was the essential piece in his plan for the succession. Any indication that Leo might be reneging on his promise would be a very serious matter for Aspar and his family.

Crowning an Emperor

Leo was less distinguished than Marcian. Croke calls him "an unusual choice."⁴² Unlike Marcian, there is no suggestion that he was a senator. However, like Marcian, he came from humble origins in the Balkans, had military experience, and was an orthodox Christian.⁴³ In 457, he was a tribune leading a unit of soldiers stationed near Constantinople and under Aspar's command.⁴⁴

A less-distinguished emperor required a more elaborate coronation, and Aspar stage-managed things to suit. A detailed description has been preserved in the *Book of Ceremonies*, a Byzantine court manual that was compiled in the tenth century but is based on a sixth-century source.⁴⁵

---

[39] Roberto 2009.
[40] See ch. I, *supra*. McEvoy 2010:168.
[41] Croke 2005:157; Brooks 1893. *V. Dan. Styl.*, ch. 65 says Ariadne. Cf. *LRE*, vol. I:317 n. 3, noting that there is no record that Aspar objected when Ariadne was married to Zeno, which might have been expected. But see ch. IX, *infra* on an exchange between Aspar and Leo.
[42] Croke 2005:150; 2021:55.
[43] He had previously been the *curator* who managed Aspar's estates and may have served with Aspar. Theophanes AM 5961; Zonaras 13.25.35; Croke 2005 n. 21, 2021:55.
[44] *LRE*, vol. I:314–15. Bury believes that Leo was from Dacia and was the commander of the *Mattiari seniores* because that unit contained Dacians. *PLRE* 2, Leo 6. Malalas refers to him as a "Bessian," a people living near the Danube frontier, perhaps with origins in Dacia. Jo. Malalas, book 14; Wood 2011.
[45] Const. Porphyr., *De ceremonis*, i., *c*.91. *LRE*, vol. I:316 n. 2; Gillett 2003:222–3; Croke 2005:151 n. 17, 2021:55 n. 24.

Leo was first acclaimed as emperor by the soldiers, the senate, and senior government officials in a ceremony at the Hebdomon, just outside Constantinople.[46] After his coronation by the patriarch, Leo spoke to his "most valiant fellow soldiers" and, to further earn their goodwill, wisely provided "five nomismata and a pound of silver to each shield."[47]

The role of the patriarch in this ceremony is of interest. As Bury points out, "[a]s there was no Augustus or Augusta to perform the ceremony of coronation, this duty was assigned to the Patriarch Anatolius, who had perhaps taken some part in the coronation of Marcian."[48] Pulcheria, as an Augusta, had been able to perform this act for Marcian in 450, but in 457 there was no one of Augustal rank in Constantinople to do the same for Leo.[49] This time the job fell to the patriarch, perhaps because he had earlier participated in the coronation of Marcian, but certainly to provide Leo legitimacy with a display of religious support.[50]

The ceremony at the Hebdomon was followed by an elaborate procession through Constantinople to the imperial palace. It is in this procession that the dominant role of Aspar in the new regime was made plain for all to see. Aspar rode in the imperial carriage with Leo, and it was Aspar who presented Leo with the traditional gold crown on behalf of the senate of Constantinople. It was a visual image whose political significance could not have been missed by anyone in the city.[51]

Leo's accession had the support of the army, the senate, the patriarch, and the people—it was not contested. At the end of that February day in 457, Aspar should have been pleased by the ease of the transition. Once again, he had made an emperor, and perhaps he had guaranteed a place for his family in the imperial house—but would his partnership with Leo last?

---

[46] *LRE*, vol. I:315.
[47] Ibid.
[48] Arnold noted to author that the See of Constantinople had recently been elevated to a patriarchate at the Council of Chalcedon in 451. See *ODB*, "Patriarchates."
[49] As we will see with Verina and Ariadne, an Augusta could create an Augustus.
[50] Gibbon, ch. XXXVI.
[51] Const. Porphyr., *De Ceremonis*; Roberto 2009; Croke 2005:152.

9

Beginnings of the Struggle with Leo (457–65)

Events at Constantinople

The new partnership between Leo and Aspar seemed to get off to a good start. Late in 457, the new consuls for 458 were named. In keeping with tradition, Leo (the new eastern emperor) took the eastern consulship for himself, while the western consulship went to the new western emperor, Majorian. When the consuls were named for 459, the western honor went to Ricimer (Majorian's barbarian "generalissimo") while the eastern honor went to Aspar's second son, Patricius.[1] The consulate for Patricius may have been a way for Leo to keep his alleged promise about the succession by honoring Aspar's son. The pattern of emperor and patrician seemed to be taking hold in both parts of the empire.[2]

The eastern consulate in the next few years also went to associates of Aspar. The eastern consul for 461 was Dagalaifus, another member of the eastern empire's military aristocracy. His father, Areobindus, had been a *magister militum praesentalis* who served as Aspar's colleague as consul in 434 and a co-commander in the Hun wars.[3] More important, Dagalaifus was married to Godisthea, a daughter of Ardaburius the Younger and thus Aspar's granddaughter.

---

[1] Bury raised the possibility that the person who became consul was Patricius, the Master of Offices, not Aspar's son. *LRE*, vol. I:317 n. 2. That Patricius was close to Leo, reading out the letters of Ardaburius the Younger in 465 (see ch. X) and conspiring with the empress Verina after Leo's death (see ch. XIII). *PLRE* 2, Patricius 8. But both *PLRE* 2, *Fasti Consulares*, 1243 and *CLRE*, 452–3 identify "Patricius" as Aspar's son. The choice of Aspar's youngest son, Ermanaric, as consul in 465 also supports this conclusion—why would they have skipped over Aspar's middle son, Patricius, especially if he was the intended heir?
[2] Stewart 2014:9 refers to Aspar at this time as a "shadow emperor."
[3] The grandfather and namesake of this Dagalaifus was an important general in the time of Julian, so his family's service in the Roman army was even longer than that of the Ardaburii. Kulikowski 2019:32, 36; Drijvers 2015:87; Lenski 2002:23, 25.

In 463, the eastern consul was a man named Vivianus. Although the connection is unclear, he appears to have been Aspar's ally since Aspar supported him in a quarrel with Leo in 466.[4] At least through late 462 (when Vivianus was nominated for the consulate), the partnership between Aspar and Leo seemed to be holding.

The only hint of evasion on Leo's part may be that Patricius had not yet been named Caesar. There was perhaps a precedent in that Anthemius (Marcian's intended successor) had never been named Caesar. However, unlike Patricius, Anthemius had married Marcian's daughter so he could make a dynastic claim.[5] Perhaps Leo pointed to Ariadne's age, arguing that it would be unseemly for them to be betrothed until the girl was older.[6] Nonetheless, in 462 (five years after Leo's accession) Patricius was still neither a Caesar nor a member of the imperial family by marriage.

As time went on, it became harder for Leo to make excuses.[7] It also seems that, despite his presumed promise to Aspar, Leo was beginning to harbor thoughts about keeping the succession in his own family.

In 462, Leo had two daughters but no son who could make a dynastic claim, a situation which suited Aspar. Yet, Leo apparently still had hopes for a son. Near the city of Constantinople there was a pillar on which lived a holy ascetic known as Daniel the Stylite.[8] In the summer of 462 Leo made his desire for a son known to Daniel, who allegedly gave him a favorable prophecy. Although Leo's wife Verina gave birth to a son in April, 463, the child died after only five months.[9]

The story of Leo's son gives us two important insights into Leo's thinking in the early 460s. First, despite the promise supposedly made to Aspar in 457, Leo had begun to develop his own independent dynastic ambitions, perhaps prompted by his wife, Verina, who would play an increasingly significant role in both his and succeeding reigns. Second, the connection between Leo and orthodox religious figures (such as Daniel the Stylite) was important and would

---

[4] Croke 2005:57, 161–2. Since Vivianus had served as *p.p. Orientis*, based in Antioch, in 459–60, it is possible that the connection was Ardaburius the Younger, who was serving as *m.m. Orientis* in Antioch at the time.
[5] The seven-year-old Valentinian III had been made a Caesar in 424. But Valentinian III had a dynastic claim by right of birth, whereas Patricius had no dynastic claim without a marriage.
[6] We do not know the date of Ariadne's birth, other than that she was born shortly before Leo became emperor in 457. A date in the very mid-450s seems plausible.
[7] Moreover, Aspar (and perhaps Ardaburius) were growing impatient. Croke 2005:159.
[8] Daniel was regularly consulted by many prominent citizens, including the emperors Leo and Zeno. He maintained his unique lifestyle for 33 years, not dying until 493. *V. Dan. Styl.*
[9] A letter from the Patriarch of Antioch suggests that the infant may have immediately been given the title of Caesar, which (if true) could not have pleased Aspar. Croke 2005:158 n. 42.

become even stronger as Leo's reign went on. As an Arian, this was a strategy that Aspar could not easily counter.

It was becoming clear that the succession would rest with Leo's two daughters and their eventual husbands. In this connection, it is interesting that both Leo and his wife began to promote the image and cult of Pulcheria, the empress who had extended her dynasty by "marriage" to Marcian.[10] The struggle over who would marry Ariadne (in the 460s, when it was decided for her, and in 491, when the choice was hers) also shows the evolving role of imperial women in the succession.[11]

The death of Leo's infant son in September, 463 was therefore a turning point.[12] Although the child's death briefly re-invigorated the prospects of Aspar and Patricius with regard to the succession, we also begin to see signs that Leo was beginning to look for allies to help him resist Aspar. Two appointments made by Leo in 463/464 seem to stand out.

One was the nomination in late 463 of Anicius Olybrius to be the eastern consul for 464. Olybrius came from an old and prestigious family in Rome.[13] At the time of the Vandal sack of Rome in 455, he was either married or betrothed to Placidia, the younger daughter of Valentinian III.[14] Although his wife, her sister, and his mother-in-law were all taken to Carthage as prisoners, Olybrius somehow escaped and later turned up in Constantinople.[15]

He seems to have arrived there some time before the empress Eudoxia and Placidia were released in 462. He may have been there earlier in 455 as part of an effort to get his wife's grandmother, the retired empress Eudocia, to renounce her support for anti-Chalcedonian positions (which shows that he had important orthodox connections).[16] An early date for his arrival in Constantinople is also supported by the *Vita* of Daniel Stylites, where the empress Eudoxia thanks Daniel for prophesying her release to Olybrius at a time "when you [Daniel] were still in the church" (i.e., before Daniel's pillar was constructed).[17] This suggests that Olybrius had been in Constantinople for some time prior to 462

---

[10] Croke, 2005:158–9; Holum 1982:227–8 n. 38.
[11] McEvoy 2019a:126 and 2016b:172–9; Herrin 2016:5–25 and 2013:306–7; Angelova 2015:198–202.
[12] Croke 2005:158.
[13] *PLRE* 2, Anicius Olybrius; Clover 1978:172–6.
[14] *PLRE* 2, Placidia 1.
[15] Clover 1966:138–43 follows O. Seeck, s.v. "Anicius," RE I, Pt. 2 (1894), 2207–08 suggesting that Olybrius was "possibly" taken to Carthage along with the Theodosian women. On efforts by the east Romans to win the return of the Theodosian women, see Clover 1966:180–2.
[16] Clover 1978:177–82.
[17] *V. Dan. Styl.*, ch. 35.

when the women captives were released. Shortly after her reunion with Olybrius in Constantinople in 462, Placidia gave birth to a daughter.[18] From a dynastic viewpoint, these women were among the last surviving members of the Theodosian dynasty. The opportunistic Vandal king Geiseric later supported the claims of Olybrius to the western empire, regarding Olybrius as a relative by reason of the forced marriage of Placidia's older sister to Geiseric's son, Huneric.[19] Geiseric's interest in inserting Huneric into the imperial family dated back to the 442 treaty between the Vandals and the west Romans. Although this plan seems to have broken down in the early 450s, Geiseric's capture of the Theodosian women in 455 allowed him to revive it by marrying Huneric to Eudocia.

Why did Leo pick this displaced aristocrat with imperial connections (and perhaps ambitions) to be the eastern consul for 464? It has been suggested that Olybrius' consulship "may be interpreted as both a statement of recognition by Leo and a concession to [Olybrius'] influence."[20] However, other than his imperial and senatorial connections in Rome, what "influence" did Olybrius have in Constantinople that would have been of interest to Leo? Leo may have seen Olybrius as a possible conduit to leading figures in the Orthodox Church, who might help him gather allies for a struggle with Aspar.[21] For example, Olybrius was an early devotee of Daniel the Stylite.[22] In fact, it may have been Olybrius who instigated Leo's plea to Daniel for a son in 462.[23]

The second significant appointment in 464 was the selection of Basiliscus, the brother of Leo's wife, Verina, as the *magister militum* for Thrace.[24] Like his sister, Basiliscus was ambitious and would play a large role during the reign of Leo and beyond. Like Leo, he came from the Balkans and had served as a Roman soldier. Priscus calls him "a successful soldier, but slow-witted and easily taken in by deceivers."[25] His appointment to one of the five senior east Roman military commands struck directly at Aspar's power base. Not only did it put one of the key commands into the hands of a close relative of Leo, but the command in

---

[18] This daughter would eventually marry the son of Dagalaifus, and their child would become one of the richest and noblest women in Constantinople in the time of Justinian. Since one grandmother was descended from Aspar, and the other was a Theodosian, this child was the descendant of both Aspar and Theodosius II. Unusually, she apparently held the title of *patricia* in her own right. PLRE 2, Anicia Iuliana 3; McEvoy 2016:504–5.

[19] This marriage would have long-term effects on Roman/Vandal relations. Conant 2012:22–30; Croke 2015:105–6 (rev. Croke 2021:35); Clover 1966:96–102.

[20] Croke 2005:159.

[21] If Olybrius was in the east c. 455 to persuade the dowager Augusta Eudocia to change her religious views, this might may also be evidence of his important religious connections.

[22] *V. Dan. Styl.*; PLRE 2, Olybrius 6.

[23] Croke 2005:159.

[24] PLRE 2, Fl. Basiliscus 2.

[25] Priscus, fr. 43 (*FCH*), Elton 2018:242.

question covered the area where Aspar's allies, the Thracian Goths, had settled.[26] Any military conflict between Constantinople and the Thracian Goths would therefore be initially handled by Basiliscus, not by the Ardaburii. The promotion of Basiliscus might therefore be seen as a move by Leo to curtail the military power of Aspar and his family. From a political viewpoint, it also raised Basiliscus as another candidate, and possible alternative to Patricius, in the eventual contest to succeed Leo.

All of these moves were probably of concern to Aspar. Several sources report an undated incident in which Aspar grabbed Leo's imperial cloak and allegedly said that "It is not fitting that the one who wears this cloak should lie." To which Leo is said to have angrily replied, "Nor is it fitting that he should be driven like a slave."[27] Scholars disagree on the nature and date of the "lie" referred to and have suggested several disputes between Aspar and Leo in the 460s that might provide the context for this exchange.[28]

However, it is possible that the dispute was caused by Leo's failure to fulfill his promise to appoint Patricius as Caesar and marry him to Leo's daughter. There are several times in the struggle between Aspar and Leo when this exchange could have happened, but a date in late 464 or early 465 is possible. It is a moment when Leo's antagonism towards Aspar had become more obvious, and when Aspar's resentment may have increased because of the appointments of Basiliscus and Olybrius. An earlier date for this exchange seems unlikely since relations between Aspar and Leo still seemed cordial. However, in 464 or early 465 these appointments may have concerned Aspar enough to try to force the succession issue. Later dates for this exchange have been suggested, but a date between 465 and 468 would fall in a period in which Aspar's political leverage with Leo had weakened (although that itself might explain the outburst).

By 464 it had been seven years since Leo's accession—if a promise about Patricius had in fact been made by Leo in 457, nothing had been done about it (other than Patricius' consulship in 459, which did nothing to secure a dynastic claim). Moreover, both Aspar and Leo were getting on in age and must have felt increasing pressure about the succession issue. As we will see, Aspar may also

---

[26] It is possible that Basiliscus received this command because he came from that area. Still, the timing seems strategic, and perhaps reflects the growing influence of Verina.
[27] Cedrenus, 607.17–18 (Bekker 1838); Zonaras, 14.1 (122–3); Croke 2005:162–3.
[28] Croke 2005:162–3 (rev. 2021:65–6). It is often connected to the murky dispute as to whether Tatianus or Vivianus should receive the consulship for 465.

have been under pressure from his son, Ardaburius the Younger, to take some action. For these reasons, a date for this exchange sometime around 464 might be a possibility.[29]

Leo was developing an independent streak that Aspar probably found both unexpected and difficult to deal with. The basic issue between them was that they had different ideas about the succession. This made compromise difficult, but Leo was not yet ready for a complete break.

Leo may have therefore tried to appease Aspar in late 464 in a way that paid honor to the Ardaburii while still evading his promise about Patricius. This might explain why the eastern consulship for 465 went to Ermanaric, Aspar's third and youngest son. Ermanaric must have been very young at that time, and he does not seem to have any record of military or civil accomplishments that would justify such recognition. Of course, neither did Patricius when he received the same distinction from Leo in 459. The reason for Ermanaric's consulship was simply that he was Aspar's son, and the only one who had not yet held the consulship. As the *missorium* shows, Aspar took pride in the chain of consuls in his family, a great honor for any non-imperial family.[30]

Although Ermanaric received a consulate, Leo also did something that sent a mixed message. Apparently due to the continuing upheaval in the west, the east had the opportunity to appoint both consuls for 465. Although one was Ermanaric, Leo's other choice was his brother-in-law, Basiliscus.[31] The honor came very close in time to Basiliscus' promotion to *magister militum per Thracias*. Added together, they seem to show Leo enhancing the profile and status of his brother-in-law as a potential counterweight to the Ardaburii.[32] Seen in this way, the selection of Ermanaric could have been an attempt by Leo to mollify Aspar, while balancing the advancement of Aspar's family with new honors for Leo's own.

Leo's careful approach in limiting Aspar's influence was partly a result of Aspar's strong position in the government and society of Constantinople in the late 450s and early 460s. This position had developed over many decades, and reflects the assimilated, Roman part of Aspar's identity. For example, and despite his Arian faith, in the 450s and 460s Aspar actively corresponded with key Christian religious figures of all persuasions. We know that around 450 the

---

[29] McEvoy 2016:489–90 on age as a factor.
[30] Note also the consulship of Dagalaiphus, son-in-law of Ardaburius the Younger, in 461. *CLRE*: 456–7. The Anthemii had an even longer record of consuls. McEvoy 2019a:122.
[31] *PLRE* 2, Basiliscus; *CLRE*:464–5.
[32] Croke 2005:159–60, 2021:63.

heterodox bishop Theodoret wrote to thank Aspar for his help in getting Theodoret released from exile. Also, as early as 457 Pope Leo had asked Aspar to end his support for Timothy Aelurus, the violent and heterodox patriarch of Alexandria. This shows that Aspar was perceived as having major influence in the religious politics of the eastern church.[33] It was not unusual for fifth century bishops to correspond with Roman generals, but it has been observed that "Aspar's involvement in ecclesiastical politics was unusually intensive."[34] Aspar was participating in this process as a traditional senior Roman government official.

However, religious issues appear to have become a growing point of contention between Aspar and Leo. There appears to have been a dispute over the appointment of an Urban Prefect for Constantinople, where Leo rejected Aspar's Arian candidate.[35] However, in the late 450s, Aspar had been successful in persuading Leo not to attack Bishop Amphilocus of Side. On the other hand, Leo ignored Aspar's advice not to depose the heterodox patriarch of Alexandria, Timothy Aelurus.[36] This may again suggest Leo's desire to align himself with the orthodox.

Early in his reign, Leo and his family (especially his wife, Verina) began to publicly demonstrate their devotion to the memory of the empress Pulcheria, who was regarded as a champion of orthodoxy. Pulcheria had been especially devoted to the developing cult of the Virgin, the *Theotokos*, and Leo's family made a point of showing their support for this cause. A striking example of this was a church mosaic he commissioned with a portrait of his family and the words: "By showing reverence here to the *Theotokos*, they secured the power of their *basileia*." Nothing could more explicitly demonstrate the way in which Leo connected his orthodox piety to his legitimacy.[37] It was his best, and often his only, card.

While Aspar could not effectively compete with Leo on religious issues, he was able to court popular support by advertising his civic virtues.[38] There are several indications in these years of Aspar acting as a responsible Roman official

---

[33] Croke 2005:163.
[34] McEvoy 2016:95–6; Croke 2005:151 n. 15. See also Arnold 2016:503–32 (Cohen); McLaughlin 2014:253–79; Schor 2009:286, 290.
[35] Croke 2005:162, identifies this as the occasion for the cloak-tugging incident. It is interesting that the dispute was over a civil appointment, showing the extent of Aspar's influence in the government.
[36] Croke 2005:163; also Allen, *CAH XIV*, 815–6. On Aspar's involvement in the Orthodox Church, see Arnold 2016:503–32 (Cohen); Elton 2000:402.
[37] Holum 1982:227; Croke 2021:77.
[38] McEvoy 216:498.

in Constantinople. In 459 work was begun on a new cistern for the city's water supply.[39] It became known as the Cistern of Aspar, presumably because he sponsored or paid for its construction. This shows Aspar playing a traditional Roman role as a benefactor of his city. Aspar was wealthy, and could engage in acts of civic benevolence.[40] It was a part of the "civilian seriousness" that was expected of a leading senator.[41] For others, it might be shown by building churches or monasteries, but that avenue was closed to Aspar because of his Arianism and the limits placed on Arian churches.[42] This accumulation of "cultural capital" made it more difficult for his enemies to make the "barbarian" attack stick.[43]

Another event in Constantinople in late 464 also strengthened Aspar's popularity. On September 2, 464, a fire began that spread across the city.[44] By the time it was over, eight of the city's fourteen districts had been severely damaged. While fires were a constant menace in Constantinople, this one was especially severe and caught the attention of our sources. Malalas says it was "a great conflagration ... such as had never been experienced before."[45] Modern historians have called it a "massive conflagration" and "the most devastating of all the early Byzantine infernos."[46]

The contrast between the reactions of Aspar and Leo to this calamity is clearly noted in our sources. Aspar (then probably in his 60s) ran about the city directing fire-fighting efforts, handing out money to encourage the firefighters, and reputedly carrying buckets of water himself. The contemporary historian Candidus refers to "the measures which Aspar took for the public good on this occasion."[47] In contrast, the Easter Chronicle says that the emperor Leo "departed in terror to the far side [of the Bosporus]."[48] Similarly, Malalas says that the

---

[39] *Chron. Pasch*, 85, n. 278. The similar fifth century Cistern of Aetius was not named for the western general, but rather for an Urban Prefect of the same name who supervised its construction. It was sponsored by the empress Pulcheria, whose palace was in the area. Ibid. On this and the fire, see McEvoy 2016:498; Wickham 2005:158; Mathisen 2006:1034.

[40] Gibbon, ch. XXXVI. On his wealth see McEvoy 2016:494–5; Lee, in Kelly (ed.) 2013:90–108.

[41] For another cistern constructed by Pulcheria, Angelova 2015:157.

[42] However, the Ardaburii also made important donations to the orthodox "Anastasia" church in Constantinople. Laniado 2015:19–20; Snee 1998:157–86. Laniado cites the *Vita Sancti Marciani oeconomi*, which shows that even a high orthodox official and saint could speak kindly of the Ardaburii for their contributions to his church, in exchange for which the scriptures would be read there "in their language" [i.e., Gothic] on holy days.

[43] Wickham 2005:158 n. 13, 165–6.

[44] As both Croke and the Whitbys note, the fire should properly be dated to 464, not 465. Croke 2005:179, n. 45; Whitby & Whitby: 87, n. 285 (*Chron Pasch*, 91 mistakenly dates it to 469).

[45] Jo. Malalas book 14, ch. 43.

[46] Croke 2001:103; Croke 2005:159; *LRE*, vol. I:321–2.

[47] Candidus fr. 1 (*FCH*).

[48] *Chron. Pasch.* (Whitby & Whitby:91).

emperor Leo "fearing for the palace" fled to his summer palace on the Bosporus.⁴⁹ He stayed there for six months, using his time to construct a new harbor and portico.⁵⁰ The contrast between the behavior of the two men stands out in our sources and it could not have failed to be noticed by the citizens of Constantinople.⁵¹

Events in the Balkans

Throughout Leo's reign, there was turbulence in the Balkans as a result of the continuing fallout from the collapse of Attila's empire. While Marcian had resettled several groups of Goths inside the eastern empire, other groups (including mixed Hun/Gothic raiding parties) continued to be a problem. Sometimes this involved the Romans in wars between feuding groups; at other times, the Romans conducted their own campaigns against groups of raiders.

Marcian had settled two groups of Goths in the Balkans under federate treaties. The Pannonian Goths had entered into a treaty with the east Romans in 455/456, under which they received annual payments of three hundred pounds of gold from Constantinople. When Leo became emperor in 457, he stopped these "usual yearly payments," much as Marcian had stopped the payments to Attila in 450. The Amal leader, Valamir, patiently waited for two years for the payments to resume and finally sent an embassy to Constantinople. His ambassadors were not successful, but they reported that the Thracian Goths seemed to be in favor.⁵²

The Pannonian Goths responded by invading some adjacent parts of the eastern empire, getting as far as Epirus before Leo agreed in 459/460 to a new treaty that renewed their payments, at which point they returned to Pannonia.⁵³ It was a provision of this treaty that sent Valamir's nephew, Theoderic the Amal, to Constantinople as an honored hostage.⁵⁴ Although this treaty lasted for some

---

⁴⁹ Malalas, 14.43. Leo's refuge is identified as the palace of St. Mamas, which is significant because the date of the fire was also the day dedicated to St. Mamas. Croke 2005:179, n. 46 suggests that Leo went there to propitiate the saint. However, Malalas refers to Leo's trip as a *"processus"* which would be a regular imperial excursion. Perhaps it was his way of putting a more dignified face on Leo's departure from the city.
⁵⁰ *Chron.Pasch*, 91; Angelova 2015:154.
⁵¹ McEvoy 2016:503.
⁵² Wolfram 1998:262.
⁵³ The east Roman forces who resisted these Goths apparently were led by Marcian's son-in-law, Anthemius, perhaps as *m.m. per Illyricum*. PLRE 2, Anthemius 3; Wolfram 1988:263.
⁵⁴ Arnold 2014:144.

time, late in the 460s there would be renewed turbulence in the Balkans that would require Aspar's attention. In the meantime, Theoderic the Amal resided in Constantinople, and "is said to have enjoyed the emperor's [Leo's] favor."[55] One wonders if Leo was already courting the young man as the future leader of a people who might be a counterweight to Aspar's Thracian Goths.

Relations with the Western Empire

The murder of Valentinian III in 455 led to a chaotic situation in the west. A Gallo-Roman senator named Avitus briefly became emperor, but was never recognized in the east and was deposed by his military in late 456.[56] He was eventually replaced in late 457 by the more vigorous Majorian, who was duly recognized by Leo (ignoring any potential Theodosian claims by either Anthemius or Olybrius).[57] But real power in the west now lay with the "barbarian" Ricimer, commander of the western armies, who became the western consul for 459.

However, Majorian was not content to be a figurehead for Ricimer.[58] Like several Roman officers who had served under Aetius, he had ideas of his own about what needed to be done to restore the western empire. Initially, this was not a problem since both Majorian and Ricimer had some common goals, chief of which was doing something about the Vandals. In 460, Majorian went to Spain to prepare for an attack on the Vandals in Africa. However, the Vandals staged a pre-emptive raid that destroyed most of his fleet. This setback seems to have seriously weakened Majorian's position in the west, and perhaps he had neglected Italy for too long.[59] When he returned there in August, 461, he was seized by Ricimer and executed.[60]

One could say that with the death of Majorian the balance between emperor and patrician in the west irreversibly shifted against the emperor in a way that

---

[55] Wolfram 1988:262–3.
[56] Avitus was sensitive about the lack of any dynastic basis for his legitimacy. In a panegyric, his son-in-law Sidonius Apollinaris addressed this issue by attacking the failure of the Theodosians (especially Valentinian III) to protect the western provinces. Gillett 2003:95; Kulikowski 2019:216; Harries 1994:78–9.
[57] *CAH XIV*, 20–3; *PLRE* 2, Maiorianus, 702–3. MacGeorge 2002:196–299; O'Flynn, 1983:106–7; Mathisen 1979:597–627.
[58] Heather in *CAH XIV*, 23. Leo never tried to be a "soldier-emperor" like Majorian. His biggest military effort was led by Basiliscus.
[59] The latter point has been suggested to author by J. Wijnendaele.
[60] Cassiodorus, s.a. 461; Priscus fr.35(2) (*FCH*:339).

was never realized in the east. In addition, since Majorian had been recognized by Leo, this again ruptured relations between the two halves of the empire. Ricimer's new candidate, a senator named Livius Severus, was never recognized as a legitimate Augustus or as a consul by the eastern court.[61] Following his (apparently natural) death in 465 there was yet another western interregnum. This lasted until April 467 when Ricimer and Leo finally agreed on a plan for dealing with the Vandal threat.[62] However, it is necessary to first return to the political situation that suddenly developed in Constantinople in early 465.

---

[61] MacGeorge 2002:216–17.
[62] Ibid., 32–5. See ch. XI, *infra*.

10

The Rise of Zeno (465–7)

At the start of 465 Aspar's position in the east Roman empire was strong, although it was now clear that Leo and his family had their own dynastic ambitions. While Aspar's youngest son, Ermanaric, would be one of the consuls for the new year, the other would be Leo's brother-in-law, the general Basiliscus. However, in addition to the military power of his family, Aspar was the *princeps* of the senate of Constantinople.[1] As a result of his civic activities, including his actions during the great fire of 464, he also had considerable popular support in Constantinople despite opposition to his Arianism from the orthodox monks and clergy. His long years in the upper reaches of east Roman society had made him "a courtly grand seigneur."[2]

All this was about to change.

Ardaburius the Younger and the Persian Letters

At some point after March, 465, Leo finally returned to Constantinople and called a meeting of the east Roman senate. Aspar was there, in his role as *princeps* of the senate. His youngest son, Ermanaric, would probably also have been there since he was a consul for the year, plus his consular colleague, Basiliscus. Aspar's middle son, Patricius, may also have been there since he was both an ex-consul and a senator. However, Aspar's oldest son, Ardaburius, was likely at his military headquarters in Antioch as *m.m. per Orientem*.

At the meeting, Leo dramatically called upon the Master of Offices to read out certain letters which had been brought to the emperor by an army officer of

---

[1] Const. Porphyr, *De ceremoniis* 1. 91; Marcell. *comes*, *Chron*, s.a. 471; John Malalas, XIV 40; *Chron. Pasch.* s.a. 467; Roberto 2009.
[2] Goffart 2006:276 n. 43.

Isaurian background who would take the name Zeno.³ The letters were from Ardaburius to the Persians, and apparently contained an offer to collude with them in an attack on Roman territory. According to the *Vita* of Daniel Stylites, Leo said that he was (or pretended to be) horrified, and asked Aspar what he thought should be done. Aspar supposedly responded that he had warned Ardaburius about his behavior, but no longer controlled him. He was therefore prepared to accept whatever punishment Leo thought Ardaburius deserved.⁴ Leo promptly removed Ardaburius from his position as *magister militum per Orientem* and deprived him of his title of *patricius*.⁵

This important turning point in Aspar's struggle with Leo raises several questions: (1) Was Aspar really surprised by the letters? Did he know or suspect what Ardaburius was planning? (2) Was Ardaburius acting on behalf of Aspar, or on his own? (3) Why would Ardaburius think that collaboration with the Persians was a good idea? Was this the result of resentment at the choice of Leo as emperor in 457, rather than Aspar or perhaps even Ardaburius himself? Or did it stem from frustration over Leo's increasing independence and failure to make Patricius his heir?

As to the first point, this account in the *Vita* does not indicate that Aspar even questioned the authenticity of the letters; his reaction seems more resigned than surprised. If accurate, it suggests that Aspar knew or believed the letters were genuine.

There are at least two explanations for how Aspar might have known about Ardaburius' letters prior to their disclosure to the senate by Leo. One is that he may have known or suspected what Ardaburius was doing, whether he agreed with it or not; the second is that Leo may have shown Aspar the letters before the *conventus* and arranged an outcome with him. It is striking that, despite this hard evidence of high treason, Ardaburius was not executed or imprisoned, but merely relieved of his military post and recalled to Constantinople. In fact, he continued to serve in the east Roman army in military campaigns in the Balkans, and perhaps elsewhere. Is it possible that Leo had shown the letters to Aspar in

---

³ *V. Dan. Styl.*, ch. 55; *PLRE* 2, Patricius 8; Croke 2005:165. The Master of Offices was Patricius (not Aspar's son of the same name), who was part of Leo's circle. After Leo's death, he conspired with the empress Verina to overthrow Zeno. *PLRE* 2, Patricius 8, citing Candidus = Phot. Bibl. 79 and John of Antioch fr. 210. As for Zeno, his Isaurian name was Tarasicodessa. He is to be distinguished from the earlier Isaurian general called Zeno who had been a *magister militum* under Theodosius II and Marcian. *PLRE* 2, Fl. Zenon 7.
⁴ *V. Dan. Styl.*, ch. 39. The sixth-century *Vita* is generally sympathetic to the orthodox Leo and to Zeno, but not to Arians like Aspar.
⁵ Croke 2005:160.

a private meeting before the *conventus*, and that Aspar agreed to have Ardaburius punished but not in a more severe fashion? In the *Vita* of Daniel Stylites, Aspar appears to leave the punishment to Leo, but then immediately tells the emperor what the punishment should be. While it could be the result of the author of the *Vita* writing with knowledge of the outcome, does it suggest that the *conventus* followed a pre-arranged script?[6]

It may also be significant that the *Vita* places the blame for this treachery on Ardaburius but not on Aspar. Indeed, he has Aspar saying that he had advised against his son's plans and no longer controlled him. If so, it could suggest that the relationship between Aspar and his son was changing and that a new dynamic was developing within Aspar's family.

The most difficult question is why would Ardaburius even write such letters? Unfortunately, we have no information as to what the letters actually said or what explanation, if any, Ardaburius offered. It has been suggested that Ardaburius' intent might have been to lure the Persians into an attack, so that he could gain additional renown and influence by defeating them. Alternatively, the letters could have been badly worded but about matters in which the two empires were legitimately cooperating, such as the Caucasian defenses or unrest in the border principalities. We simply do not know.[7]

Since Ardaburius the Younger became an important figure in the struggle with Leo, it is worth taking a closer look at him. By 465, he was probably about forty-five years old, and had mainly pursued a military career, possibly serving with his father in the Hun wars in the 440s. He had also served as consul in 447. Under Marcian, he had fought well in the Balkans in the early 450s and was then promoted to *m.m. per Orientem*. He had a long tenure in this post from 453 to 465. Priscus, who visited him in Antioch in the 450s, praises his success in the Balkans but also accuses Ardaburius of having "turned to self-indulgence and effeminate leisure" while in Antioch.[8] An ornate silver chalice has been found at Antioch, and is currently in the Dumbarton Oaks collection in Washington. Its inscription identifies its owners as Ardaburius and his wife, Anthusa.[9] Although

---

[6] Crawford 2019:51–2.
[7] Ibid., 50.
[8] Priscus fr. 19 (*FCH*:305); Jo. Malalas 14.37; LRE, vol. 1:316 n. 4. This may be a trope about "barbarians" and luxury. It is similar to Procopius in describing the Vandals after their conquest of Africa. Procopius, *Wars*; Conant 2012.
[9] *PLRE* 2:100–1, identifies two women named Anthusa. Anthusa 2 is the daughter of the Isaurian general, Illus. Despite a suggestion that she might have been married to Ardaburius as part of the Ardaburii marriage strategy, this has been dismissed as unlikely since it would have attracted comment in our sources. Croke 2021:58.

it is unknown where or when it was made, it shows the wealth and taste of its owners.¹⁰

Like his father, Ardaburius was occasionally involved in religious matters, including those of the Orthodox Church. While in Antioch, he is reported at one point to have "shot at" the resident stylite, St. Symeon, but later provided a military escort when the man died.¹¹ On another occasion, Ardaburius helped the orthodox "Anastasia" church of St. Gregory Nazianzus in Constantinople, which was near a residence owned by the Ardaburii, to obtain certain relics.¹² Although St. Gregory had been an opponent of Arianism, the *quid pro quo* was that this orthodox church agreed to read the Scriptures in Gothic on certain feast days.¹³ Ardaburius (like his father) remained a faithful Arian, and this perhaps is an example of the family acting as patrons of the Arian community in Constantinople.

While the career of Ardaburius to 465 thus seems very much like that of his father, there seems to be a recklessness that distinguishes him from Aspar. The fact that Ardaburius wrote *letters* detailing his proposed treachery shows something of this difference. Nor would it be the last time that Ardaburius would write compromising letters that his opponents would be able to use against him. He seems to have learned nothing from this incident.

Perhaps this was the result of generational change—in 465, Aspar was probably in his mid-sixties, while Ardaburius was likely in his mid-forties, the prime of life. Ardaburius might have resented that neither he nor his father had become emperor in 457 when his father had the opportunity to do so. Perhaps this made him impatient at his father's indirect (and increasingly unsuccessful) efforts to control Leo or to have Leo fulfill the promise about Patricius. And perhaps Ardaburius was also aware of the contrasting model being provided at this time in the west by Ricimer. From this point on, we need to constantly consider how much of what happened should be attributed to Ardaburius as opposed to Aspar. In some cases, we have a basis to distinguish the two, but in

---

¹⁰ Similarly, Matthews has noted a mosaic floor from Antioch that depicts a private bathhouse "belonging to or provided by Ardaburius." Matthews 2006:88 (my thanks to Prof. J. Osgood for this). Although it is unlikely, some have suggested that this Anthusa was a daughter of the Isaurian general Illus. *PLRE* 2, Anthusa 2; Croke 2021:81:Crawford 2019:43, 62.

¹¹ McEvoy 2016:495. The escort is said to have consisted of his Gothic retainers. In the attack on the palace in 471, the Goths of Ostrys are said to have been "shooting with bows." Evagrius, *HE*, book 1, ch. XIII; *Chron. Pasch.* s.a. 464; Jo. Malalas, 14.37. Some of Symeon's relics were later brought to Constantinople by Leo, perhaps to strengthen his relationship with the stylite Daniel. See *V. Dan. Styl.*, ch.58 and the comment by Dawes & Baynes:81.

¹² Snee 1998:157–86.

¹³ Ibid.; McEvoy 2016:496–7.

many cases our sources obscure the distinction by referring to them collectively as the "Ardaburii" or by simply referring to "them both."[14]

Zeno and the Isaurians

There is a another set of questions that arise from the Persian letters which requires us to consider things from Leo's viewpoint. In late 465 or early 466, Zeno was promoted by Leo to be the commander of the *domestici* guard unit. If Zeno was already an officer of the *domestici*, as Croke believes, then giving him this promotion as a reward for the Persian letters was a logical next step in Zeno's career, and often a prelude to one of the *magister militum* commands.[15]

But was this the beginning of an "Isaurian" faction at court? There is some basis in our sources for viewing Aspar's feud with Leo as a contest between "German" and "Isaurian" court factions.[16] Some modern historians have adopted this model, seeing the Persian letters as the spark which led Leo to form an "Isaurian faction" at his court as a counterweight to the "German faction" of Aspar and his family.[17] However, this view may have been influenced by nineteenth-century ideas about ethnicity and nationalism. In recent years, Croke and others have disputed this model and set forth a more nuanced chronology and explanation.[18]

The fact that the letters were brought to Leo by an Isaurian (Zeno) does not necessarily mean that Leo had a prior plan to create an alliance with Isaurians. The threshold question is how did Zeno came to have copies of those letters?[19]

Croke suggests that Zeno was not an Isaurian tribal leader who suddenly appeared in Constantinople, but an officer who had already served for some time in the east Roman army. While it is possible that he came to Constantinople with other Isaurians in 447, he seems to have become integrated into the military and civilian society of east Rome in the 450s.[20] In 465, Zeno was apparently an

---

[14] e.g., *V. Dan. Styl.*, ch. 66; Hydatius s.a. 468 (an entry of controversial origin and inaccuracy, but interesting in that it refers to different punishments for Aspar and Ardaburius).
[15] Croke 2005:172.
[16] Candidus fr. 1 (*FCH*) mentions Leo's emerging favoritism to "the Isaurian people," and to Zeno in particular. Cf. Croke 2005:165, Kaldellis 2018.
[17] Brooks 1893; *LRE*, vol. 1; Kaldellis 2018; Burgess 1992. Kaldellis suggests that Leo was recruiting Illyrians as a counterweight to Aspar's Goths, whereas the usual model is that he was recruiting Isaurians through Zeno. See also Burgess 1992-875. There may be some truth to this if Leo was looking for soldiers who were not Goths. See the story of Titus, *infra*.
[18] Croke 2005:160, 163–75; McEvoy 2016a; Elton 2000.
[19] Croke 2005:166-7.
[20] Zeno is believed to have had a first wife named Arcadia (possibly of Roman origin) who died around 466. *PLRE* 2, Arcadia 2; Croke 2005:168.

officer of the *domestici*. Although primarily based in Constantinople, selected *domestici* were stationed with each of the five senior *magistri militiae*, presumably to keep an imperial eye on them. Croke suggests that Zeno may have been one such officer, assigned to the Antioch headquarters of Ardaburius. It is even possible that Ardaburius had tried to include Zeno in whatever he was trying to do with the Persians—Leo is said to have emphasized Zeno's "loyalty" to the emperor, thereby suggesting that Zeno had made a choice.[21]

However, even if Zeno had become assimilated into east Roman affairs, this does not mean that he wholly abandoned his Isaurian identity or failed to retain ties to Isauria.[22] On two occasions when he had to flee Constantinople, he sought safety in Isauria, a place where he apparently felt secure and had friends. His identity was therefore not unlike that of Aspar, who had become an assimilated Roman but still was able to form strong personal ties with the Thracian Goths and other "barbarians." One difference is that Zeno seems to have had a geographical "refuge" in Isauria in times of trouble, whereas Aspar had no "Alan homeland" to which he could flee.[23] Perhaps more important was that Aspar was a second-generation "barbarian," who had been born and lived his life within the east Roman empire, whereas Zeno appears to have been born in semi-"barbaric" Isauria. In this sense, Zeno might perhaps be viewed as more of a "barbarian" than Aspar.

The concept of ethnic "factions" has also been criticized.[24] As we saw in the revolt of Gainas in 400, people did not necessarily take sides based solely on their ethnicity.[25] It has sometimes been argued that the dividing line was based on religion, so that Arians tended to line up with other Arians. Yet we have ample evidence of situations where Arians fought other Arians (such as in the empire's wars against the Vandals). It has also been pointed out that religious allegiance could and did change.

An example of such a change at this time was the general Jordanes. As we saw earlier, Jordanes was the son of John the Vandal, a Roman general and apparent ally of Aspar. Given his heritage, it is no surprise that Jordanes was an Arian, and as late as 450 was a supporter of Aspar. However, at some point in the mid-460s,

---

[21] Croke 2005:168–9.
[22] On the background of the Isaurians, see Shaw 1990, especially part 2.
[23] The Thracian Goths might perhaps have served this purpose, as shown by the flight of Ostrys to them after Aspar's murder.
[24] Croke 2005:148–9. See also Wood 2011 citing Elton for the point that "ethnic solidarity was not the prime motivator of allegiance and ... political factions did not represent specific policies or ethnic solidarities."
[25] See ch. III, *supra*.

when Jordanes held the post of *comes* of the Imperial Stables, Leo was thrown from his horse while visiting Daniel the Stylite.[26] According to Daniel's *Vita*, Leo blamed Jordanes for the accident. Jordanes fled to Daniel's pillar to seek refuge and agreed to convert to orthodoxy. While it is hard to say whether this showed Jordanes' understanding of Leo, or the persuasiveness of Daniel, the *Vita* reports that Leo and Jordanes were thereafter "reconciled." Not surprisingly, it was Jordanes who was named by Leo to replace Ardaburius as *m.m. per Orientem*. With this move, in addition to the earlier appointment of Basiliscus, Leo's allies now controlled at least two of the top five commands in the east Roman army. As a reclaimed heretic, Jordanes also became a protégé of Daniel.[27] Both of these considerations probably had weight with Leo, for whom political calculation and authentic religious piety were always intertwined.

Another conversion story, which is undated, comes from a hagiographic story about two brothers named Galbinus and Candidus, apparently military officers. They are said to have been former associates of Aspar and Ardaburius, perhaps even sons-in-law of Aspar, who for some reason had renounced their Arianism.[28] They were apparently sent (by Leo?) to Palestine to acquire a relic of the Virgin, which was then installed in a church in Constantinople in a great ceremony attended by both the emperor and his wife. The cult of the Virgin had been a central concern of the late empress Pulcheria, and this became an occasion for Leo and his family to associate themselves with it.[29]

Earlier historians maintained that this was also the moment when Leo created a special Isaurian guard unit, the *excubitores*, as a check against Aspar's Gothic soldiery. However, this has been questioned.[30] Croke points out that the two sources alleging that Zeno recruited Isaurian guards are talking about events later in Zeno's reign, not Leo's. He also notes that the guard unit of *excubitores* was not an innovation of Leo but had existed since the first century (although Leo may have upgraded its status). A sixth century source does not mention the recruitment of Isaurians for this unit, although several modern historians have made this assumption as part of their re-construction of an Isaurians v. Germans conflict.[31]

---

[26] *V. Dan. Styl.*, ch. 49; *PLRE* 2, Fl. Iordanes 3; Croke 2005:160. One wonders whether this was a ploy by Leo to detach him from Aspar's group.
[27] *V. Dan. Styl.*, ch. 55.
[28] Croke 2005:174 n. 86.
[29] Angelova 2015; Holum 1982.
[30] Croke 2005:155, 169–71; Croke 2005a:117–51 (rev. Croke 2021:108–33); McEvoy 2016:488 ff.; Elton 2000:394.
[31] Jo. Lydus. For support of the ethnic view, see Candidus fr.1 (*FCH*). But cf. Elton 2000:397.

Other evidence suggests that Leo was recruiting widely and generously at this time and was not limiting his efforts to Isaurians. The *Vita* of Daniel Stylites tells us about a man named Titus, supposedly recruited from Gaul, and coins of Leo have been found as far away as Sweden.[32] However, these efforts by Leo may have been part of his extensive recruiting for the Vandal expedition of 468, not specifically for a struggle with Aspar.[33]

Nonetheless, the Persian letters shifted the balance of power in Constantinople in Leo's favor. From 465 to 468, Leo seemed more confident about his position, and began to take a more assertive position. In late 465, he did several things which can be viewed as challenging the interests of Aspar.

Candidus refers to a dispute in which Leo nominated an elderly official named Tatianus for consul whereas Aspar supported a rival candidate named Vivianus.[34] Tatianus had befriended Marcian when the latter fell ill during the Persian War of 421, and Marcian later appointed him to the important post of Urban Prefect of Constantinople (450–2).[35] However, Tatianus apparently was an opponent of Aspar, showing that one cannot simply assume that Marcian's friends were always Aspar's friends. When Leo sent Tatianus as an ambassador to the Vandals around 462, Tatianus is reported to have made remarks that disparaged Aspar and offended Geiseric.[36]

Sometime in late 465 Leo nominated the elderly Tatianus as the eastern consul for 466. This led to a serious quarrel with Aspar, who supported the candidacy of Vivianus.[37] It has been suggested that Aspar had committed to

---

[32] *V. Dan. Styl.*, ch. 60. In communication with the author, Prof. Arnold has raised a question as to whether Titus came from Gaul or Galatia. The phrase "en tais Gallais" ("in the Gauls") has usually been translated to mean "Gaul" (Dawes & Baynes) but nearby Galatia could be a possibility. On coin finds in Sweden, see Kulikowski 2019:224.

[33] See ch. XI, *infra*. Stewart 2014:17 connects the recruitment of Titus to the expansion of the *excubitores* but suggests that it may reflect a desire by Leo to *avoid* having all of his guards from a single ethnic group. Croke suggests that Titus and his men might have been recruited for the Vandal expedition. Croke 2005:180

[34] Candidus fr. 1 (*FCH*:467); *PLRE* 2, Tatianus 1; Fl. Vivianus 2. This was a year when the east chose both consuls, the other one being Leo. *CLRE*, 466–7 suggests the possibility that Vivianus may have been the western consul. Since these were to be the consuls for 466, the debate over their nomination would have occurred in late 465.

[35] As Urban Prefect, he dedicated the Column of Marcian in Constantinople. Angelova 2015:157. He was also present at the Council of Chalcedon, which may reflect his role as Urban Prefect and also shows his orthodoxy. If he had strong religious feelings, this could explain his opposition to the Ardaburii.

[36] *PLRE* 2, Tatianus 1; Priscus fr. 41 (*FCH*); Libanius, *Ep.* 899; Merrills & Miles 2010:118–19; Clover 1966:191–6. Were the remarks about the fact that Aspar was an Arian? Tatianus was the grandson of a high official under Theodosius I (also named Tatianus) who was dismissed after Theodosius's death and seems to have held strong anti-barbarian views. The younger Tatianus was educated by this grandfather. We can only speculate, but was this the basis for his anti-barbarian, anti-Arian views?

[37] Candidus, fr. 1 (*FCH*).

support Vivianus for a second consulship *before* the disclosure of the Persian letters in March 465 and it was Leo's decision later in the year to instead nominate Tatianus that angered Aspar.³⁸ This is possible, but does not explain why Aspar committed to Vivianus in the first place.³⁹ Vivianus had just served as consul in 463, and repeat consulships (except by reigning emperors) were uncommon.⁴⁰ In the end, while a few western consular lists include Tatianus (with Leo) for 466, his name does not appear elsewhere. It is unclear whether this omission was due to Tatianus' death or Aspar's opposition.⁴¹

There seems to have been another conflict around this time over the appointment of a new Urban Prefect, with Aspar supporting an Arian candidate who Leo rejected. Leo's candidate may have been Dioscorus, the tutor for Leo's daughters, who was appointed as Urban Prefect sometime before 467.⁴²

However, neither of these quarrels was the biggest blow to Aspar's grand strategy. Candidus says that "as a result of" the Tatianus/Vivianus dispute, Leo "allied himself with the Isaurian people through [Zeno], who he made his son-in-law."⁴³ With this marriage, Leo struck directly at Aspar's dynastic plans. Another important result was that, from this point on, Leo's dynastic hopes no longer ran through his brother-in-law Basiliscus, but through Ariadne and his new son-in-law, Zeno.⁴⁴

The marriage of Zeno and Ariadne apparently took place in early/mid-468.⁴⁵ If Ariadne had been the intended bride for Aspar's son, Patricius, then this move by Leo clearly showed his intention to frustrate Aspar's dynastic plans in favor of his own. Absent the scandal of the Persian letters, Leo might not have had the confidence to take such a bold action. Aspar presumably understood the implication—a male child of Zeno and Ariadne would have a very strong claim

---

³⁸ Croke 2005:161–2.
³⁹ *PLRE* 2, Vivianus 1 shows nothing that would seem to justify a second consulship, although comments suggest that Vivianus was a respected and popular civil official. Jo. Lydus comments that his consulship was remembered for its extravagance. *CLRE*, 460–61.
⁴⁰ *PLRE* 2, *Fasti*; Croke 2005:162.
⁴¹ *PLRE* 2, Tatianus 1; note comment that Tatianus "possibly was a victim of Aspar"; *CLRE*, 466–7; Croke 2005:161 at n. 51; Basic & Zeman 2019.
⁴² *PLRE* 2, Dioscorus 5, list of Urban Prefects for Constantinople at 1256. Croke 2005:162–3 says this was the dispute that led to the cloak-pulling scene, although Zonaras 14.1 places it even later, with the appointment of Patricius as Caesar in 470.
⁴³ Candidus, fr. 1 (*FCH*:467). The death of Zeno's first wife around this time made him available as a husband for Ariadne. Zeno's son by his first wife soon died. *Suda* Z 84 (*FCH*:415).
⁴⁴ Basiliscus may have already had a son named Marcus. Zeno also had a son by his first marriage, but a son of Zeno and Ariadne would presumably have taken precedence over either *PLRE* 2, Fl. Basilicsus 2, Fl. Zenon 7. See ch. XI, *infra*.
⁴⁵ Croke 2005:172–3 (revised marriage date, Croke 2021:76, 135–7, 157).

to the succession.⁴⁶ And, in fact, the newlyweds soon had a son, named Leo, in mid- to late 469.⁴⁷

The struggle between Aspar and Leo over the succession was far from over, but the line between them was now clearly drawn.⁴⁸ Both Aspar and Leo had their respective bases of support. On Aspar's side, he had his extended family and many friends in the government, much of the east Roman army, and the Thracian Goths. On Leo's side, he had both Basiliscus and Zeno, a portion of the army (parts of which were now commanded by Basiliscus, Jordanes, and Zeno), and the less tangible but very significant aid of the Orthodox Church (including the clergy, many monks, and Daniel the Stylite). The period of Aspar's dominance was over for now—in 467, the opposing forces of Aspar and Leo were in a precarious and unstable equilibrium. However, a decisive military success might allow Leo to secure his position.⁴⁹ Events were about to present Leo with an opportunity.

---

⁴⁶ Croke 2005:173. However, there were still the dynastic claims of Anthemius and Olybrius. An attempt by Anthemius' sons to overthrow Zeno in 479 narrowly failed. Similarly, in the early sixth century, there was the accession of Justin I over the nephews of the emperor Anastasius.
⁴⁷ *PLRE* 2, Leo 7. Croke 2003 (rev. Croke 2021:136–8, 157) for the date.
⁴⁸ Croke 2005:173; Clover 1978.
⁴⁹ Stewart 2014:11.

11

Leo's African Gamble (467–8)

Balkan Prelude

The relative stability achieved in the Balkans under Marcian was eventually disturbed in 466 when the Sciri went to war against the Pannonian Goths.[1] After it appeared that neither side was able to win, they both sent embassies to seek assistance from Constantinople. This situation led to yet another dispute between Aspar and Leo.[2] Aspar's position was that the east Romans should not support either side, perhaps hoping that they would destroy or weaken each other. Possibly encouraged by the early success of the Sciri in killing the Gothic king Valamer, Leo instead decided to support the Sciri. However, the Pannonian Goths eventually managed to defeat the Sciri, which gave them yet another grievance against Constantinople.

Possibly taking advantage of this situation, Hun remnants re-appeared on the scene, perhaps in early 467.[3] They were now led by sons of Attila named Dengizich and Ernach, each of whom ruled a different territory. Apparently in need of food and a Roman trading post, they sent an embassy to the east Romans offering to negotiate a new treaty. However, they were initially rebuffed by Leo.[4]

Although Ernach was not inclined to press the matter, Dengizich invaded Thrace and was confronted by the local Roman commander, Anagastes, probably a *comes rei militaris*. He was also the son of the east Roman general Arnegisclus, who had died dramatically near the end of the Hun war of 447.[5] Dengizich would not negotiate with a mere *comes* like Anagastes, but decided that another

---

[1] Croke 2005:175, 2021:79; Wolfram 1998:264.
[2] Priscus fr. 45 (*FCH*:353 and 396–7, n. 168); Wolfram 1998:264; Goffart 2006:204.
[3] Priscus fr. 46 (*FCH*:353) merely says "at this time." See Heather 1996:152; Heather 1991:254–63; Stewart 2014:10; Burns 1984:53–4.
[4] Priscus, fr.46 (*FCH*:353).
[5] See ch. VI, *supra*. This shows the multi-generational nature of the eastern military aristocracy.

embassy should be sent to Leo.[6] Surprisingly, this second embassy, perhaps sent in late 467 or early 468, received a completely different response—Leo now said he was "ready to do everything if they would remain obedient to him ..."[7] Why did Leo change his position so dramatically?

Several answers have been proposed. One view is that this reflects the interests of Aspar, who was anxious to protect his Thracian Goth allies from a Hun invasion.[8] However, as with the Sciri, Leo was probably not taking Aspar's advice at this time. Indeed, Leo may have seen a Hun presence on the Danube as a useful check on Aspar's support from the Thracian Goths. However, if so, why had it not occurred to Leo at the time of his initial reply to Dengizich?

A more plausible view is that Leo now wanted to appease the Huns because he had more pressing matters elsewhere. This is a pattern we have seen before. As in 440, east Rome wanted peace with the Huns in the Balkans because it was about to make a major military effort against the Vandals in Africa. A Balkan war with the Huns was the last thing that Leo wanted at this moment.[9]

It is unclear whether there were further negotiations with the Huns. The situation in the Balkans soon became very confused, with the east Romans fighting various bands of Goths and Huns. The date of this fighting has been debated, with some scholars arguing for 467 and others for 468 or 469. Because events in this war are precursors to the "revolt" of Anagastes, and because Anagastes' revolt was probably triggered by Leo's choice of consul for 469 (a decision made in late 468), I would place this war in late 467 or early 468.[10] Regaining control of the Balkans apparently required a major effort by the east Roman army in the latter part of 467. The Romans eventually managed to defeat and trap their enemies, although Dengizich escaped. The campaign involved several Roman generals, including Basiliscus, who was presumably still *m.m. per Thracias*.[11] Our sources also identify a separate unit as "Aspar's men," although it

---

[6] This is reminiscent of the multiple embassies sent by Attila, partly so that favored associates could receive the "gifts" that were usually bestowed by the Romans on ambassadors.

[7] Priscus fr. 48 (*FCH*:355).

[8] Croke 2005:176–7; Maenchen-Helfen 1973:166; Gordon 1960:135.

[9] Maenchen-Helfen 1973:166 draws an analogy to the events of 376 on the Danube but I believe the analogy to 440 is closer and would have been fresher in the minds of the east Romans. Blockley notes Leo was dealing with a series of natural catastrophes that occurred at this time. Priscus, fr. 48 (2) (*FCH*:355, 397 n. 172).

[10] Croke 2005:177 dated these events to 467, whereas Wolfram 1998 dated them to 469. However, recent scholarship suggests it may have been sometime in 468. Croke 2021:136–7, 157; Kosinski 2008:210–11. As in 440, Aspar had an important military role in the Balkans, but was not sent against the Vandals. Wolfram 1998:265–6.

[11] Priscus fr. 49 (*FCH*:357). This also helps us date the campaign to 467 or very early 468 because it was before Basiliscus was promoted and given command of the Vandal expedition.

does not mention Aspar himself being present.[12] Surprisingly, one source reports that Ardaburius took part in this campaign, and that he killed a Hunnic/Goth leader, Bigelas.[13] His presence may show that Ardaburius was not completely disgraced by the Persian letters, and perhaps that he had become a surrogate in the field for the aging Aspar.

The successful campaign by the east Romans in late 467–early 468 temporarily brought peace to the Balkans. It also allowed Leo to go forward with the great gamble that he believed would bring him a decisive military victory. The seeds for this effort had been planted by Leo as early as 465. However, to understand Leo's plan, we first need to look at the situation faced by Ricimer after he executed the western emperor Majorian in 461.

Ricimer's Vandal Problem

Ricimer, now the *de facto* ruler of the western empire, faced a shrinking base of potential soldiers and the means to hire them. Of his several enemies, the most dangerous was the Vandal kingdom in Africa.[14] In addition to possible personal enmity between Ricimer and Geiseric,[15] the Vandal fleet continued to disrupt seaborne trade in the western Mediterranean and raided coastal towns in southern and central Italy. After Majorian's proposed invasion failed, Geiseric simply ignored Ricimer, since he knew that the remnant of the western empire no longer posed a serious threat.

Ricimer also had enemies among the western Romans. Several former subordinates of the murdered general Aetius simply refused to accept Ricimer's regime, especially after the execution of Majorian.[16] While many of their soldiers were "barbarian," these officers were viewed as "Roman" unlike the "barbarian" Ricimer. They included the west Roman generals Aegidius and Marcellinus.

Aegidius was based in northern Gaul, trying to protect what was left of that region from the Franks and the Visigoths. After Majorian's execution, he refused

---

[12] Maenchen-Helfen 1973:167; Priscus fr. 49 (*FCH*:359, 397 n. 175).
[13] Jordanes, *Rom*. 336; *PLRE* 2, Ardabur iunior 1, Bigelis; Crawford 2019:60–1; Croke 2005:177 n. 93, 2021:80–1. However, this could be a reference to a separate campaign in 468.
[14] Jacobsen 2012:150–1; Merrills & Miles 2010; Clover 1966:182.
[15] Ricimer's grandfather had led the attack on the Vandals and Alans in Spain in 418. Kaperski 2015:226 n. 93 (citing Fredegar) suggests that Geiseric envied Ricimer because he had double royal parentage, i.e., "two kingdoms [Sueves and Visigoths] called him to kingship," whereas Geiseric was illegitimate. Kaperski 2015:226 n. 93; MacGeorge 2002:238.
[16] *PLRE* 2, Aegidius; Priscus, fr. 39 (*FCH*:343). LRE 2, Marcellinus 6; MacGeorge 2002:67, 92–3.

to recognize Ricimer's puppet-emperor Livius Severus, and instead set up a local government. However, Aegidius had a sense of the larger strategic picture. He may have claimed the emperor in Constantinople as his legitimate overlord.[17] He also threatened to invade Italy, although he never did. However, in May 465 he sent ambassadors to Geiseric to propose an alliance against Ricimer.[18] Shortly thereafter, in late 465, he apparently was murdered by poison or in an ambush. While we have no proof of his culpability, Ricimer certainly had a motive to remove Aegidius before he could combine against him with the Vandals.[19] The death of Aegidius eliminated one of the threats to Ricimer's rule.

Marcellinus had begun his revolt earlier, after the murder of Aetius in 454.[20] At that time, he was the commander of the west Roman forces in Dalmatia, perhaps a *comes rei militaris*. The regime that he set up in Dalmatia was essentially independent of Ricimer's regime from 454 until sometime around 457 when he agreed to recognize the authority of Majorian.[21] The coastal character of the Dalmatian command meant that Marcellinus had ships, and this would have made him particularly valuable in any campaign against the Vandals. As the ruler of Dalmatia, Marcellinus was also anxious to keep the Vandals from gaining control of the southern entrance to the Adriatic.[22]

Majorian promoted Marcellinus to the rank of *magister militum* and in 460 sent him to clear the Vandals from Sicily, a task which he apparently accomplished. However, from Ricimer's point of view, Marcellinus was perhaps a little too successful. After Majorian's execution, Ricimer bribed many of Marcellinus' troops in Sicily to desert to him, which caused Marcellinus to return to Dalmatia.[23]

Marcellinus rapidly rebuilt his forces to again become a potential threat to Ricimer's regime in Italy.[24] The combined threats from Marcellinus and the Vandals were more than Ricimer could handle, especially without a fleet to match his opponents.[25] It is interesting to read Priscus' explanation of why the east Romans declined to provide Ricimer with the ships he wanted: "The latter [i.e., the fleet] they sought from the eastern Romans but did not receive it because

---

[17] MacGeorge 2002: 93.
[18] Hydatius, s.a. 464–5; Merrils & Miles 2014:121; MacGeorge 2002:94; Clover 1966:182–3.
[19] Hydatius, s.a. 465; *PLRE* 2, Aegidius; MacGeorge 2002:66–7, 108.
[20] *PLRE* 2, Marcellinus 6; Procopius, *Wars*, I, 6.7; MacGeorge 2002:66–7.
[21] Sidonius Apollinaris, *Ep.* I, 1–1.6 refers to a *coniuratio Marcelliana* in 457, which may indicate that Marcellinus was considered as an alternative to Majorian as emperor. *PLRE* 2, Marcellinus 6; MacGeorge 2002:40–50; Harries 1994:83.
[22] MacGeorge 2002:50; Clover 1966:173–80.
[23] Priscus fr. 38 (*FCH*:341).
[24] Blockley suggests that Marcellinus may have been recruiting from the Pannonian Goths. Blockley 1992:345; cf. *PLRE* 2, Marcellinus 6.
[25] Priscus fr. 39 (*FCH*:343).

of the treaty that [the eastern Romans] had with the Vandals. Because of the division of the Empire this fact resulted in great harm for the western Romans."[26] In other words, in 462 the east Romans still felt bound by their 442 treaty with the Vandals and would not provide aid to a third party for use against the Vandals, even if that third party was the other half of the Roman empire.[27]

This refusal was prior to the Persian letters, i.e., at a time when Aspar was still dominant at Constantinople. It is also consistent with what was later alleged or suspected about Aspar's views. However, around 462 Leo was encouraged (perhaps by Olybrius) to renew diplomatic activity with the Vandals, especially with regard to the return of the Theodosian women captives.

At the same time, Ricimer's regime initiated a new diplomatic effort to try to deal with both Marcellinus and the Vandals.[28] Although Ricimer's ambassador had some success with Marcellinus, he had none with Geiseric. However, the east Romans finally made progress with Geiseric on the issue of the captives. Apparently, some payment was made to the Vandals, perhaps disguised as a dowry for Eudocia but really as a ransom for her mother and sister. One source contains an oblique (possibly sarcastic) reference to Eudocia's sister, the wife of Olybrius, describing her as "the one who had been ransomed, that is to say rescued, from captivity."[29] The return of the captives was probably too popular an issue for Aspar to oppose, especially since it was not a military action against the Vandals.

A further plea was made to Constantinople around 464, the west Romans claiming "they could not continue to resist unless the eastern Romans reconciled them with the Vandals." This appeal seems to have led to the unsuccessful embassy of Tatianus.[30]

Geiseric continued to raid Sicily and Italy in 462, 463, and 465. He also began to apply pressure against the eastern empire by extending his raids into the Adriatic and perhaps into the eastern Mediterranean. There were even rumors of a possible Vandal attack on Alexandria, which would have threatened the grain supply for Constantinople. Leo took the rumor seriously enough to consult Daniel the Stylite for advice.[31] Other than the release of the Theodosian women, all efforts at diplomacy with Geiseric had failed. Something had to be done about the Vandals.

[26] Ibid.
[27] MacGeorge 2002:233 n. 96; Clover 1966:190–1.
[28] For Ricimer's negotiations with Leo, see MacGeorge 2002:233–6. Priscus fr. 39 (*FCH*).
[29] *Chron. Pasch.* s.a. 464 (Whitby & Whitby:86, emphasis added). See also Croke 2005:180 n. 97; Clover 1966:182, 190–5.
[30] Priscus, fr. 41 (*FCH*:345–7), *PLRE* 2, Tatianus 1; Clover 1966:190–5; Mathisen 1986, 35–49; ch. X, *supra*.
[31] *V. Dan. Styl.*, ch. 56.

Clover suggests that Leo's attitude to the Vandal problem "had changed slowly" since his accession in 457.[32] However, the Persian letters allowed Leo to pursue a more aggressive Vandal policy and he may have welcomed a *rapprochement* with the west Romans. The death of Ricimer's puppet-emperor, Livius Severus, on November 14, 465 re-opened the question of the western succession.[33] Between 462 and 465, Leo slowly abandoned any idea of a diplomatic solution to the Vandal problem. After 465, he felt free to explore a military solution.

Ricimer wanted military help from the eastern empire to deal with the Vandals. Leo was prepared to provide that help, but he wanted something in return that would strengthen his own tenuous position. The solution was clever—Ricimer needed an emperor, and Leo had someone at hand with all the qualifications. As we have seen, Anthemius was so well-qualified that he might have been chosen as the east Roman emperor in 457 but for the opposition of Aspar. In fact, he could yet be a candidate should Leo die or suffer a serious reverse. For these reasons, sending him off to the west had the added benefit of removing a potential imperial claimant from Constantinople.[34] Finally, the choice honored the dynastic principle, since Anthemius could claim to be a member of the Theodosian house by virtue of his marriage to Marcian's daughter. After all, sending eastern forces to restore a Theodosian to the western throne was what Theodosius II had done in 424.[35]

Ricimer accepted this proposal as the price for east Roman assistance. However, in order to make sure of his new partner, he also wanted to reinforce his own status in the western empire by marriage to Anthemius' daughter, Alypia.[36] While their differences in age, religion, or social standing may not have been attractive to Anthemius (or Alypia), either Leo managed to convince him or Anthemius simply concluded it was worth the throne.[37] Agreement having

---

[32] Clover 1966:182–8, suggesting that Leo may have given tacit approval for Marcellinus to help Majorian against the Vandals in 460.

[33] *PLRE* 2, Libius Severus 18. *PLRE* notes an allegation by Cassiodorus that Ricimer had Severus poisoned, but a later poem by Sidonius Apollinaris "implicitly" denies this.

[34] *PLRE* 2, Anthemius 3. We do not know what Aspar thought of this. However, Aspar had frustrated Anthemius' hopes of becoming emperor in 457. Their subsequent relationship cannot have been close, especially since Aspar still hoped to see Patricius become Leo's successor. Croke suggests that Aspar may have encouraged the departure of Anthemius. Croke 2005:181. Clover 1978:169–96 agrees that Leo desired to remove both Anthemius and Olybrius from Constantinople

[35] Clover suggests that because Olybrius' daughter, Anicia Juliana (b.462) "eventually" married Aspar's great-grandson, this somehow means that Olybrius and his daughter were under the influence of Aspar in the 460s. Clover 1966:188–9. However, this seems unlikely since the marriage did not occur until 478. *PLRE* 2, Anicia Iuliana 2. Also, Olybrius was closely aligned with Leo and the Orthodox Church.

[36] MacGeorge 2002:235–6.

[37] This again shows that "barbarism" itself was not a bar to an imperial marriage. It also demonstrates the role of imperial women in establishing legitimacy.

Figure 10 *Solidus* of Anthemius with Leo I, *c.* 468 (*RIC X* 2804; wildwinds.com).

been reached, Anthemius was sent from Constantinople to Italy with a large army in the spring of 467, and was proclaimed emperor near Rome on April 12, 467.[38] Soon after this, Alypia was married to Ricimer.[39]

If the first order of business between Ricimer and Leo had been the western succession, then the next item was to plan the attack on the Vandals. This raised the question of what to do about Marcellinus. While Marcellinus had no love for Ricimer, he and his fleet would be very useful to the combined Roman forces. The solution was to give Marcellinus a role in Anthemius' new regime and in the proposed campaign against Geiseric.

Marcellinus may have already held the title of *magister militum*, perhaps *magister militum Dalmatiae*.[40] He accompanied Anthemius to Italy with troops in the spring of 467, and by 468 he is known to have held the rank of *patricius*, giving him titles very similar to those held by Ricimer. In this, Leo and Anthemius may have overplayed their hand, for the role that they gave Marcellinus was seen by Ricimer (probably correctly) not so much as that of an ally but rather as a counterweight to Ricimer's own power in the west.[41]

With the new regime in place in Italy by mid-467, Leo could start serious planning for his main objective—a military campaign against the Vandal kingdom.

---

[38] See Sidonius Apollinaris' panegyric for Anthemius: "Anthemius came to us with a treaty made by the two realms; an empire's peace has sent him to conduct our wars." *Carm.* 2.307–16.

[39] *PLRE* 2, Alypia, Anthemius 3. Anthemius would later bemoan the fact that he had agreed to this marriage as beneath his station. Cf. Sidonius Apollinaris, *Carm.*2; Ennodius, *Vita Ephiphani*; Arnold 2014:161.

[40] A title later held by Julius Nepos, his nephew and successor. *PLRE* 2, Iulius Nepos 3.

[41] *PLRE* 2, Marcellinus 6; O'Flynn 1983:117–18, 189.

The Expedition of Basiliscus Against the Vandals (468)

Leo made one final diplomatic effort with Geiseric in 467 soon after Anthemius' accession in Rome, but his message was more of an ultimatum which Geiseric rejected.[42] It may have been a diplomatic formality by Leo before going to war, or perhaps a final effort inspired by Aspar to avoid a conflict.

Given Geiseric's negative response, Leo began to gather his forces during the winter of 467/468. For once, Leo was willing to pay well for soldiers, and the word spread throughout the empire and possibly beyond.[43] Procopius tells us that Leo did this "out of fear that if he was parsimonious some obstacle would arise to his desire to punish the barbarians."[44]

The size of Leo's effort deeply impressed both ancient sources and modern historians.[45] One even called it "the Fourth Punic War."[46] It has been said that its "size and cost became a legend in antiquity."[47] Our best source for numbers is Priscus, who is said to have "set down [these events] with the greatest accuracy,"[48] and who seems to be the common source for later Byzantine historians. Theophanes tells us that Leo's fleet had 1,100 ships and that he spent 130,000 pounds of gold on the expedition.[49] One source suggests that even the disgraced Ardaburius may have accompanied the expedition.[50] It is likely that Aspar had some role in the planning, although no source suggests that he took part in the expedition.

The east Roman strategic plan involved a coordinated attack on the Vandals by several forces. The main force would be a large seaborne army that would gather in Constantinople, sail to Sicily to join with the west Roman forces there, and hopefully land somewhere near Carthage. A second east Roman force would land in Tripolitana and then march northwards towards Carthage.[51] It was

---

[42] Priscus, fr. 52 (*FCH*:361).
[43] Procopius, *Wars*, 3.6.1–2 and 5–15; Priscus fr. 53 (*FCH*). See ch. X, *supra*.
[44] Procopius, *Wars*, 3.6.
[45] For example, Theophanes AM 5961; Priscus fr. 53 (*FCH*). Crawford 2019:65–6; Heather 2005:399–407; Clover 1966:196–9.
[46] Croke 2005:179, citing Gauthier 1935:217–71. Cf. Clover 1966:219–26.
[47] Clover 1966:196–9, suggests that the fleet included about 1,000 ships and 40,000 men. Procopius, *Wars*, 3.6, adds that "this army numbered one hundred thousand men," which probably exaggerates a bit and may also include the sailors. McEvoy 2016a:252; Gibbon ch. XXXVI.
[48] Evagrius, *HE*, 2.16. See Priscus, fr. 53 (*FCH*:361–3), Crawford 2019:65–6; Croke 2005:180; Treadgold 1997:189–91.
[49] Procopius, *Wars*, 3.6.1–2; Theophanes, AM 5961; *FCH*:399 n. 184.
[50] Damascius, *Vita Isidori* (Photius Biblio. 242); Crawford 2019:67; Croke 2005:182 n. 105 (rev. Croke 2021:84).
[51] Based on Theophanes AM 5963, it has been suggested by Courtois that this campaign may have been separate and conducted later, perhaps in 470 or 471. Courtois 1955:204, n. 97. This suggestion has been adopted by Croke 2005:194–5, 2021:96. However, Lee comments that "this view has found little support". A.D. Lee, *CAH XIV*, 49 n. 99; see also Blockley 1992:76, 212 n. 37 who follows "the majority view based on Procopius."

thought that this force might gain assistance from local orthodox Christians who were being persecuted by the Arian Vandals. Assisting the orthodox was a theme that appealed to Leo and helped him to justify this war (much as Pulcheria had justified the Persian war of 421/422). It was not only consistent with Leo's efforts to champion orthodoxy, but it had the additional benefit of drawing attention to Arian oppression as he contended with Aspar.

Prior to these attacks in Africa, western forces led by Marcellinus would drive the Vandals from their bases in Sardinia, Sicily, and southern Italy.[52] Taking these three thrusts together, it would be the largest effort made by the Romans in the fifth century against any barbarian kingdom.

A critical issue was determining who would command each of these forces. Marcellinus would command the forces provided by the west Romans, which may be reflected in the new titles conferred on him by Anthemius in 468.[53] However, we hear nothing of a role for Ricimer in this plan, which again suggests that Anthemius was using Marcellinus to reduce Ricimer's influence.

The force sent to Tripolitana would be commanded by two generals, Heraclius of Edessa and Marsus the Isaurian.[54] Heraclius seems to have been the senior of the two.[55] He had previously commanded Roman forces assisting the Lazi against the Persians, and he would later campaign against the Goths in Thrace.[56] Malchus describes him as brave but reckless.[57] Little is known about Marsus, other than that (like Zeno) he was an Isaurian and (like Heraclius) a partisan of Leo.[58]

But who would command the main army and fleet that would sail from Constantinople? If Leo's aims were not already clear to Aspar, they would have become so in late 467/early 468 when Leo promoted his brother-in-law, Basiliscus, to the rank of *m.m. praesentalis* and named him as the commander of the main expeditionary force. The contrast between the commanders of Leo's forces in 468 and the expedition that had been sent against the Vandals in 441 could not be sharper—as we have seen, in 441 most of the senior Roman commanders had Germanic names; in 468, *none* of them did.

---

[52] Priscus fr. 52 (*FCH*).
[53] *PLRE* 2, Marcellinus 6.
[54] Priscus fr. 53 (*FCH*).
[55] He is said to be the son of Florus of Edessa. *PLRE* 2, Florus 3. However, he might have been the son of the person identified in *PLRE* 2 as Florus 2, the prefect of Egypt in the 450s. Conceivably, both were the same person.
[56] *PLRE* 2, Heraclius 4.
[57] Malchus, fr. 6 (*Suda*, H 466) (*FCH*:413).
[58] *PLRE* 2, Marsus 2; Burgess 1992:878. While he may have supported Zeno against Aspar, Marsus later supported the Isaurian Illus against Zeno. Both Heraclius and Marsus had connections to Isauria/Syria, so they may have been known to Zeno (or possibly Jordanes, who was now at Antioch).

The choice of Basiliscus was not illogical. In 468, there were only two men who held the rank of *m.m. praesentalis* in the east Roman army.⁵⁹ One was Aspar; the other was Basiliscus. If someone was to lead the largest expeditionary force that east Rome had ever assembled, it was logical to name one of them, much like Areobindus in 441 or Ardaburius the Elder in 424.⁶⁰ While Aspar had more experience fighting the Vandals, that had been twenty-five years earlier. Aspar was now close to seventy years old; Basiliscus was the younger man.⁶¹

In addition, Basiliscus' military reputation at the beginning of 468 was not what it would be by the end of the year. He had been a soldier for a long time, and he had fought successfully against the Goths and Huns in the Balkans. The characterization of him by later chroniclers and historians as incompetent and/or corrupt is colored by their hindsight knowledge of what happened to the expedition, as well as events during his brief reign as emperor.⁶²

With this later knowledge, our sources try to assign blame and make charges. Croke reviewed the array of opinions, noting that superior Vandal seamanship was a likely cause, but that the incompetence of Basiliscus inspired persistent claims of treason.⁶³ These charges sometimes fall on Aspar and sometimes on Basiliscus, often depending on the sympathies of the author. While a charge of treason against Aspar is found in Hydatius,⁶⁴ Brooks noted that this controversial entry did not explicitly connect Aspar's disgrace to the failure of the expedition. However, the reference is in 468 and it does refer to conspiring with the Vandals. Priscus, who wrote under Zeno (and so might have been expected to disparage Aspar) attributed the failure to bribery of Basiliscus by Geiseric, not Aspar, although he also says Basiliscus wanted to do "a favor" for Aspar. The matter is complicated by later events involving Basiliscus—Leo may have wanted to shift the blame to Aspar; but partisans of Zeno may have wanted to blame Basiliscus. Gibbon believed that the charges against Aspar were later fabricated to cover up

---

⁵⁹ Croke 2005:181. The position had become vacant when Anthemius was sent to become western emperor.
⁶⁰ Had Ardaburius not been disgraced in 465, might he have had this command? If he had accompanied his father in Africa in 431-5, he might have had the right experience. And some sources suggest that Ardaburius accompanied or otherwise assisted the expedition. Croke 2005:182 n. 105, 2021:84 n. 162. But it would have been a huge risk for Leo, since a success by Ardaburius would have seriously weakened Leo's position. For Leo, Basiliscus was the better choice.
⁶¹ McEvoy 2016:489-90 on age. However, Arnold noted to author the Byzantine general Liberius, who was sent against the Ostrogoths in 550 at age 85 and then against the Visigoths in Spain two years later. *PLRE* 2, Petus Marcellinus Felix Liberius 3 (at 677-81). Similarly, the Byzantine general Narses campaigned successfully in Italy when he was in his 70s.
⁶² Gibbon, ch. XXXVI says that the empress Verina exaggerated Basiliscus' military ability to Leo, and that "the discovery of his guilt, or incapacity, was reserved for the African war."
⁶³ Croke 2021:84-6; McEvoy 2016:489.
⁶⁴ Hydatius, s.a. 468; Theod. Lect. 1, 25; Procopius, *Wars*, I, 4; Theophanes AM 5961.

the incompetence of Basiliscus, and Jones agreed. Similarly, Roberto 2009 believes that the charges of collusion with Geiseric are "not provable" and suggests that the failure of Basiliscus' expedition only confirms the good sense of Aspar's policies. However, Bury and others have repeated the accusation that Aspar sought the failure of the expedition.[65]

How would the choice of Basiliscus have appeared to Aspar in 468 in the context of his struggle with Leo? We have little knowledge of relations between Aspar and Basiliscus.[66] Basiliscus was part of Leo's circle and was now of equal rank to Aspar. If the expedition was successful, it would strengthen the reputation and power of both Leo and Basiliscus, and weaken that of Aspar, who had opposed the effort. Aspar thus had reason to want the expedition to fail purely for domestic political reasons, quite apart from any understanding he may or may not have had with Geiseric.[67] Some have claimed that Aspar supported the choice of Basiliscus because Aspar knew him to be incompetent. However, Basiliscus had recently worked with "Aspar's men" in successfully checking the Huns of Dengizich. On its face, this does not show a lack of ability, although Aspar may have made his own judgement.

Not surprisingly, some sources charge that Basiliscus was bribed or persuaded by Aspar to see that the expedition would fail.[68] In addition to the fact that such allegations were a standard charge whenever things went wrong, the accusation of bribery makes little sense. Basiliscus knew that success against the Vandals would have made him very powerful in east Rome, second only to the emperor himself. If so, what bribe would have been great enough to make Basiliscus forfeit the exalted position he would achieve by a success?

Alternatively, it has been suggested that Basiliscus might have been persuaded that the failure would be blamed on Leo, and that things would end with a new emperor in Constantinople. In such circumstances, Basiliscus might have thought he could replace Leo (perhaps with the support of Aspar, who may have encouraged Basilicus' hopes). As later events showed, Basiliscus was certainly ambitious enough to take the eastern throne for himself, regardless of his family tie to Leo.[69] It is possible that Basiliscus (as well as Aspar) was also open to this

---

[65] Brooks 1893:209-38; Priscus, fr. 53 (*FCH*); Gibbon, ch. XXXVI; Jones 1964:22; Roberto 2009; cf. LRE, vol. I:335; Previtte-Orton 1952:465; Barker 1966:40; Salzman 2021:206.
[66] Croke 2005:182-3, 2021:84-6.
[67] Croke 2005:183.
[68] Priscus fr. 53 (*FCH*:363-5) accuses Geiseric of bribery but also says that Basiliscus' acceptance of a truce was done "as a favor to Aspar." Similarly, Theophanes *Chron*, AM 5961, Jordanes, *Rom*. 337. Modern historians tend to doubt the accusation of bribery, but the political angle remains possible. Stewart 2014:11 n. 44; MacGeorge 2002:58.
[69] See ch. XIII, *infra*. Croke 2005:183.

scenario because he saw Leo's elevation of Zeno as blocking his path to the throne. Procopius describes Basiliscus as "a man extraordinarily eager to become Emperor, which he thought he could achieve without difficulty *if he won the friendship of Aspar* ...70 so, they say that Aspar feared that if the Vandals were defeated Leo would establish his hold on the throne more securely, and so he [Aspar] repeatedly urged upon Basiliscus to spare the Vandals and Geiseric."71

Almost a millennium later, the Byzantine historian Nicephorus Callistus tried to make sense of all this by positing a conspiracy by Basiliscus to gain Aspar's backing for him to replace Leo.72 However, there are two difficulties with this theory.

First, it requires Basilicus to assume that the blame for the failure of the expedition would fall mainly on Leo, not on himself.73 However, it was Basiliscus who was the subject of popular anger when he returned to Constantinople after his defeat, anger so severe that he had to take refuge in St. Sophia. He was supposedly spared punishment only because of the intercession of his sister, the empress Verina. Nonetheless, the failure of the expedition did not stop Basiliscus from becoming emperor in 475. And Basiliscus supported Leo in the final showdown with Aspar in 471.

Another (and perhaps more critical) objection is that the replacement of Leo by Basiliscus would not have achieved Aspar's goal of marrying Patricius into the imperial family. Basiliscus had a son, Marcus, who Basiliscus would eventually name as Caesar, as well as an ambitious nephew named Armatus, both of whom could have taken precedence over Patricius even if Patricius had already been married to one of Leo's daughters (which he was not in 468).

However, a simpler explanation is also plausible—if Aspar conspired in the expedition's failure, the object was to weaken Basiliscus, which in turn would weaken Aspar's main opponent, Leo.74 Aspar might have encouraged the "slow-witted" Basiliscus to think that he would gain if the expedition was defeated, even if Aspar knew better. In short, Aspar had sufficient political reasons in 468 to welcome a failure by Basiliscus without any need to attribute this to an "understanding" he had supposedly reached with Geiseric in the 430s.75

Nonetheless, the circumstances of the defeat looked suspicious. It was inevitable that a defeat would be attributed to treachery, and Aspar must have

---

70 Procopius, *Wars*, 3, 6, 2 (emphasis added). See also Priscus, fr. 53 (*FCH*:363 and n. 186).
71 Procopius, *Wars*, 3, 6, 3–4. See also Stewart 2014:11; MacGeorge 2002:57.
72 Nicephorus Callistus, *HE*, 15.27 (PG 153.80); Croke 2021:85–6.
73 Stewart 2014:12.
74 Croke 2005:183.
75 Crawford 2019:72–4.

known that he was likely to be a target of such accusations. The story about Marcian's eagle may have been an effort by Chalcedonians to justify the legitimacy of Marcian, but the details of his capture and promise to Geiseric in the 430s may have been added by later sources as an oblique attack on Aspar and an attempt to "explain" the disaster of 468 as the result of a conspiracy by Arian barbarians.

Whatever the politics of the situation, by early 468 Basiliscus had received the command of the expedition, and the fleet sailed from Constantinople. Initially, things went well for the Romans. Marcellinus successfully drove the Vandals from Sardinia, and then apparently went to Sicily to await the arrival of the east Romans.[76] In the early naval actions, the Romans were successful, and the Vandals withdrew their fleet to Carthage.[77]

The force advancing from Egypt had even greater success. It landed in Tripolitana and captured several cities before the army began marching overland towards Carthage.[78] Procopius claims that these early successes greatly alarmed Geiseric.[79]

After linking up with the west Romans, Basiliscus arrived at Cape Bon, not far from the Vandal capital at Carthage. At this point, Geiseric apparently requested a five-day truce, in which time he "might take counsel and do those things which the emperor most desired."[80] Basiliscus accepted the offer, a fatal decision which became the object of much criticism.

During this truce, Basiliscus apparently landed at least some troops and anchored his fleet close inshore. Procopius (writing in the sixth century with a different agenda) believed that the truce was "the result of cowardice or treachery," which he attempted to explain as follows:

> Basiliscus, either as a favor to Aspar as promised, or because he had sold the opportunity for money, or because he thought it the best course, granted their request, did not stir from his camp and conceded the initiative to the enemy.[81]

It appears that Procopius did not really know what had happened but was repeating various allegations that had subsequently been made. Familiar explanations are alleged—cowardice, treachery, politics, and bribery. However,

---

[76] Clover suggests that Marcellinus may also have made a raid on Africa that disrupted efforts by Geiseric to form a Vandal/Sueve/Visigothic alliance against the Romans. Clover 1966:195–6.
[77] Clover 1966:196–9.
[78] Priscus, fr. 53 (*FCH*:365); Procopius, *Wars*, 3.6, 9. Although the majority view is that this campaign occurred in 468, there is a minority view that it occurred in 470. Cf. Clover 1966:199.
[79] Procopius, *Wars*, 3.6; Priscus fr. 53 (*FCH*).); Gibbon, ch. XXXVI.
[80] Priscus, fr. 53; Gibbon, ch. XXXVI.
[81] Priscus fr. 53 (*FCH*, 365); Procopius, *Wars*, 1, 2, 5–27; Gibbon, ch. XXXVI; Jacobsen 2012:154.

his first point is quite specific, i.e., accepting the truce might have been done "as a favor to Aspar as promised." This is consistent with Procopius' statements that Aspar had "repeatedly urged upon Basiliscus to spare the Vandals and Geiseric," and that acceptance of the truce was done "as a favor to Aspar."[82]

These comments in our sources are the most serious bases for the allegation that Aspar "suborned" Basiliscus to have the expedition fail. Taken at face value, they suggest that Aspar was secretly acting in Geiseric's interest by giving Basiliscus bad advice. But might there be an alternate interpretation of these comments?

From our prior discussion of Aspar's campaign in Africa in 431–5, we know that there were two pitched battles in both of which the Romans were defeated by the Vandals.[83] And yet the eventual treaty in 435 was a compromise between the Romans and the Vandals. It was previously suggested that, following the two defeats, Aspar may have engaged in a war of attrition that brought Geiseric to the bargaining table. Was the advice Aspar gave to Basiliscus that he should avoid a pitched battle with the Vandals, because the Vandals might agree to reasonable terms if given a chance to negotiate?[84] In such circumstances, Basiliscus could return to Constantinople claiming a "victory." Is this why Basiliscus granted the truce, especially since Geiseric's message suggested he was willing "to do those things which the emperor most desired"?

There is one final possibility. Only in his last clause does Procopius suggest that Basiliscus might have actually thought this was "the best course."[85] One can think of several reasons why a brief truce might have seemed to Basiliscus to be "the best course." The fleet may have needed to refit before a climactic sea battle with the experienced Vandals. Similarly, the seaborne army may have needed a few days ashore. Also, Basiliscus may not have known where the army of Heraclius was, and whether it was in a position to assist him in an assault on Carthage. Scouts sent out during the truce could bring him that intelligence.

Of course, Geiseric used the time to prepare the main Vandal fleet, including a number of fireships. The Vandals' knowledge of the local weather suggested an imminent change which would give them the windward advantage. Sending the fireships into the Roman anchorage caused panic as the Roman ships attempted

---

[82] Priscus, fr. 53 (*FCH*:365).
[83] See ch. V, *supra*.
[84] Geiseric's message might also support this. However, the weakness of this argument is that Basiliscus probably knew that Geiseric had broken his word by capturing Carthage in 439.
[85] Procopius, *Wars*, 5–27; Croke 2005:182; Gibbon, ch. XXXVI. Elton 2018:201, 242 believes the cause was most likely a "military failure" by the Romans and the superior leadership of Geiseric, rather than a betrayal by either Aspar or Basiliscus.

to escape the flames. Those that were able to do so immediately found themselves confronted by the main Vandal fleet. Although some Roman ships were able to reach Sicily, a large portion (perhaps half) of their fleet was destroyed. It was the unhappy end of Leo's great gamble, and the last time that the west Romans were able to mount any significant military offensive.

Learning of this disaster, the force led by Heraclius and Marsus retreated to Tripolitana, which was later returned to the Vandals by treaty in 471.[86] Similarly, Marcellinus returned to Sicily, only to be assassinated by one of his officers. It is assumed that this was the work of his western rival, Ricimer.[87]

One of the survivors of the battle was Basiliscus himself, who apparently was aboard a ship anchored at the far end of the anchorage. He returned in disgrace to Constantinople. Knowing the fury he would face from Leo and the people of the city, he immediately sought sanctuary at St. Sophia, where he remained for some time until Leo finally allowed him to leave. Angry as Leo was, he still had need for Basiliscus in his ongoing duel with Aspar and perhaps now more than ever.

---

[86] Courtois 1955:202–4 reads Theophanes AM 5963 to suggest that a force under Basiliscus, Heraclius, and Marsus made a second attempt to take Carthage in a campaign in 470/471 but was withdrawn from Africa in 471 because Leo needed them for the show-down with Aspar. Croke 2005:194–5, 2021:96. Lee and others disagree. *CAH XIV*, 49 n. 99; Crawford 2019:84–5; Blockley 1992:75–6, 212. See also Priscus fr. 53 (*FCH*); Procopius, *Wars*, 3.6. Blockley 1992:76 believes Heraclius and Marsus withdrew initially only to Tripolitana, which they evacuated in 471 when Leo made a new treaty with Geiseric. Leo may have given up Tripolitana to prevent the Vandals from coming to Aspar's aid. Merrills & Miles 2014:122.

[87] *PLRE* 2, Marcellinus 6; Gibbon, ch. XXXVI; MacGeorge 2002:58–60.

12

Aspar's Apogee and Defeat (469–71)

Just as the disclosure of Ardaburius' letters to the Persians in 465 had swung the political balance in Constantinople in Leo's favor, the catastrophic defeat of Basiliscus' expedition against the Vandals in 468 now swung the balance back towards Aspar and Ardaburius.[1] It did not take long for Ardaburius to launch an intrigue that was probably aimed at eliminating Zeno.

The Revolt of Anagastes (469)

Anagastes had played a major role in suppressing the Hun/Goth raids into Thrace in 466/67. He probably replaced Basiliscus as *m.m. per Thracias* in 468, when Basiliscus was promoted and sent to Africa.[2] His father was Arnegisclus, a Roman general who had died in the Hun war in 447. As discussed, in the earlier Hun war in 441, Arnegisclus had apparently been responsible for the death of John the Vandal, a Roman general who seems to have been an ally of Aspar.[3]

The fuse for Anagastes' "revolt" was lit in late 468 or early 469 by the reappearance in Thrace of Dengizich. Having escaped the massacre of the Huns by "Aspar's men," Dengizich returned from beyond the Danube with new forces on a raid into Thrace. He was probably motivated by a desire for revenge, and perhaps by knowledge that the east Romans had again weakened their position in the Balkans by sending troops on an African expedition. The latter would have been true even if he did not yet know of the disastrous outcome of that expedition. A military response by the Romans was required, and Anagastes, as the *m.m. per Thracias*, would initially lead it.[4]

---

[1] John Lydus, *De Magistratibus*, 3.43–4; Stewart 2014:12.
[2] Croke 2005:184, n. 113. Cf. *PLRE* 2 which suggests that Zeno replaced Basiliscus in 468 but see *infra*.
[3] See ch. VI, *supra*.
[4] Croke believes that Zeno may have been involved in the Balkan fighting of 468/469, but probably as *comes domesticorum*, not yet as *m.m. per Thracias*. Croke 2005:178. Cf. Stewart 2014:10. Zeno was probably appointed *m.m. per Thracias* in 469 to replace and suppress Anagastes, Croke 2005:184–7, 2021:86–9.

Since the memory of Attila's invasions still lingered among the east Romans, any attack by the Huns was taken seriously. However, Anagastes defeated and killed Dengizich, thus ending the last major Hun threat against the empire.[5] Dengizich's head was paraded through Constantinople and put on display.[6] This success came at an opportune time for Leo's regime, now reeling from the disaster of the African expedition.

Anagastes apparently basked in his victory, and felt he deserved a higher award, such as a consulship.[7] However, when the consuls for 470 were chosen in late 469, he was disappointed to learn that he had not been selected. Worse, the emperor Leo's choice was Jordanes, the *m.m. per Orientem*.

The choice of Jordanes was particularly galling to Anagastes, because of the bitter history between their families.[8] Priscus believed this was the main reason why Anagastes decided to revolt. However, he also noted that Anagastes was an epileptic who might not have been able to perform consular duties. As usual, he mentions that "others" suggested that the revolt was for "money."[9] We are not exactly sure what Anagastes did, but certain of his actions in late 469 were taken as a "revolt" against Leo.[10]

Leo mobilized a force to suppress the revolt under the command of Zeno, who was now appointed *m.m. per Thracias* in place of Anagastes.[11] However, in addition to the military response, Leo also sent officials who negotiated with Anagastes and dissuaded him from any further action. According to Priscus, Anagastes then "revealed that Ardabur, the son of Aspar, was responsible for the revolt and [Anagastes] sent Ardabur's letters to the Emperor."[12]

The first astonishing thing is that, once again, there were letters.

This really makes one wonder about Ardaburius. While Blockley says "he appears to have had a penchant for plotting,"[13] he was not very good at it. After

---

[5] "Huns" is used to mean the peoples led by Attila and his sons, not the much later raid of 559 by the so-called "Kotrigur Huns."
[6] *Chron. Pasch.* s.a. 468 (90, especially n. 294). See also Marcell. *comes* s.a. 469; Maenchen-Helfen 1973:168; Croke 2005:179 n. 95.
[7] He may also have suppressed a revolt by another Goth named Ulith or Oullibus. See Priscus fr. 54 (*FCH*:369 and n. 190); McEvoy 2016:490.
[8] See ch. VI, *supra*.
[9] Priscus, fr. 56 (*FCH* 369).
[10] Priscus fr. 56 (*FCH* 369) Jo. Antioch. fr. 206, 2. PLRE 2, Anagastes.
[11] PLRE 2, Armatus; Croke 2005:184–6; see *V. Dan Styl.* ch. 65. Some sources suggest that Armatus, the nephew of Basiliscus, was the *m.m. per Thracias* who commanded the force sent against Anagastes. It seems Armatus was in this post in 471, and it is possible that he may have held it earlier. The explanation may be that Zeno was initially named *m.m. per Thracias* in 469 but was replaced by Armatus after the attempt on Zeno's life and his transfer to Antioch.
[12] Priscus fr. 56 (*FCH*:369).
[13] Blockley 1992:76.

the disgrace of the Persian letters, one would have expected Ardaburius to exercise some discretion in his intrigues. Yet, we again have written letters to his intended co-conspirator that could be used against him. This renews the question of how much Aspar knew about what his son was doing, and whether he still had any control over him. Another possibility is that the aging Aspar may have become more anxious to achieve his dynastic ambitions, and perhaps willing to tolerate less cautious measures.[14]

The second astonishing thing is that Ardaburius chose to plot with Anagastes, whose family history does not suggest that he would be a likely ally of the Ardaburii. Aspar had been aligned with Jordanes, not Anagastes, at least until Jordanes changed sides in 465. However, in 469 the key factor seems to be that Leo was the common enemy of both the Ardaburii and Anagastes. It also shows how little we know about the shifting political currents among these people, and how misleading it may be to assume too rigid a model of "factions." Perhaps Ardaburius had developed a good personal relationship with Anagastes during their campaigns in the 460s. Or perhaps the real purpose of the "revolt" of Anagastes was to lure Zeno out of the city and into a more vulnerable position. This will not be the last time that we will see Ardaburius attempting to detach supporters from Leo. His final intrigue may have proved fatal for him.

The third astonishing thing is that neither Ardaburius nor Aspar appear to have suffered for this conduct.[15] Our sources contain nothing that indicates that Ardaburius, or Aspar, were penalized in any significant way for this second attempt at treason. Instead, the Ardaburii were about to reach their political apogee, driving Zeno from Constantinople and finally achieving their dynastic dream. However, nothing further is heard of Anagastes.

The Plot Against Zeno (469)

A good question about the revolt of Anagastes is "why did Ardaburius instigate it at all?" Croke's hypothesis is that it was only the first step in a plot by "Ardaburius and Aspar" to isolate Leo in Constantinople by having Zeno sent out to suppress the revolt. Aspar may even have suggested it, perhaps saying that Zeno knew Anagastes from the earlier campaign.[16] Leo may have seen it as a way for his regime to regain some of the military prestige that it had recently lost in the

[14] McEvoy 2016:489–90.
[15] Ibid. 2005:187.
[16] Ibid. 2005:187.

Vandal expedition and an opportunity to showcase Zeno. However, for the Ardaburii, the real reason may have been to get Zeno out of the capital and into a setting where a kidnapping or assassination could more easily occur.[17]

As the new *m.m. per Thracias*, Zeno set out for the Balkans from Constantinople (where he was serving as consul). Accompanying him was a unit of the *domestici* guards. Although Zeno had been a member and then commander of the *domestici*, it was apparently men from this unit who were bribed or otherwise persuaded by "Aspar" to take Zeno prisoner. However, Zeno was warned about the plot (by one of the *domestici*?) and managed to escape.

Initially, he fled to the Balkan city of Serdica, but then took a very roundabout route to Chalcedon, across the Bosporus from the capital. Significantly, he avoided returning to Constantinople.[18] While at Chalcedon, Zeno received a new appointment from Leo to go to Antioch as *m.m. per Orientem* to replace Jordanes, who would become consul for 470. Zeno first went to Isauria where he was joined by his wife, Ariadne, and his infant son.[19] Zeno eventually arrived at his new headquarters in Antioch, where he remained until 471.[20]

There are a number of questions about this plot and its aftermath. It has been suggested that references in our sources to "Aspar" mean *both* Aspar and Ardaburius.[21] However, the letters produced by Anagastes are described by Priscus as coming from "Ardabur, the son of Aspar" and it was "Ardabur's letters" that were sent to Leo. There is nothing in the sources to indicate that the letters came from Aspar, or that Aspar was responsible for them, although it is possible that he was. It is also possible that Ardaburius acted independently.

Whether the aim was to kill or capture Zeno, this plot represents an escalation of violence in the struggle between the Ardaburii and Leo.[22] In 465, Leo had had sufficient reason to order the execution of Ardaburius over the Persian letters, but he did not do so. However, in 469 there was a very good reason why the

---

[17] Ibid. Unlike Croke 2005:178, 187 n. 120, 2021:81–2, 90 n. 183, I tend to believe that Ardaburius' plot with "the Isaurians" came later than 469, but it is possible.
[18] *V. Dan. Styl.*, ch. 65.
[19] Croke 2005:187–8. Zeno would again flee to Isauria during his brief overthrow as emperor in 475–6. These actions emphasize the Isaurian side of Zeno's identity. It also undercuts the idea that in 469 he already had an Isaurian force in Constantinople (the *excubitores*) that would protect him. Croke 2005:186. It is possible that Zeno fled to Isauria first, and then returned to Chalcedon, but this seems unlikely. Croke 2005:189; Jo. Malalas, *Chron.*, 15.12.
[20] Priscus, fr. 57 (*FCH*); Jo. Antioch fr. 206, 2. The suppression of the bandits occurred while Zeno was still consul, i.e., in 469. Croke 2005:194. On his appointment as *m.m. per Orientem*, see *PLRE* 2, Fl. Zenon 7.
[21] Croke 2005:187 who "presumes" the involvement of Aspar.
[22] Theophanes, *Chron.*, AM 5962 points to the attempt to assassinate Zeno as being the event which "incurred Leo's suspicion" about the Ardaburii. *FCH*:399, n. 189. This event may have made Leo worry that the Ardaburii were now prepared to use violence against him and his family.

Ardaburii would have wanted to kill Zeno—if Zeno was dead, then Ariadne would be a widow, and she would again be available for marriage to Patricius.[23]

Zeno's route after he escaped the plot has also been extensively discussed.[24] There seems little doubt that he deliberately avoided the more direct route to Constantinople through Adrianople. Why did he do so, and why did he not join Leo in Constantinople?

As to the first question, it is likely that he considered the direct route too dangerous, most likely because it would have taken him through a region inhabited by Aspar's allies, the Thracian Goths.[25] As to the second question, Zeno appears to have avoided Constantinople because it was also dangerous for him to return to the imperial capital.[26] If so, the wisest thing was to get his family to safety in Isauria or to distant Antioch. In short, Zeno's response to the plot was flight, not fight. It is telling that he apparently felt he had so little support among the military forces he was supposed to be leading that flight was his best option.

The disclosure of Ardaburius' letters to Anagastes should have been another embarrassing fiasco for the Ardaburii, similar to what had occurred after the disclosure of the Persian letters. The fact that it was not, and that none of the Ardaburii were punished, may indicate the weakness of Leo's position. However, Leo presumably still had forces available to him—e.g., his guards, and the eastern army (perhaps still under the influence of Jordanes, and now commanded by Zeno). But most important, he still had the support of the Orthodox Church. Although he had become unpopular due to his military defeats, he could still use the power of the church to rally his supporters among the people of Constantinople. Leo was weakened, but probably not quite ready for a final confrontation with the Ardaburii. And perhaps Aspar had offered him a compromise.

Here we may come to the heart of the difference between Aspar and Ricimer.[27] Unlike Ricimer, Aspar never used his power to kill or overthrow an emperor. Aspar's standard preference was to negotiate a solution, and he did not overplay his hand at this point.[28] The deal he seems to have made with Leo preserved the

---

[23] Matters might have been complicated by the fact that Ariadne already had a son by Zeno. However, given the rate of child mortality in the fifth century, things could change (in fact, young Leo II did not live very long).
[24] See Croke 2005:187-90.
[25] Ibid., 188.
[26] Ibid., 187-90.
[27] Lot 1927:218.
[28] Other examples include the settlement with Aetius and his Huns in 424; the settlement with the Vandals in 435; the initial truce with the Huns in 441; the accession of Marcian in 450 and that of Leo in 457; and possibly the settlement of the Goths in Thrace in the 450s.

precarious equilibrium between them. Zeno and his family went to Antioch, far from the capital and from Leo. This was not dissimilar to the type of internal exile that Leo had allowed to Basiliscus after his defeat. The anger of the Ardaburii was primarily directed against the advancement of Zeno into the imperial family because it threatened their own dynastic plans. It has even been suggested that the Ardaburii may have agreed to stop plotting against Leo, provided that Zeno stayed far away. And in exchange, Leo would finally honor the promise that he had made to Aspar in 457, and which had always been Aspar's greatest objective—Leo would allow Aspar's son, Patricius, to marry into the imperial family and to have the title of Caesar, thus endorsing him as Leo's heir apparent.

Patricius Caesar (470)

The transfer of Zeno to Antioch, following on the disgrace of Basiliscus, undermined Leo's authority and put the Ardaburii back in a dominant position in Constantinople.[29] While we have few details about this period,[30] the one thing that is clearly reported in our sources is that in 470 Patricius was finally given the title of Caesar.[31] McEvoy rightly calls this "a spectacular triumph" for Aspar, and the fulfillment of the promise that was probably extracted from Leo in 457.[32]

"Caesar" at this time usually meant the presumed successor to a reigning Augustus. Under the Constantinian and Theodosian emperors, a Caesar was normally a son of the reigning Augustus. However, there were some variations on this general rule. For example, Anthemius, the son-in-law of Marcian, was presumably intended as a successor, but never received the title of Caesar. Moreover, when Anthemius was later made an Augustus in the west by Leo, he did not first become a Caesar. The succession to Leo himself was unique—shortly

---

[29] Croke 2005:190–1, 194; MacGeorge 2002:267. While succession had been an issue since 457, MacGeorge is right that it became paramount in 470/471.
[30] There is a peculiar story from 470 when the general Jordanes was consul. While Leo was away, Jordanes is said to have toured Leo's private chambers. When Leo returned, he was furious and Jordanes was thought to be "in extreme danger." Since Jordanes had become a favorite of Leo by his conversion, why was Leo so enraged? Did he think that Jordanes was seeking to become emperor? Elton 2018:202. This may demonstrate Leo's edgy and "suspicious" state of mind at this time. Priscus, fr. 63 (*FCH*:373); John of Antioch, fr. 209, 1.
[31] Croke 2005:190–5.
[32] McEvoy 2016:490. See also Evagrius, *HE*, 2.16; Zonaras 14.3; Theophanes, *Chron.*, AM 5963; *V. Marcelli*; Croke 2005:191–3.

before his death in 474, he made his young grandson (the son of Zeno and Ariadne) his Caesar and then his co-Augustus.[33] After Leo's death, this enabled the child to make his father, Zeno, a co-Augustus, who then became the sole Augustus when the boy died. Like Anthemius, Zeno never held the preliminary title of Caesar.[34] In the east, Patricius was unusual in receiving this title without being a relative of the reigning emperor by either blood or marriage.[35] However, he may have set a precedent—Armatus, the nephew of Basiliscus, later forced Zeno to name his son as Caesar, although the boy was neither Zeno's son nor someone with a marriage connection to an imperial woman.[36]

Leo did not make Patricius his Caesar willingly but was forced by circumstances to do so. Our sources describe Patricius as someone who Leo "made Caesar in order to win Aspar's favor."[37] In other words, Leo could no longer resist Aspar's demand that Leo fulfill the promise that he had apparently made in 457.

Patricius not only received the title at this time but may also have at least been betrothed (but not yet married) to one of Leo's daughters. The name of the daughter is not given in our sources. However, it is assumed by historians that this was Leontia, the younger daughter of Leo, since Leo's older daughter (Ariadne) was already married to Zeno.[38] Leontia was still very young at this time (perhaps barely thirteen), so it is questionable whether there was a marriage or even a "betrothal" ceremony.[39] However, the reaction in the Hippodrome tells us that many people in Constantinople saw the elevation of Patricius as the prelude to an eventual imperial succession.

---

[33] There were examples of emperors who made their very young *sons* a co-Augustus (Valentinian I/ Gratian and Valentinian II; Theodosius I / Arcadius and Honorius; Arcadius / Theodosius II; Basiliscus/Marcus) but not a child *grandson*. Arcadius, the short-lived son of Theodosius II and Eudocia, was never named a Caesar, either because the child died or because there were doubts about his paternity. Other variations had occurred when Theodosius II made his *cousin*, Valentinian III, an Augustus; when he made his *sister*, Pulcheria, an Augusta; and when Galla Placidia made her *daughter* an Augusta.

[34] Croke 2021:139–40; McEvoy 2019b. This may have been due to the unpopularity of Zeno in the capital. Candidus, fr. 1 (*FCH*) tells us that Leo wanted to make his son-in-law Zeno a co-Augustus but "his subjects would not accept him." There was anti-Isaurian rioting at this time. Marcell. *comes* s.a. 473.2; Crawford 2019:100; Croke 2021:140. See also Priscus, fr. 55 (*FCH*:369).

[35] This assumes that Patricius never actually married Leo's daughter.

[36] Although Armatus' aunt was the dowager empress Verina. In the west, this pattern ended with the death of Valentinian III. In the east, it continued through the reign of Anastasius. However, there was the Augusta Verina's coronation of Leontius as an Augustus, although he was not related to her family and was regarded as a usurper by Zeno. See ch. XIII, *infra*.

[37] Priscus, fr. 53.5 and 61 (*FCH*:369, 371); Evagrius, *HE*, 2, 16; Theophanes, AM 5963; Marcell. *comes*, s.a. 471.

[38] Suggestions have been made that Ariadne was forced to temporarily divorce Zeno in order to marry Patricius, but there is no real support for this. Ariadne likely remained with Zeno and their son, possibly in Antioch, until after the murder of Aspar in 471. Croke 2021:95–6, n. 208.

[39] Croke 2005:195; cf. Handley 2010:117.

We know very little about Patricius' activities during the year or so when he was Leo's Caesar. The only public activity of Patricius that we know of (and from a much later source) is a visit to Alexandria sometime in 470 where he was allegedly recognized and treated as a Caesar. If it happened, it has been suggested that this trip may have been an effort to buttress imperial control in that turbulent city in view of religious conflict and continuing threats from the Vandals.[40]

However, Leo showed in other ways that he was not entirely comfortable with his prospective son-in-law. For example, there does not appear to be any coinage clearly showing Leo as Augustus and Patricius as Caesar, something that is known for earlier Augustus/Caesar pairings and which Leo would do later for his grandson.[41] In addition, there was the lingering problem of Patricius' religion, and here Leo showed his skill at shaping popular opinion.

It is important to note that we have only have one source for this story, a life of St. Marcellus, who at the time was the abbot of the Studion monastery in Constantinople and a man who had had prior brushes with the Ardaburii. As so often in the history of Constantinople, the action involved a popular demonstration in the Hippodrome while Leo was presiding over the races. The choice of location is important—historians have long noted "the importance of the Hippodrome as the setting for Constantinopolitan political theatre."[42]

In order to understand Leo's behavior, it is useful to examine two earlier instances where Leo staged a political drama before the Constantinopolitan crowd. In both cases, the drama may have also been designed to show Leo's support for orthodoxy.

The first instance involved a prefect of the City Watch named Menas, who in 465 was accused of unspecified "evil deeds." He was "questioned in the Hippodrome by the senate," after which he was knocked down at the command of Leo and dragged through the streets by the crowd until he was killed near the Studion monastery.[43] Since the senate was apparently present, and since Aspar was its *princeps*, this means that both Aspar and Leo were there.

The fact that Menas was taken from the Hippodrome and killed at the "estate of Studius" may suggest that there was a religious context to this drama. Studius was a wealthy ex-consul who had built a church and a monastery in the western part of Constantinople. By Leo's time, this monastery was home to as many as a

---

[40] Croke 2005:193 n. 136, citing Theophanes AM 5961. It is also possible that Aspar's support for the controversial bishop Timothy Aelurus might have been a factor.
[41] Croke 2005:194, 2021:95, 143 n. 47; Kent 1994:102.
[42] *Chron. Pasch.*, s.a. 465, 87 n. 46.
[43] *Chron. Pasch.*, s.a. 465, 87.

thousand monks known as the *Akoimetoi* ("sleepless" monks, who prayed in shifts around the clock) under the strong leadership of their abbot, Marcellus. These "Studite" monks became the shock troops of orthodoxy, leading demonstrations against those they regarded as pagans or heretics.[44] The fact that Menas was killed at this monastery may suggest that the Studite monks were somehow involved in the fall of Menas. If so, Leo's participation might suggest that he was demonstrating support for their cause.[45]

Religious motives (in this case, an attack on paganism) also appear to be behind another public drama that involved Leo. It concerned a man named Isocasius, who was a senior judicial official. He was arrested on two charges—first, that he was "a Hellene" but also "because of the rioting then current in Constantinople."[46] The charge of "Hellenism" indicates he was being accused of paganism. However, it is unclear why there was "rioting then current in Constantinople" or what connection Isocasius had to it. Given the anti-pagan emphasis in our source, the rioting may have been religious in nature.

Although Isocasius was initially sent to Bithynia for questioning about his paganism, the case was transferred to Constantinople after a plea from a popular doctor known as "Jacob the Cooler" because of Isocasius' rank as a *quaestor*.[47] The trial was held in public before Leo and the people of Constantinople "who were standing and watching" and who "acclaimed the emperor many times." The acclamation was a traditional way in which the crowd made its desires known to the emperor. In this case, although it is not specified, the crowd was apparently calling on Leo to show mercy to Isocasius. Leo eventually complied, although on the condition that Isocasius converted to orthodoxy.[48]

Leo may have used the trial to win orthodox support by a renewed attack on pagans, although he acceded to the people in granting some leniency. It may be relevant that at about this time Leo issued laws imposing further restrictions on pagans that excluded them from the legal profession.[49] Leo had to tread more

---

[44] *PLRE* 2 Studius; Mango 1978:115–22. If this event came after the Persian letters, one wonders whether it was pointed at the Ardaburii. We know of an incident where Ardaburius' men pursued a fugitive to this monastery but were stopped by the intervention of Marcellus. *Vita Marcelli* 32; McEvoy 2016:491; Croke 2005:191–2. Perhaps Menas had somehow been involved in that matter. It is said that he was finally killed by a "Goth."

[45] Cf. Van Nuffelen 2018:234–58, who suggests that the "tripping" of Menas was a mistake by Leo that caused him to lose control of the crowd's actions.

[46] *Chron. Pasch.*, s.a. 467, 87–8, especially n. 287; Jo. Malalas 369; Theophanes 115.9–18. However, Pickett suggests that the trial occurred in 469 and thus after Leo's edict. Pickett 2021: 395 n.104; 397, n.109.

[47] So-called for his use of ice baths. He was so popular that the senate had set up his statue, appropriately enough at the Zeuxippon public baths. *Chron. Pasch.*, 87–8.

[48] Pickett 2021:397 n.108 suggests that Isocasius later reverted to paganism; Greatrex 2020:402–3.

[49] *Cod. Just.* i.4.15; *Chron. Pasch.* s.a. 467, 88 n. 287.

carefully against the Arians because of Aspar and the many Arian soldiers in the east Roman army, but that would come after Aspar's death.[50]

The trials of Menas and Isocasius show Leo's efforts to gain popular support through public events that mixed political and religious messages. The reaction to the elevation of Patricius in 470 did not involve a trial, but it would again show Leo's use of religion to gain a political objective.

According to the *Vita* of Marcellus, when the appointment of Patricius as Caesar was announced in Constantinople, there was a strong orthodox reaction. Two of the most powerful orthodox leaders in Constantinople were Gennadius, the orthodox Patriarch, and Marcellus, the Studite abbot. Both promptly led a march to the Hippodrome, where they began a demonstration against Patricius' appointment.[51] The protesters are said to have included "the people, monks, and clergy." Gennadius provided the clergy; Marcellus provided the Studite monks. Who were "the people"? Surely some were following their orthodox leaders. However, it is tempting to believe that Leo encouraged this demonstration as a way to limit the political consequences of Patricius' appointment.[52]

The *Vita* describes a dramatic scene.[53] The crowd came to the Hippodrome on a day when Leo was presiding over the races, and supposedly chanted "for hours" that Patricius should not be made Caesar nor marry Leo's daughter, since they wanted an orthodox emperor. Since Leo was unlikely to have disagreed, the fact that the chants went on "for hours" suggests either some stage-management by Leo, some exaggeration in our source, or possibly both. Zonaras further suggests that the appointment of Patricius was also not welcomed by the east Roman senate who feared it would lead to Arian persecution of orthodox Christians, as had happened in Africa after its conquest by the Arian Vandals.

The sources suggest that Leo eventually said something to the crowd which ended the disturbance and satisfied them. Exactly what Leo said remains unclear. The *Vita Marcelli* and Theophanes both report that Leo told the crowd that Patricius had agreed to abandon his Arianism and convert to orthodoxy. Although Zonaras does not say this, he does report that Leo ended the demonstration "by both his words and his deeds." If Patricius later made a state visit to Alexandria where he was honored as Caesar, then he apparently did

---

[50] *Chron. Pasch.* s.a. 467, 89, n. 290; Jo. Malalas, 14.41.
[51] *V. Marcelli*, 34; Theophanes AM 5961; Zonaras, 14.5–14.7; Croke 2005:192.
[52] McEvoy 2016:491–2, citing Snee, who emphasizes that their objection was about religion, not ethnicity.
[53] *V. Marcelli*, 35; Theophanes AM 5961; and Zonaras, 14.5-7 (the latter two may be drawing on Priscus, who may have been present). See also Croke 2005:192 2021:94; Wood 2011:308; Alan Cameron 1976:292; *LRE*, vol. I:319.

receive the title, as Priscus also tells us.[54] However, whether he actually converted to orthodoxy or merely promised to do so remains unclear.

There are several things that we can learn from these accounts. First, it is significant that the crowd's complaint was about religion, not about barbarians or barbarian descent. Even though Patricius was the son of Aspar, the complaint was about the family's Arianism, not about whether a barbarian father or grandfather disqualified you from becoming emperor.

Second, if Patricius did convert at this time, there is no indication that anyone else in his family was required to convert. There is no record that either Aspar or Ardaburius ever converted, and several sources allege that they were later murdered precisely because of their Arianism. Either Aspar's position in Constantinople was too strong for Leo to require this of him, or else Aspar refused out of concern that it would alienate his Arian supporters, especially the Thracian Goths. In addition, Aspar's devotion to his creed appears to have been sincere, so even the promise of the imperial succession might not have been sufficient for him to abandon his faith.

Finally, the Hippodrome demonstration against Patricius again shows the intertwined nature of Leo's political and religious strategies. Although he could no longer prevent Patricius from becoming Caesar, Leo ensured that Patricius would do so on terms that were more palatable to him. And if Patricius ever did become emperor, at least Leo would have the satisfaction of knowing that he had been succeeded by a nominally orthodox emperor.[55]

Leo's orthodoxy was an important source of his political strength. Moreover, it was a strength that Aspar could not counter so long as he remained an Arian. Religion and politics were always close companions in east Rome.

Final Moves (471)

At the beginning of 471, Leo was in a precarious position.[56] Both of his main supporters, Basiliscus and Zeno, had been forced to leave Constantinople after suffering military setbacks. And with Patricius as Caesar, the issue of the imperial succession was becoming very clouded, since the title gave Patricius a claim that could not be ignored. Even though Zeno had a son, neither the boy nor his father

---

[54] Croke 2005:193, n. 136. See also Priscus fr. 53 and 61; Evagrius *HE* 2, 16; Theophanes AM 5963.
[55] Although there was no guarantee that he would remain orthodox, as in the earlier case of Constantius II and later with Basiliscus and Anastasius. Kulikowski 2019:23, 46.
[56] Roberto 2009.

had that title in 471. While their dynastic claim to the throne as members of Leo's family might be strong, their status in the succession might soon be weaker than that of Patricius. A son of Patricius and Leontia might have had a stronger claim, since Leontia (unlike Ariadne) had been born "in the purple."[57]

Another factor was that Leo was getting older.[58] Aspar and Ardaburius were also getting older and may not have been able to resist the temptation to remove Leo, especially now that Patricius was Caesar.

Leo's desperation was understandable—all of his succession strategies since 457 had failed and he now had one of the Ardaburii as a son-in-law. His initial hope had been that he and Verina would have a son. Although they did in 463, the child did not survive, which put the focus on his two daughters. However, the scandal of the Persian letters in 465 allowed Leo to evade his promise to Aspar by marrying Ariadne to Zeno. Their young son then became the center of Leo's dynastic hopes. There may also have been a back-up plan (perhaps pushed by the empress Verina) for a collateral dynastic succession through her brother, Basiliscus, and his son. Unfortunately for Leo, by 471 the futures of both Zeno and Basiliscus had been seriously tarnished. While his best hope was still Ariadne's son, he might lose that advantage if Patricius and Leontia also had a son.

Our sources for 471 are not very good but we have some evidence of where the key players were. Zeno remained in Antioch until at least the beginning of June.[59] Later in 471, Zeno left Antioch (most likely at Leo's summons) and travelled to Chalcedon, still not daring to enter the capital, but close to it. Similarly, Basiliscus remained close by at Heracleia. He had apparently retained his rank of *magister militum praesentalis*, and apparently had some troops at his disposal.[60] Leo was not only gathering his supporters but trying to avoid a Vandal intervention on Aspar's behalf. To this end, a truce with the Vandals was reached in 471, which was proclaimed as a "victory" by Leo although it was really a recognition of the status quo that had existed in Africa since the defeat of

---

[57] This point was not idle, as it was raised during a revolt against Zeno in 479. *PLRE* 2, Fl. Marcianus 17; see also a panegyric noting that Honorius (unlike his older brother, Arcadius) had been born while his father was emperor. Claudian, *Panegyric on the 3rd Consulship of Honorius*; Gillett 2003:93; Omissi 2018:293. This idea had roots in Sparta and Achaemenid Persia. Herodotus 7.3.

[58] Malchus, fr. 1 (*FCH*) says that Leo became seriously ill in 473. *PLRE* 2, Leo 6. This may explain the sudden elevation of Leo II to Caesar and consul-designate in October, 473. *PLRE* 2, Leo 7; Croke 2021:139.

[59] Croke 2005:194–5.

[60] Cf. Croke 2005:194, 196, who suggests that Basiliscus "now led a new expedition against the Vandals, which reached Sicily." This seems unlikely. After the disaster of 468, and the contempt shown in the sources for its commander, a second attempt against the Vandals by Basiliscus seems doubtful, even if the eastern empire still had the financial and material resources to make such attempt. Theophanes AM 5963, 5964.

Basiliscus.[61] However, it allowed Leo to withdraw Heraclius, Marsus, and their troops from Tripolitana for possible use at home.[62]

Tensions between Leo and the Ardaburii continued to rise in the latter half of the year. Finally, something happened that convinced Leo that he had to strike first.

And this takes us back to Ardaburius' "penchant for plotting."

Several of our sources report that Leo learned that Ardaburius was intriguing against him with "the Isaurians." There has been much dispute over exactly what this means. Those who view the Leo/Aspar struggle as a fight between ethnic factions, and the *excubitores* as an "Isaurian" force, see this as evidence that Ardaburius was trying to tamper with the loyalty of the *excubitores* as a prelude to a physical attack on Leo.[63] However, as discussed, this was not primarily an ethnic struggle nor were the *excubitores* an exclusively "Isaurian" unit.[64]

We get a better sense of the situation from this summary of Candidus, who was a near-contemporary and an Isaurian:

> how Ardabur, who was himself plotting to oppose the emperor, planned to bring the Isaurians over to his side; how Martinus, an attendant of Ardabur, told [Zeno] what Ardabur was contriving against the Emperor; and how, their intentions against one another having for this reason grown more savage, the Emperor Leo destroyed Aspar and his sons Ardabur and the Caesar Patricius.[65]

There are several points worth noting. First, the plot is by Ardabur, not "Aspar and Ardabur." In particular, it was by "Ardabur, who was *himself* plotting to oppose the Emperor."[66] As with the Persian letters and the letters to Anagastes, it raises the question of whether Ardaburius was intriguing on his own, or whether Aspar knew about it. One cannot rule out the possibility that Ardaburius had contacts with individual Isaurians in Leo's guards

Second, it is worth noting that once Leo knew about this intrigue, the level of anger and potential violence clearly increased: "their intentions against one another having for this reason *grown more savage*."[67] Leo was now afraid for his life. Several other contemporary or near-contemporary sources' entries refer to the "savagery" and "anger" of Leo's personality.[68]

---

[61] Gillett 2003:43 n. 24 citing McCormick 1986:47–64.
[62] Croke 2005:194–7.
[63] Brooks 1893; *LRE*, vol. I:319; Jones 1974:223; Previtte-Orton 1962:471.
[64] Croke 2021:74–5.
[65] Candidus, fr. 1 (*FCH*:467).
[66] Ibid. (emphasis added).
[67] Ibid. (emphasis added).
[68] Malchus, fr. 16 (*FCH*:422–3); and anonymous source (*FCH*:475).

Other sources are similar to Candidus, although they mention Aspar. Procopius says that Leo murdered both Aspar and Ardaburius "when he suspected that *they* were plotting against his life."[69] Both John Malalas and the Easter Chronicle refer only to Aspar, but both say that he was murdered because he was "planning a rebellion" or "usurpation."[70] The *Vita* of St. Marcellus alleges that "Aspar and his sons stirred up a rebellion."[71] Zonaras (possibly drawing on Priscus) also refers to Leo's discovery of a plot against himself by Aspar and Ardaburius, and Leo's concerns about the succession.[72] The reference to "concerns about the succession" is telling—as McEvoy has suggested, Leo resorted to violence because the Ardaburii had finally succeeded in positioning themselves to control the succession.[73]

Having decided to strike, Leo planned his moves carefully and with secrecy. Basiliscus was close by at Heraclea, and some excuse was found to bring Zeno to Chalcedon.[74] Aspar's youngest son, Ermanaric, was friendly with Zeno and was apparently moved out of the way.[75] Some historians claim that the Ardaburii were asked to attend a dinner at the palace, but it was more likely that it was a *conventus*, a meeting of the senate.[76] Aspar, as *princeps* of the senate would necessarily have attended, and probably two of his sons, the ex-consul Ardaburius and the Caesar Patricius. None of them would have thought it strange to be summoned to such a meeting.

The attack was carried out by Leo's eunuchs, apparently *cubicularii* of the sacred bedchamber. Notably, Leo did not use his *excubitores* for the assassination, perhaps because he did not completely trust them.[77] Aspar and Ardaburius were immediately killed. Their bodies were allegedly mutilated and dumped into rubbish baskets.[78]

---

[69] Procopius, *Wars*, 3, 6, 27 (emphasis added).
[70] Jo. Malalas, 14, 40; *Chron. Pasch.* s.a.467.
[71] V. Marcelli, ch. 65.
[72] Zonaras, 14.8 and 14.29; Croke 2005:195–6.
[73] McEvoy 2017:500–6; Croke 2005:147.
[74] Some believe that Zeno entered Constantinople immediately after the murders, although others believe that he was so unpopular in the city that he did not feel safe to enter it until much later. Croke 2005:198 at n. 150; *V. Dan. Styl.*, ch. 66.
[75] Apparently, Zeno had a friendship with Ermanaric, as much later we find Ermanaric commanding Rugian troops in Zeno's army. *PLRE* 2, Herminericus; Candidus, fr. 1 (*FCH*:467); Theophanes AM 5964; Jo. Antioch, 214, 4; Brooks 1893.; *LRE*, vol. I, 320 n. 3; Kulikowski 2019:242; Crawford 2019:186. This again shows the complex patterns of identity and alliance among the key players.
[76] Jo. Malalas, *Chron.*, 14.40 has the best account; he is also the source for the *Chron. Pasch.*, although he gets the date wrong, *Chron. Pasch*, s.a. 466; see Croke 2005:197, n. 146.
[77] Elton 2000:397. A parallel is the murder of Aetius by Valentinian III, where only the emperor himself and a single eunuch took part. Jo. Ant., fr. 201 (2).
[78] Jo. Malalas, *Chron.*, 14.40; Croke 2005:197.

The fate of the Caesar Patricius is a bit murkier. John Malalas lists him among the victims of the assassination, as do most other sources, and we have no evidence of any activity by him after this date. However, while the summary of Candidus says that Leo "destroyed" Patricius along with his father and brother, it also adds that: "the Caesar unexpectedly survived his injuries and lived on."[79] This may mean that Patricius lingered before dying of his injuries, although "lived on" may mean more than that.[80] A letter from Leo supposedly sent to the western emperor Anthemius in 472 refers to the murder of Aspar and Ardaburius but does not mention Patricius, which could suggest that Patricius was still alive.[81] If Patricius did survive, he was clearly deprived of his title of Caesar and any plan for his marriage to Leontia was definitely off.[82] The succession, and the future, now lay with Leo's grandson and the child's father, Zeno.

However, even with both Aspar and Ardaburius dead, the day was not over, and there would be one final attempt to shake Leo's hold on the throne. Malalas provides us with the best account:

> A riot began in Constantinople, for the victims had a large band of Goths and *comites* and other followers, and a large band of supporters. Then a Goth who was one of Aspar's associates, a *comes* named Ostrys, entered the palace with some other Goths, shooting with bows. A battle broke out between the *excubitores* and Ostrys, and there were many casualties. He [Ostrys] was surrounded and saw that he was beaten, so he fled, taking Aspar's concubine, a beautiful Gothic girl, who escaped with him on horseback into Thrace, where he plundered many estates.[83]

This suggests that two things happened that day, in quick succession or perhaps simultaneously. First, there was a riot in the city.[84] As Malalas says, this certainly included many Goths who served the Ardaburii as soldiers, as well as Arian or Gothic citizens who viewed them as patrons.[85] Although the Ardaburii

---

[79] Candidus, fr. 1 (*FCH*:467). Hydatius s.a. 468 also does not mention Patricius, but Evagrius, a later writer, does.
[80] The suggestion that Patricius was deliberately spared because he was Leo's son-in-law, Croke 2005:197–8, seems unlikely. The whole point of Leo's action was to remove Patricius from the line of succession.
[81] Croke 2005:197 n. 147.
[82] Leo named his grandson (the son of Zeno and Ariadne) as Caesar in October, 473, which suggests that the position was open at the time. Leontia was soon married to a son of Anthemius. *PLRE* 2, Leontia.
[83] Jo. Malalas, *Chron.*, 14.40. See also *Chron. Pasch*, s.a. 467 (Whitby & Whitby, 89).
[84] Croke 2005:198.
[85] Although "Goths" certainly included Thracian federates, it probably included other "barbarians" in Aspar's service and possibly some non-Gothic Arians.

had enemies (especially the orthodox monks and clergy), they were also popular and generous benefactors who had lived in the city for three generations. While Leo and Verina had made great efforts to associate themselves with the memory of Pulcheria, some people might also recall the long association between Pulcheria and Aspar despite their religious differences.

However, *after* the rioting began (and while it was continuing), there was an attack on the palace by Ostrys. He was a Goth who likely had the Roman rank of *comes rei militaris*, and it is probable that he was leading federate troops from the Thracian Goths.[86] Some historians have identified him as Triarius, the father of Theoderic Strabo, but that seems unlikely since the Thracian Goth who claimed to be Aspar's heir was not Triarius, but his son, Theoderic Strabo.[87] Although Ostrys fled to safety with the Thracian Goths, Strabo did not immediately seek revenge for the murder of Aspar (who was probably a relative by marriage) but instead sought to inherit his rank and property in the empire.[88]

As to the battle in the palace, it is only after the assassination and the attack by Ostrys that the *excubitores* are said to have defended Leo. Perhaps with both Aspar and Ardaburius safely dead, Leo finally felt that he could trust them. Or perhaps they were more willing to fight in defense of Leo against an attack by the Gothic federates. No mention is made of the *domestici* or any other military unit at Leo's disposal, and the struggle in the palace has encouraged the notion that this was a struggle between "Germans" and "Isaurians."[89] However, the retreat of Ostrys marked the end of the upheaval. Leo apparently had little trouble thereafter in regaining control of the city, especially once Basiliscus appeared on the scene with loyal troops.[90]

However, there was one final scene to be played, and it was in a setting that should have appealed to Leo—the Hippodrome. According to Malalas: "The Byzantines chanted an acclamation about him [Aspar], 'The dead man has no friend—except Ostrys.'"[91]

The fact that it is described as an "acclamation" suggests that it was intended as an organized chant in praise of Leo. But was it?

One way to read this, as most people have, is that the point of the chant was to emphasize that no one except Ostrys had been willing to fight for the

---

[86] *PLRE* 2, Ostrys; Laniado 2015, n. 16; Heather 1991: 260.
[87] *Chron. Pasch.*, at 89, n. 289.
[88] Croke 2005:199. See ch. XIII, *infra*.
[89] *Chron. Pasch.*, 89 n. 289.
[90] Croke 2005:198.
[91] Jo. Malalas, *Chron.*, 14.40.

Ardaburii, or that the Ardaburii had little support.[92] While Croke agrees, he also adds the qualifier "if that is the point of the acclamation."[93] Did this reference to Ostrys reflect a subtle admiration for someone who had opposed Leo?

We have no alternative history of Leo's reign that overtly champions the Ardaburii. This is presumably because many of the Byzantine sources that have survived were written by those with an orthodox viewpoint. In these accounts, Leo was generally praised as a champion of orthodoxy against heresy and paganism. In fact, the very next chapter of Malalas after the death of Aspar makes the connection between the defeat of the Ardaburii and the anti-Arian policies of Leo explicit: "The emperor Leo carried out a persecution of the Exakionite Arians *because of Aspar and Ardaburius*, sending decrees everywhere to prevent them possessing churches or gathering together."[94]

Marcellinus *comes* is even harsher, disparagingly referring to the murders as the elimination of "Aspar ... an Arian, together with his Arian brood."[95] To Leo, the defeat of the Ardaburii was not just a political victory, but a victory that could be portrayed as a triumph over Arianism. It was an image that served both his political objectives and the religious legacy he wanted to leave.

However, there are hints in some sources that the popular opinion of Leo was not universally favorable.[96] For example, the Byzantine historian Evagrius summarized Priscus' account of the assassination as follows:

> [Priscus the rhetor also tells] how Leo *by the use of treachery rewarded Aspar, as it were*, for his [Leo's] own promotion *and destroyed the man who had made him Emperor* together with his sons Ardaburius and Patricius, the latter of whom he had earlier made Caesar in order to win Aspar's favor.[97]

This is hardly praise of Leo.[98]

Malchus also did not have a favorable view of Leo. Although he first says that Leo "seemed to be the most successful" of the emperors, he continues:

> But I do not consider it success if someone plunders the possessions of his subjects, continually pays informers to this end, himself brings accusations when

---

[92] Wood 2011:304–5; Stephenson 2022:171; Kaldellis 2019: n.67.
[93] Croke 2005:198.
[94] Jo. Malalas, *Chron.*, 14.41 (emphasis added). "Exakionite" refers to an Arian church outside the walls of Constantinople. See *Chron. Pasch.*:50 n. 157 and 89 n. 290; Wood 2011:305.
[95] Marcell. *comes*, s.a. 471; Croke 2005:199; 2001:96. Cf. Stewart 2014:6.
[96] Stewart 2014:13.
[97] Evagrius, *HE*, 2, 16 (emphasis added); Priscus, fr. 61; Theophanes AM 5963 (*FCH*:371).
[98] Gibbon, ch. XXXIX (vol. 4, 32–3, 184).

he cannot find another to do it for him, collects the gold from every land and lays it up for himself alone, and so thoroughly empties the cities of their former wealth that they could no longer easily pay the taxes which were assessed.[99]

The same summary concludes that "Malchus asserts that he [Leo] was a lodging place of every vice."

Other sources also suggest an unflattering view of Leo in Byzantine memory. A description of the emperor Zeno, again apparently based on Malchus, contrasts Zeno's personality with that of Leo:

> Zeno, the Roman Emperor, did not have in his character the same cruel streak as Leo, nor did he have the constant, inexorable anger that was in Leo ... He was not so frantically eager as Leo for wealth and profit, and he did not fabricate charges against wealthy men, although he was not wholly above such activity.[100]

The point about Leo's anger is also mentioned in a Byzantine comment about the orthodox Patriarch Acacius, who was said to have observed Leo's "savagery" towards "those who annoyed him at all."[101] Only by constant praise was Acacius able to keep Leo "docile and easily restrained his anger."

While we have many sources (particularly orthodox ones) that praise Leo and condemn Aspar as a barbarian and a heretic, a modern study suggests that Malalas subtly presented Leo as a "barbarian" whose claims to "*Romanitas*" were undermined by his "cruelty and untrustworthiness."[102] By introducing Leo as "the Bessian," Malalas may be suggesting that Leo was an "internal barbarian" of the empire, much like his Isaurian ally Zeno, and of questionable legitimacy.[103] In contrast, Aspar was far more culturally assimilated in Constantinople than either Leo or Zeno. However, Leo had the advantage of being orthodox in his religion –and religion became the weapon that Leo wielded to greatest effect in their struggle.[104]

There is one final piece of evidence that relates directly to the death of Aspar and which shows that popular memory gave Leo a sobriquet that probably would *not* have been chanted in the Hippodrome. There are at least two entries in the *Suda* that refer to Leo with the name "*Makelles*." One is the above-quoted entry about the patriarch Acacius, which refers to "the savagery of Leo *Makelles*."[105]

---

[99] Malchus, fr. 3; *Suda* L 267 (*FCH*:409).
[100] Malchus, fr. 16; *Suda* Z 83 (*FCH*:423–4).
[101] *Suda*, A 783 (*FCH*:475).
[102] Wood 2011:299.
[103] Wood 2011:309–10.
[104] Wood 2011:310–11; Arnold 2014:146, 159.
[105] *Suda*, A 783 (*FCH*:475).

The other is an entry about Leo himself, apparently based on Malchus, which is entitled "Leo, Roman Emperor, *Makelles*."[106] As it happens, we also have a fragment of Malchus that begins "In the seventeenth year of the reign of Leo *Makelles* . . ."[107] These references show us that Leo's nickname, as remembered in our Byzantine sources, was "*Makelles*"—"The Butcher."[108]

---

[106] *Suda* A 267; Malchus fr. 3 (*FCH* 409). See also *PLRE* 2, Leo 6; Kulikowski 2019:242; McEvoy 2016:91–2; MacGeorge 2002:267; *LRE*, vol. I:320.

[107] Malchus fr.1 (*FCH*:405).

[108] Leo is the only fifth-century emperor to be remembered in this way, even though Valentinian III killed Aetius and Zeno is culpable in several deaths, including the family of Basiliscus.

13

Aftermath (471–91)

Leo's murder of Aspar and Ardaburius in 471 ended the fourteen-year struggle between the emperor Leo and the Ardaburii for control of the east Roman government and the succession. However, it was not the end of the story. While the murder of Aspar and his sons ended their plans, it did not resolve the succession issue.[1] Leo's claim of legitimacy had never been strong, and his dynastic plan would be severely contested over the next two decades.

The purpose of this chapter is to complete our story with an overview of events from 471 to 491, when a new order was achieved in the Roman world. We began in 395 with the death of Theodosius I; we will end in 491 with the turmoil in the east largely ended by Leo's daughter's choice of a new emperor ("a Roman emperor, an orthodox emperor!") who would lay the foundation for an imperial resurgence under Justinian.[2]

The Balkans (part I)

After Aspar's murder, the most pressing problem for Leo's government was the reaction of the Thracian Goths. This powerful people was settled close to Constantinople and had strong ties to the family of Aspar. They were led by Theoderic Strabo, who was a relative (probably a nephew by marriage) of Aspar. Strabo's Goths were anxious to continue the terms of their settlement in Thrace, during which they had become dependent upon Roman supplies and money for a life of relative peace and comfort.

Strabo did not immediately rise in revolt. He instead opened negotiations with Leo in which he claimed to be speaking as both the leader of the Thracian

---

[1] Nor did it end the story of the Ardaburii, although their imperial dreams were over. McEvoy 2016:492–506.
[2] On the re-conquest by Justinian, Heather 2018, 2013; Wickham 2009, 2005; O'Donnell 2008; on Anastasius' long reign, Kulikowski 2019; Haarer 2006.

Goths and the heir of Aspar. This was not contested, even though there should have been other heirs. Even if Patricius had not survived, there was still Ermanaric. Also, Aspar apparently had two daughters and Ardaburius had both a wife and a married daughter. Finally, there was the Gothic wife or "concubine" of Aspar, although Strabo may have been speaking for her.[3] While Leo readily agreed to let Strabo take Aspar's place as a *m.m. praesentalis* (with its salary), he balked over claims to Aspar's property and a demand that Strabo "be allowed to live in Thrace."[4] The first objection may have been due to Leo's reputed greed; the second may have been a concern that Strabo was asking for an independent enclave, similar to the Visigoths in Gaul.[5]

At about this time, Leo also released his hostage, Theodoric the Amal, to return to the Pannonian Goths. Probably the treaty between Constantinople and the Pannonian Goths required that he be returned at a certain age. However, one might consider whether Leo already viewed him and his people as potential allies in a struggle with Theoderic Strabo.[6]

Because Leo rejected his proposals, Strabo led his Goths in a limited military campaign against the Romans in the Balkans and then, having made his point, resumed negotiations.[7] Although it took eighteen months, a treaty was finally concluded in 473. Strabo received Aspar's old rank of *m.m. praesentalis*, recognition as the sole ruler of the Goths, and an annual payment of 2,000 pounds of gold.[8] This is also the treaty that contains the provision that Strabo would fight any foe of Leo "except only the Vandals."[9] Heather believes that Strabo wished to replicate Aspar's role as a senior general with influence and access at an imperial level; however, Strabo lacked Aspar's network in Constantinople and was constrained by rivals such as Zeno, Armatus, and Basiliscus.[10]

The treaty of 473 between the Thracian Goths and the east Romans did not last long, because things soon changed in Constantinople—on January 18, 474, the Emperor Leo I died.[11]

---

[3] Croke 2005:199.
[4] Malchus, fr. 2 (*FCH*:407–9).
[5] Heather 1991:267 translates the claim as "to possess Thrace," which would make this more likely.
[6] Jordanes says that he was sent back to his family with gifts, which suggests that Leo was trying to show good will. Moorhead 1992:14, n. 35; Heather 1991:265.
[7] Malchus, fr. 2 (*FCH*:409). Strabo's opponent seems to have been the general Heraclius, now the *m.m. per Thracias*, who Leo had brought back from his campaign against the Vandals. *PLRE* 2, Heraclius 4.
[8] Heather 1991:253–63, 267–70; Wolfram 1998:269.
[9] See ch. V, *supra*. Wolfram 1998:269 n. 144.
[10] Heather 1991:270.
[11] *PLRE* 2, Leo 6.

Leo's Final Years, the Accession of Zeno, and the Reign of Basiliscus (473–6)

Leo's death was not unexpected. He was seventy-three years old, and several sources refer to an unspecified "illness" and his declining health.[12] In the months prior to his death, perhaps spurred by health concerns, Leo had taken several steps regarding the succession. By October, 472 he had given the title of Caesar to his young grandson and namesake, the child of Zeno and Ariadne.[13] The child was also named as the intended east Roman consul for 474.[14] However, Leo was in a hurry, so near the end of 473 he made his grandson his co-Augustus, with the imperial name of Leo II. Thus, when Leo I died, his grandson became the sole Augustus of the eastern Roman empire. In an unusual (and possibly unique) ceremony on February 9, 474, the child then crowned his father, Zeno, as co-Augustus.[15] The coronation was held in the imperial box in the Hippodrome (no doubt for maximum public attention) and the child was held during the ceremony by both his mother (Ariadne) and his grandmother (Verina), thus reinforcing the dynastic image. However, only ten months later (November, 474), young Leo II died, leaving Zeno as the sole ruler of the eastern empire.[16]

Zeno has been called "the most politically successful general in the fifth-century east."[17] He had achieved something that even Aspar had never sought for himself. And he would reign (with an interruption) from 474 to 491, a period of seventeen years, equal to the length of Leo's reign and exceeding that of Marcian by a decade. However, he was never popular in Constantinople and was forced to spend much of his reign dealing with multiple revolts, conspiracies, civil wars, religious controversies, and threats from Gothic armies in the Balkans.[18] After the death of Aspar, he apparently remained at Chalcedon for some time. One source says that it was not until the coronation of his son as co-emperor that he felt secure enough to return to the capital, but that seems unlikely.[19]

---

[12] *PLRE* 2, Leo 6; Malchus, fr. 1 (*FCH*:at 403).
[13] Cf. the dates in *PLRE* 2, Leo 6; Croke 2005:198, n. 150; Croke 2003 (rev. Croke 2021:138–43); The point is that in the last two years of his life, Leo was conferring the highest titles on his young grandson. Unlike Patricius, there are coins for Leo II as both Caesar and co-Augustus. Kent 1984:103.
[14] *PLRE* 2, *Fasti*, 1244. There was no western consul for 474. Croke 2021:143–9.
[15] *PLRE* 2, Leo 7; McEvoy 2019b. This supposedly was done after consultation with the senate. Croke 2021:145; Kulikowski 2019:243. Theophanes, *Chron.*, 120, 1.
[16] *PLRE* 2, Leo 6, Leo 7, Fl. Zenon 7. Gibbon, who is hostile to Zeno, states that the child's death "soon excited the public suspicion," Gibbon, ch. XXXIX. However, Greatrex disagrees: "The sources do not even hint at any suspicious circumstances surrounding young Leo's death, a silence of considerable import given Zeno's subsequent unpopularity." *CAH XIV*, 49 n. 105. Croke 2021:149–50.
[17] Greatrex in *CAH XIV*:49.
[18] On Zeno's continuing unpopularity, Elton 2018:209.
[19] *V. Dan. Styl.*, ch. 55; Croke 2005:198, n. 150.

It is difficult to say how much of this unpopularity was specific to Zeno and how much of it arose from his identity as an Isaurian. Modern historians have suggested that Zeno was simply a soldier in the east Roman army who came from Isauria, and whose role in the power struggle between Leo and Aspar was not based on his ethnicity.[20] However, several of our sources make specific reference to Zeno's ethnic background.[21]

The Isaurians were often regarded as "internal barbarians" with a reputation as dangerous brigands.[22] Several incidents suggest that this reputation had not been lost in the fifth century. Priscus writes of a group of Isaurians en route to join Zeno, "the son-in-law of the Emperor," who "turned to robbery and murder" at Rhodes and then caused more trouble in Constantinople.[23] There was also a Hippodrome riot in 473 in which a number of Isaurians were targeted and killed by the crowd.[24] It is therefore not surprising that Zeno's initial grasp on the throne was weak, and that within three months after becoming the sole eastern Augustus he would be overthrown, albeit temporarily.

We have seen several figures from the fifth century who had multiple identities and allegiances and were able to use these multi-faceted personalities to succeed within the east Roman state. Aspar was a prime example of this, and Zeno was similar—in his view, there was no contradiction between being an Isaurian and being a Roman general.[25] However, many people in Constantinople may not have seen it that way, just as there were those who always saw the Ardaburii as barbarians.

Another factor in Zeno's unpopularity may have been concerns about his religious views. In contrast to Leo, Zeno came from the east, a region that was often more receptive to heterodox views.[26] It is possible that some in Constantinople may have viewed Isaurians as potential heretics. However, Zeno

---

[20] McEvoy 2016a:501–2; Croke 2005:200–2.
[21] Candidus, fr. 1 (*FCH*:467); Priscus fr. 55 (*FCH*:369, Jo. Ant. fr. 206); Jo. Malalus 14.47. See Brooks 1893, Gibbon, ch. XXXIX; Greatrex in *CAH XIV*, 50; Burgess 1992:874.
[22] Marcell. com. s.a. 405 on Isaurians causing "huge damage"; Arnold 2014:159–60 on the *limes isauricus*; Gadddis 2005:213–14 on John Chyrsostom's fear of Isaurian brigands; Shaw 1990. Kulikowski 2019:239–40, objects to the term "internal barbarians," but concedes "that they posed challenges to law and order is not in doubt."
[23] Priscus fr. 55 (*FCH*:369).
[24] Marcell. *comes*, s.a. 473, 2; Greatrex in *CAH XIV*, 50 n. 107, Alan Cameron 1976. This may be related to Zeno's accession. Croke 2003:564. It was followed by a further riot against Isaurians in Constantinople after Zeno's expulsion in 475. Lenski, 1999:427–8.
[25] See also ch. VI on the earlier Isaurian general, Zeno, and *infra* for the later careers of the Isaurians Illus and Longinus.
[26] In 471, Leo had rebuked Zeno for allowing the anti-Chalcedonian monk Peter to replace the orthodox Patriarch of Antioch. Croke 2005:194–5; Elton 2000:402.

was helped to some extent by the undoubted orthodoxy of his wife, Ariadne, and the friendship of people like Daniel the Stylite.[27]

Zeno's legitimacy was also weakened by the presence of other potential claimants. For example, Julius Nepos had been crowned by Leo as the western Augustus in 473. It was highly unlikely that Nepos had the means or desire to seek the eastern throne, but he might have found support from the empress Verina, who was apparently a relative of his wife.

Closer to home, and much more serious, were potential dynastic claims by Anthemian and Theodosian candidates. Although the western emperor Anthemius had been killed in 472, three of his sons survived and resided in Constantinople. Because their mother was the daughter of Marcian, they were "Theodosians-by-marriage" as well as Anthemians. Moreover, the oldest son, Marcianus, had married Leo's younger daughter, Leontia. In 479, Marcianus would lead an attempt to overthrow Zeno, and come very close to success.[28] An even stronger Theodosian claim could have been put forward by the children of Olybrius, who had briefly succeeded Anthemius as the western emperor. Their mother was the younger daughter of Valentinian III, the last Theodosian emperor in the west, and their grandmother was the daughter of the eastern emperor, Theodosius II. Although they do not appear to have made a bid for the eastern throne, the memory of their ancestry persisted in Constantinople for a very long time.[29]

This list does not include other senior military officers who did not have a dynastic claim but who might have had the military power to oust Zeno. These included the Isaurian general Illus, as well as Basiliscus and his nephew, Armatus. And then there was Theoderic Strabo, who definitely had an interest in holding high Roman office and exerting power in Constantinople.

However, the proximate cause of Zeno's temporary overthrow in 475 was frustrated dynastic ambition within Leo's family. The shift of attention to Ariadne and her family did not sit well with the ambitious dowager empress Verina. Since Zeno and Ariadne had no further children after the death of Leo II in late 474, Verina would not have an imperial grandchild. As to Zeno, it should be recalled that Verina, like her husband, was fervent in her support of orthodoxy. If she had doubts about Zeno's religious stance, that could have been another reason why she did not want him on the throne. She did have a second daughter, Leontia, who had married Marcianus. Yet, when they made a bid to overthrow Zeno in

---

[27] *V. Dan. Styl.*, ch. 55, 65, 66, 67, 69, 85, and 91. His later attempt at religious unity, the *Henotikon*, was criticized by both sides. Crawford 2019:162–87.
[28] *PLRE* 2, Fl. Marcianus 17. Malchus, fr. 22 (*FCH*).
[29] McEvoy 2016a:492–4, 497, 505.

479, Verina seems to have stuck with Zeno and Ariadne, although it would not be surprising if she was involved on both sides.

In early 475, after the death of young Leo II, Verina organized a conspiracy to overthrow Zeno. Zeno was warned and fled to Isauria. However, Verina and her candidate were soon pushed aside by someone else who wanted the throne—her brother, the disgraced general Basiliscus.[30] His supporters included his nephew, Armatus; Leontia's husband, Marcianus; the Isaurian general, Illus; and possibly Theodoric Strabo. There appears to have been little or no opposition to this coup which is further testament to the unpopularity of Zeno at this time.

Basiliscus soon proved himself to be as incompetent an emperor as he had been a general. He antagonized many of his allies and gradually lost their support. However, his biggest mistake was to attempt to modify the Chalcedonian creed in a way that offended the Orthodox Church and suggested that he might have heterodox sympathies.[31] This quickly brought him into conflict with Acacius, the Patriarch of Constantinople, which led to a mass protest by monks and clergy—plus a surprise appearance by Daniel the Stylite, who came down from his pillar to confront Basiliscus. Given this massive popular demonstration, Basiliscus was compelled to issue a statement confirming his support for orthodoxy.[32]

Seriously weakened by this religious dispute, Basiliscus soon had other problems. The empress Verina was embittered by the way Basiliscus had hijacked her attempted coup, as well as by the elevation of Zenonis, Basiliscus' wife, as an Augusta. Ever flexible, Verina soon began communicating with Ariadne to plot Zeno's restoration.[33]

The regime of Basiliscus had become very shaky by October, 476. It would also be a momentous year in the west.

The End of the Western Empire (470–6)

The instability of Basiliscus' regime at Constantinople was exceeded by the even greater instability of the imperial regime in the west.

---

[30] Crawford 2019:110–11 suggests that they worked together to overthrow Zeno.
[31] *PLRE* 1, Basiliscus 2 notes several sources who call him a "monophysite." The *V. Dan. Styl.*, ch. 71 has the holy man accusing him of "Jewish" ideas. The heterodox monk Peter the Fuller supported Basiliscus, who had restored him as Patriarch of Antioch, even though Peter had earlier been associated with Zeno. Jo. Malalas, 15, 5.
[32] *PLRE* 2, Basiliscus 2; *V. Dan. Styl.*, ch.70–85; Crawford 2019:113–21; Elton 2018:204.
[33] Elton 2000:401–2.

The partnership of Anthemius and Ricimer had never been easy. The failure of the Vandal expedition and the assassination of Marcellinus had frustrated Anthemius' efforts to establish his legitimacy. One could speculate on whether a victory over the Vandals would have reinforced Anthemius' authority to a point where, backed by Marcellinus, he might have successfully challenged Ricimer but this was not the case.[34]

After Basiliscus' defeat, Ricimer and Anthemius began to quarrel, with Ricimer establishing his headquarters in Milan while Anthemius remained at Rome.[35] By February 472, tensions between them had erupted into civil war, with Ricimer's barbarian troops besieging Anthemius in Rome.[36]

Seeing that Anthemius' position was weakening, Leo sent the ex-consul Olybrius to make peace between Anthemius and Ricimer, following which Olybrius would try to negotiate a treaty between the west and his "relative," Geiseric. Sending Olybrius to arbitrate between Ricimer and Anthemius was either a very shrewd move by Leo or a very foolish one.[37] Given that Olybrius himself was suspected of having imperial ambitions, he was a poor choice as a peacemaker; however, if Leo's real aim was to rid himself of a possible Theodosian rival (as he had with Anthemius), then the move may have been a shrewd one, although Olybrius' sons remained in Constantinople as potential threats (or perhaps hostages) to Leo.

Malalas tells us that Leo actually distrusted Olybrius and feared that he would seek support from Geiseric for an attack on Constantinople. Leo allegedly sent a secret letter to Anthemius, telling him to execute Ricimer and Olybrius ("as he had Aspar and Ardaburius"). However, Ricimer's guards discovered the letter, and it was shown to Olybrius.[38] Whether this story is true or not, in April 472, while still besieging Anthemius in Rome, Ricimer proclaimed Olybrius as the new western emperor. Ricimer may have had enough of fighting a losing war with the Vandals, and perhaps thought that Geiseric's support for Olybrius could lead to a rapprochement.[39]

---

[34] After the failure of Basiliscus' expedition, Anthemius could expect little or no further help from the east Romans. Leo and Geiseric entered into a truce in 471, which was followed by a long-lasting treaty in 473. *CAH XIV*, 26 n. 67; Merrills & Miles:121–2; Blockley 1992:76; Conant 2012:32–4, but date of 468 is wrong.

[35] MacGeorge 2002:246 n. 150, 251, 253. Milan may also have put Ricimer closer to the barbarian peoples from whom he recruited and to possible invasion routes. See also Arnold 2014:15–20, 25; MacGeorge 2002:247–52 on Ennodius and Cassiodorus.

[36] Priscus fr.64 (*FCH*); MacGeorge 2002:244.

[37] Jo. Malalas, book 14, ch. 45; *PLRE* 2, Olybrius 6; *CAH XIV*, 26; MacGeorge 2002:239–67; O'Flynn 1983:120–1.

[38] Ibid.; Wood 2011. Since Malalas is the only source for this story, some historians have expressed doubts as to its authenticity. See O'Flynn 1983:121; MacGeorge 2002:256–7.

[39] Clover 1966:201–8 sees this as an "excellent compromise" for Ricimer if he could have achieved it.

Anthemius' position in besieged Rome continued to deteriorate, and the city finally fell to Ricimer on July 11, 472. Anthemius was killed, possibly by Ricimer's nephew, the Burgundian prince Gundobad.[40] However, Ricimer and Olybrius had little time to enjoy their victory. Ricimer died about a month later, on August 18/19, 472. Olybrius then appointed Gundobad as *patricius*, making him Ricimer's successor and the real ruler of whatever was left of the Roman west. However, Olybrius then died on November 2, 472.[41] Gundobad soon left to become king of the Burgundians.

The last few years of the Roman empire in the west are a sad and well-known story that has been treated in greater detail elsewhere.[42] After the deaths of Anthemius and Olybrius in 472, the west went through three emperors and three "patricians" in under four years.

In 476, the largely "barbarian" western army declared Odovacer, a Scirian/Thuringian "barbarian" as its king (*rex*). Odovacer sent envoys to Constantinople who argued that there was no need for a separate western emperor, and that Odovacer should simply be recognized as a *patricius* by the east. By this time, Zeno was again emperor in Constantinople. In his view, the legitimate western emperor was Julius Nepos, now living in Dalmatia, but who had been made an Augustus by Leo in 473 and whose claims were supported by the dowager empress Verina.[43] In addition, the status proposed by Odovacer was ambiguous, providing only a tenuous allegiance to the emperor in Constantinople.[44]

Zeno would eventually find a solution to the problem of Italy.[45] But for the next half century, the west would be of little concern to the emperors at Constantinople.

The Return of Zeno (476)

By late 476 the regime of Basiliscus at Constantinople had become highly unstable. Basiliscus had not only managed to antagonize the orthodox residents

---

[40] Jo. Ant. Fr. 209; MacGeorge:260, n. 193. Priscus, fr. 64 (*FCH*); Cassiodorus, *Chron.*, s.a. 472; *PLRE* 2, Anthemius 3; Gundobadus 1.
[41] *PLRE* 2, Olybrius; Priscus fr. 65 (*FCH*). Theophanes, AM 5964; MacGeorge 2002:261, n. 199, 270.
[42] See e.g., *CAH XIV*, 25–32 (Heather); Crawford 2019:207–10; Elton 2018:217–21; Heather 2006:425–30; *LRE*, vol. I:404–11.
[43] Malchus, fr. 14 (*FCH*:421); *PLRE* 2, Odovacer, Iulius Nepos 3.
[44] Arnold 2014; MacGeorge 2002:291–3; O'Flynn 1983:137–42.
[45] See generally Arnold 2016 and 2014; Moorhead 1992; Amory 1997. Arnold suggests that Theodoric essentially revived the western Roman empire and effectively ruled as its emperor, although with nominal deference to Constantinople.

of the capital but had also lost many key former supporters.[46] One of his worst mistakes was to entrust command of the army pursuing the fugitive emperor Zeno to the ambitious Isaurian general, Illus.[47]

In order to get Illus to take this command, Basiliscus had needed to make extensive promises. Predictably, Basiliscus failed to deliver on his promises, and Illus decided to switch sides and support Zeno. Basiliscus then turned to his nephew, the *m.m. praesentalis* Armatus, to lead a second army against the forces of Zeno and Illus.[48] However, Basiliscus did not trust his nephew either. He first made Armatus "swear by his holy baptism as a recent convert not to betray him,"[49] perhaps knowing that Armatus had already rescued the empress Verina after Basiliscus discovered that she was helping Zeno and Ariadne.[50]

Basiliscus' concerns were well-founded, for Zeno soon made Armatus a better offer. Zeno promised to make Armatus *m.m. praesentalis* for life, and to make Armatus' son the new Caesar.[51] Rather than breaking the oath he had given to Basiliscus, Armatus simply led his army on a route that avoided an encounter with Zeno's army, thereby leaving the road to the capital open.[52]

The sudden arrival of Zeno and his army at the palace in Constantinople in August, 476 apparently took Basiliscus by surprise and there was little opposition. Basiliscus and his family took sanctuary in St. Sophia. Although Basiliscus readily gave up the imperial insignia, he refused to leave the church without a guarantee that neither he nor his family would be "beheaded or put to death."[53] This guarantee was given, but the family was taken to a remote fortress in Cappadocia where they were starved to death.[54] In this fashion, the promise not to execute them was kept.[55]

Once Zeno was restored in August 476, his two most important supporters were Illus and Armatus. Zeno tried to balance their honors, since they were both

---

[46] *Suda* B 164 (on Basiliscus' greed and taxation); Malchus fr.9(4) (*FCH*:417); Elton 2018:203–4.
[47] *PLRE* 2, Illus 1; Elton 2000:398ff.
[48] *PLRE* 2, Armatus.; Malalas 15.5.
[49] Malalas 15.5; *Suda*, A 3970 (*FCH*:477). Does "recent convert" suggest Armatus had been a pagan?
[50] Candidus, fr. 1 (*FCH*:467–69).
[51] Malalas, book 15, ch. 5. Illlus' son was named Basiliscus. This is confusing, but perhaps suggests Illus seeking favor. Based on coinage, he may have taken the name "Leo" when he became Caesar. *PLRE* 2, Basiliscus 1. Zeno kept his word, but the arrangement did not last. Malalas, 15.7.
[52] Malalas, 15.5; *PLRE* 2, Armatus.
[53] Malalas, 15. 5; Elton 2018:204.
[54] *PLRE* 2, Basiliscus 2; Malalas, 15.5 says that "he" (Zeno) gave the promise. However, Candidus, fr. 1 (*FCH*), attributes it to Armatus. Procopius, *Wars*, 3.8.22, attributes it to the Patriarch Acacius, which could well be true given the conflict between the Church and Basiliscus. However, the final responsibility must rest with Zeno.
[55] This seems at odds with the comment in the *Suda* that Zeno "did not have in his character the same cruel streak as Leo," *Suda* Z 83; Malchus fr.16 (2) (*FCH*:423); *Chron Pasch*. s.a. 477.

ambitious and did not like each other. However, in 477, Illus persuaded Zeno to eliminate Armatus.[56] Malalas describes Zeno's reasoning: "'How,' he asked, 'will he [Armatus] stay faithful to me as an emperor? For in a little while, if his son the Caesar grows to manhood, it is certain that he will wrong me.'"[57] Zeno then had Armatus killed on the ground that he had violated his oath to Basiliscus, but he spared his son (who he seems to have liked), although he removed him as Caesar.[58]

The history of Zeno's regime over the next decade is filled with intrigues, revolts, and betrayals, all of which Zeno managed to overcome until only he and Ariadne remained. This period represents the high-water mark of Isaurian influence in the politics of fifth-century Constantinople.

Having removed Armatus, the issue for Zeno was how to deal with Illus. Illus had provided crucial support to Zeno in defeating Theoderic Strabo's attacks on Constantinople in 478 and 480, and in suppressing a dangerous revolt in 479 led by the sons of the deceased western emperor, Anthemius. However, Illus remained suspicious, which was not entirely unreasonable since there were at least three attempts on his life. The first was made in 477 by a slave of Zeno, and the second in 478 by a man who revealed that the dowager empress Verina was behind the attempt.[59] Verina was handed over to Illus, who imprisoned her in Isauria.[60] However, Verina soon lobbied her daughter, the empress Ariadne, for her release. When Illus refused, agents of Ariadne attacked him outside the Hippodrome, costing him an ear.[61] Illus then asked to return to the east, so Zeno appointed him *m.m. per Orientem* in 481 and sent him to Antioch.

However, Illus seems to have had another plan in mind. He later received a delegation of senators in Isauria, including the patrician and *m.m. Thracias*, Leontius. Illus then temporarily released Verina—but only so that on July 19, 484 she could crown Leontius as an Augustus and send out numerous rescripts attacking Zeno and ordering local authorities to accept Leontius as the new

---

[56] *PLRE* 2, Illus 1; Evagr. *HE* III, 24.
[57] Malalas, 15.7.
[58] Malalas, 15.7; *PLRE* 2, Armatus, Basiliscus 1. Re Armatus, Malchus claims that "the citizens were overjoyed at his execution." Malchus fr. 9(4) *Suda* A 3968; (*FCH*:417; *Suda* A 3968). An anonymous source says that Theoderic Strabo could not stand him. (*FCH*:477; *Suda* A 3970).
[59] It is interesting that the latter assailant is described as "a certain Alan," which makes one wonder whether he had been connected to the Ardaburii. Candidus, fr. 1 (*FCH*:469).
[60] Zeno may have been happy to be rid of her, even if his wife was not. In exchange, Zeno obtained the release of his brother, Longinus, who had been taken prisoner when Illus was fighting against Zeno in 475 but, curiously, was still in the custody of Illus. Malalas, 15.12. *PLRE* 2, Illus 1, Paulus 25.
[61] Malalas, 15.13.

emperor.⁶² Illus also released the rebel, Marcianus, and sought assistance from the Persians, the Armenians, and even Odovacer in Italy.⁶³ This looked like a serious threat to Zeno's rule. However, in September, 484 an army sent by Zeno under John the Scythian decisively defeated Illus' army near Antioch. Illus, along with Verina and Leontius, fled to a fort in Isauria⁶⁴ where they were besieged by Zeno's forces for four years. During the siege, Verina died. The fort was finally captured in 488, and both Illus and Leontius were executed.⁶⁵

This should have been enough excitement for any emperor, and there were no serious revolts during the remaining three years of Zeno's reign. The final years of Zeno's rule saw him trying to achieve concord between the orthodox and heterodox views of the Chalcedonian creed, but as usual few people were satisfied.⁶⁶

In this section, we have focused on the politics of the imperial court under Zeno but have paid little attention to foreign policy. Not surprisingly, it was dominated by unresolved matters in the Balkans involving the two Theodorics.

The Balkans (part II) (473–88)

In the late 470s, the Balkans had become a battleground for the east Romans, the Thracian Goths (Theoderic Strabo), and the rival Pannonian Goths (Theoderic the Amal). As discussed, Theoderic Strabo initially sought to take Aspar's position at Constantinople. After a brief war between his Goths and the Romans, he achieved most of his aims in a treaty signed in late 473, shortly before the death of the emperor Leo.

Things changed with Zeno's accession in early 474.⁶⁷ As a supporter of Aspar, Strabo had been an opponent of Zeno, and may have even taken part in the plot to assassinate Zeno during the Balkan campaign of 469. It is significant that supporters of the Ardaburii such as Ostrys fled to the Thracian Goths after

---

⁶² Ibid. Burgess 1992:878, suggests that Leontius was "perhaps an Isaurian." See also *PLRE* 2, Leontius 17 which gives his birthplace as a town in Isauria but fails to consider Burgess' point that there was a town with the same name that was not in Isauria. See also Crawford 2019:196–8; Elton 2000:399. Illus never sought the throne for himself, and he may have originally intended to support Marcianus. Burgess 1992:875, n. 4.

⁶³ *PLRE* 2, Illus 1.

⁶⁴ Malalas, 15.13.; Jo. Ant., fr. 206, 2; Priscus, fr. 57 (*FCH*:371); *PLRE* 2, Zenon 17; Crawford 2019:196–201.

⁶⁵ Malalas, 15.14. *PLRE* 2, Illus 1, Leontius 17; Candidus, fr. 1 (*FCH*:at 471). Zeno's forces included a troop of Rugians commanded by Ermanaric, Aspar's youngest son. *PLRE* 2, Herminericus; Jo. Ant. fr. 214.

⁶⁶ Kulikowski 2019:248–9; Crawford 2019:162–89; Elton 2018:205–6.

⁶⁷ Heather 1991:272.

Aspar's murder. Now that Zeno was emperor, he controlled the payment of Strabo's salary as a *m.m. praesentalis*, which was a key provision of the treaty of 473 and essential to Strabo's position as paymaster for his Gothic followers.[68]

An incident in 474 may have contributed to rising tensions between Zeno and Strabo. The pro-Leo general Heraclius had been captured by Strabo but was murdered by some Goths after payment of a ransom.[69] It has been suggested that Strabo may have inspired this killing, after first obtaining the ransom.[70] This may have revived Zeno's suspicions about Strabo. It is also believed that Zeno may have reneged on some parts of the treaty of 473, possibly the payments to Strabo and the grant of the rank of senior *m.m. praesentalis* previously held by Aspar. By late 474, fighting between Strabo's Goths and Romans had resumed.

Given his problems with Zeno, it is not surprising that Strabo welcomed the coup of Basiliscus in January, 475. He may have come to know Basiliscus in the Balkan campaigns of the late 460s and perhaps had better relations with him than with Zeno. During Basiliscus's short reign, Strabo again held the rank of *m.m. praesentalis*, although this time he received the junior of the two praesental commands, while Armatus received the senior one.[71] However, Strabo resented the greater influence of Armatus, who he considered vain.[72]

Nonetheless, Strabo apparently had some influence under Basiliscus, bringing more Gothic soldiers into Constantinople, particularly into the palace guards.[73] However, it does not seem that any of the Goths actively defended Basiliscus when Zeno returned in August, 476, and it is odd that Strabo reacted so passively. Either Strabo's rivalry with Armatus had lessened his enthusiasm for Basiliscus or perhaps Strabo was distracted by something else, such as the activities of the Pannonian Goths.[74] With Zeno back, Strabo soon lost his position as *m.m. praesentalis*, as well as the subsidies that went with it. But more worrying was the fact that the restored Zeno now favored Strabo's rivals, the Pannonian Goths.

Soon after Aspar's murder, Theoderic the Amal had returned to his family and in 474 had become the leader of his people.[75] Realizing that they occupied an

---

[68] Ibid., 273; Meier 2017:42–61.
[69] Malchus, fr. 6(2) (*FCH*:413). A similar story involves Armatus. Malchus, fr. 9 (4), 15 (*FCH*:423 n. 25; Suda A 3968). Either Heraclius was acting under Armatus or these stories were conflated.
[70] Heather 1991:273. Elton 2018:203 suggests that this was a revenge killing for Aspar.
[71] Heather 1991:273.
[72] Suda A 3970 (*FCH*:477); Heather 1991:274.
[73] Malchus fr. 15 (*FCH*). Zeno (exaggerating the situation) later claimed that Strabo had suggested that Basiliscus should disband his guards and just rely on the Goths.
[74] Heather 1991:274–5.
[75] Theoderic may have become so "Romanized" by his stay in Constantinople that he had difficulty in establishing his authority with his own people. If so, he may have sought to "prove" himself by taking an aggressive attitude towards the east Romans. Arnold 2014:147.

untenable position in Pannonia, he made contact with the exiled Zeno and is said to have provided support for Zeno's restoration in August, 476.[76] In late 475 or early 476, Zeno may have encouraged Theoderic to move his people from Pannonia to Novae on the Danube. This bracketed the Thracian Goths of Strabo between their Gothic rivals to the north and the east Romans to the south.[77] The Amal then offered Zeno his further services.[78]

Zeno quickly showed his gratitude. Theoderic the Amal replaced Strabo as *m.m. praesentalis*, receiving the annual payments previously intended for the Thracian Goths. In addition, the Amal received extraordinary honors from Zeno, including the rank of *patricius* and being acknowledged as Zeno's "son-in-arms" and "*amicus*."[79]

Strabo was now in an awkward position, facing an alliance between Zeno and the Pannonian Goths. In early 477, he sent an embassy to Zeno that (unlike his earlier embassies to Leo) did not convey a sense of strength. Strabo offered to give up his Roman titles; live "a life of peace" (i.e., as a private citizen) in Thrace; and give his son to Zeno as a hostage. Zeno rejected his offer.[80]

With that, some level of fighting began. Theoderic the Amal was at Marcianopolis around the end of 477, which suggests a movement towards Strabo's territory. However, Strabo seems to have done well in the initial fighting, even winning over some of the Amal's people. In early 478 he withdrew the terms he had previously offered to Zeno.[81] Zeno then asked the Amal to join him in an attack on Strabo's base at Hadrianopolis.[82] However, Zeno may have been playing a double game in order to pit the Goths against each other. When the Amal arrived with his army at the designated meeting place, he did not find any of Zeno's promised imperial troops; instead, he found Strabo and his army in a strong defensive position.[83] After some negotiation, the two Gothic armies agreed not to fight each other.

Now it was Zeno who found himself confronted by the two Gothic leaders. The Amal, believing that Zeno had betrayed him, led his forces to Constantinople,

---

[76] Ennodius, 42; Arnold 2014:33–6, 152–6.
[77] Heather believes Theoderic acted on his own. Heather 1991:277.
[78] Malchus, fr. 20 (*FCH*:444). Heather 1991:278.
[79] Arnold 2014:152–4; Heather 1991:278.
[80] Malchus, fr. 15 (*FCH*:423), *PLRE* 2, Illus 1. Strabo had partisans in the city who were providing him with intelligence, and even engaging in a disinformation campaign. Several of these people were tried and punished by Zeno in 478.
[81] Malchus, fr. 18 (*FCH*:427).
[82] Heather 1991:284–5.
[83] Malchus, fr.18(2) (*FCH*:429).

but was repulsed. He then withdrew with his people to the city of Epidamnus in Epirus, which became his new base.[84] Zeno now changed position again, negotiating a new treaty with Strabo, restoring him to his former rank of *m.m. praesentalis* and granting him other honors, while also providing food and supplies.[85] By the end of 478, it seemed that Strabo and the Thracian Goths had regained their position in the eastern empire, whereas the Pannonian Goths held only a tenuous position on the coast of Epirus.

With good reason, Strabo may not have trusted Zeno to keep his word, which could explain his support for the attempted coup against Zeno by Marcianus in 479.[86] Once the coup was under way, Strabo and his army suddenly advanced on Constantinople. However, they arrived too late, and Strabo then had to make the embarrassing excuse that they had come to protect Zeno. This looked particularly thin since several of the leading conspirators had fled to Strabo for refuge.[87] Strabo may have considered an assault on the city, thinking (as Malchus tells us) that "the whole populace would side with him out of hatred for the Isaurians," but Zeno dissuaded him with a sizable bribe.[88]

Once things were under control, Zeno swiftly retaliated. Strabo was stripped of his title as *m.m. praesentalis* and replaced by Trocundes, the brother of Illus. Zeno also enlisted the Bulgars, newly arrived on the Danube, to attack the Thracian Goths. Strabo defeated this attack, but he was frustrated in several further attempts on Constantinople. He initiated an invasion of Greece in 481, but his career came to a sudden end when he was accidentally thrown from his horse and killed.[89]

Strabo was succeeded by his son, Recitach. The ever-flexible Zeno soon made peace with Recitach, who came to live in Constantinople. However, in late 483 or early 484, Zeno had Theoderic the Amal arrange the assassination of Recitach. This was the end of the Thracian Goths as a political force in the eastern empire.[90] One could go a bit further—with Recitach's death, the Ardaburii claim to political power (which Strabo had claimed to inherit) came to an end. Although descendants of the Ardaburii maintained a position of wealth and influence in

---

[84] Malchus, fr. 20 (*FCH*); Heather 1991:292–3.
[85] Ibid., 290. Malchus fr. 22 (4) (*FCH*).
[86] Malchus, fr. 22 (*FCH*).
[87] Heather 1991:294, n. 2.
[88] Malchus, fr. 22 (*FCH*).
[89] Heather 1991:296–9.
[90] Heather 1991:297–8; Jo. Ant. fr. 214.

Constantinople well into the sixth century, they were never again a political force in east Rome[91]

This left Zeno with the Goths of Theoderic the Amal as his only major Balkan issue. Without Strabo or his son, it became easier for Zeno to deal with them, although they had absorbed much of Strabo's former military strength. In 483, Zeno made a treaty giving the Pannonian Goths new land to settle near the Danube. Theoderic the Amal was given high honors, including the post of *m.m. praesentalis* and the consulship for 484.[92] However, the relationship between Zeno and Theoderic was never entirely secure. Although some of Theoderic's Goths were among the troops sent by Zeno to suppress the rebellion of Illus in 484, they were later withdrawn when Zeno began to suspect their loyalty.[93]

The old pattern soon began again, with Theoderic the Amal rebelling in 486, and attacking Constantinople in 487. However, using the Amal's sister as an intermediary, Zeno finally found the solution to this long-standing problem—in 488 the Amal would get imperial help to leave the Balkans with his people, and go to Italy to displace Odovacer

Ariadne Chooses an Emperor (491)

The aging emperor Zeno became increasingly concerned about who might succeed him. In 490, he supposedly consulted a mystic named Maurianus, who told him that he would be succeeded by a former *silentiarius*. Zeno promptly had the former *silentiarius* Pelagius executed.[94] Although the charge against Pelagius was paganism, the real reason may be that he had become critical of Zeno.[95] Similarly, the *Vita* of Daniel the Stylite claims that Zeno had begun to receive warnings of his impending death from Daniel.[96]

One possible successor for Zeno was his brother, Longinus. After years of imprisonment by Illus, he had been released in 485. In 486, Zeno made him a *m.m. praesentalis* and a consul, and later gave him the unusual honor of being a

---

[91] McEvoy 2016a:493-94504-06. During a rebellion against Anastasius in 512, there was an effort by the crowd in Constantinople to give the throne to Areobindus Dagalaiphus Areobindus, a general who was the great-grandson of Aspar and the husband of a Theodosian descendant. However, he had no interest, and the revolt soon collapsed. *PLRE* 2, Fl. Areobindus Dagalaiphus Areobindus 1.
[92] Arnold 2014:63
[93] Jo. Antioch. fr. 214; Brooks 1893:225 ff.
[94] *Chron. Pasch.*, s.a. 490; Marcell. *comes* s.a.490; Malalas 15.16; *PLRE* 2, Pelagius 2.
[95] Zonaras, XIV.2; Cedrenus I, 621; *PLRE* 2, Pelagius 2. Typical of these stories, which the Romans enjoyed, Zeno killed the wrong *silentiarius*.
[96] Daniel did not die until 493.

Figure 11 *Solidus* of Aelia Ariadne (*RIC X* 933, var. 2; wildwinds.com).

consul for the second time for 490. Longinus also made some important public appearances, such as the one in 490 where he awarded new dancers to the Hippodrome factions. Given these high-profile roles, Longinus probably had expectations that he was the favorite as Zeno's successor.[97] However, his situation was like that of Anthemius in 457—although Longinus had been advanced to a favored position, Zeno had never named him as a Caesar or co-Augustus. And, unlike Anthemius, he was an Isaurian.

Zeno died on April 9, 491.[98] Once again, an eastern emperor had died without a natural or chosen successor, which was always a perilous moment for the empire. The senate and officials probably recalled that this problem had last arisen in 457, when Aspar had dictated the accession of Leo. However, in 491 there was no one in Constantinople with Aspar's power and influence. Longinus probably had the support of other Isaurians who had been appointed by Zeno, but Isaurians continued to be unpopular in the capital. For these reasons, the better precedent was the crisis of 450, which had ended with a dynastic solution and a new emperor who was both Roman and orthodox. While the influence of Aspar had been important in 450, the thing that had made the choice of Marcian truly acceptable to the people and the Church was the willingness of the empress Pulcheria to convey legitimacy by becoming Marcian's wife.

As it happened, in 491 there was again an Augusta who could play this role. This was the empress Ariadne, daughter of Leo I, mother of the deceased

---

[97] Malalas, 15.12; *PLRE* 2, Longinus 6; Elton 2018:246. On the Hippodrome appearance, see Elton 2018:246–7; Cameron 1976:19, 46.
[98] *PLRE* 2, Fl. Zeno 7.

child-emperor Leo II, and now widow of the emperor Zeno. Just as Aspar and Pulcheria had saved the Eastern Empire in the succession crisis of 450, Ariadne would do the same forty years later.[99]

Ariadne may have been in her 40s at this time. As Leo's daughter and Zeno's wife, she had extensive imperial experience and provided a link to prior emperors. Like her father, she was strongly orthodox, and she had the support of key religious figures such as Daniel the Stylite, who supposedly predicted to his followers that "the Christ-loving Empress Ariadne would reign over the empire because of her perfect faith in the God of her fathers."[100] Daniel would turn out to be mostly right.[101]

The day after Zeno's death, and perhaps using skills learned from her father, Ariadne dramatically appeared before the people of Constantinople in the imperial box in the Hippodrome. She was well-received with friendly acclamations. Significantly, she wore the imperial cloak, a subtle reminder of her status as an Augusta and her inherent power to crown a new Augustus. As with Pulcheria, during the brief time between the death of Zeno and the accession of the new emperor the imperial power resided with her as an Augusta. Ariadne announced that she had replaced the unpopular (and possibly Isaurian) Urban Prefect,[102] and assured the people that she would soon announce a new emperor. Since the crowd called for "an orthodox emperor" and a "Roman" emperor, she also told them that she had asked the senate and officials "to select a Christian [i.e., orthodox] and Roman Emperor." However, the senate left the final choice up to her.

Of course, there must have been a great deal of bargaining by various candidates and factions, most of which is lost to us. Nonetheless, the people in the Hippodrome had made their views known—they had had enough of the Isaurians, and they wanted a Roman emperor. Most of all, they wanted an orthodox emperor.

---

[99] On Ariadne generally, see Croke 2015 (rev. Croke 2021:153–68, esp. 162–6); Haarer 2006; Angelova 2015:198–202 and 2004:10–15.

[100] *V. Dan. Styl.*, ch. 91. Their concern may have been about Longinus, whose religious views are unknown but may have been suspect to the Orthodox Church. Alternatively, it may reflect concern about Anastasius' religious views. See the next note, *infra*.

[101] He was right in the sense that Ariadne and her consort would rule for many years. However, Daniel probably would not have been happy with the religious positions of Anastasius. Because of the strong concern in the Church about Anastasius' religious views, he was required to sign a statement of orthodoxy before the patriarch would crown him. Kulikowski 2019:250–1; Crawford 2019:229–34; *LRE*, vol. I:430–2. While Anastasius' position would later change, Ariadne would always remain orthodox.

[102] The crowd had called for his dismissal, saying that they wanted "no foreigner [to be] imposed on the Romans." *LRE*, vol. I:430 n. 1; Cameron 1976:153. This could be taken as a reference to Isaurians.

Ariadne seemed to give them both. She chose as the new emperor and her husband an experienced civil official (and former *silentarius*) named Anastasius. He was certainly Roman, but there were (and would later be) questions about his religious views. The patriarch was initially opposed to the choice, and only relented when Anastasius agreed to sign a confession of orthodoxy. Anastasius was proclaimed as emperor the next day and crowned (reluctantly) by the patriarch, as Leo had been in 457. To further secure popular support, Anastasius wisely gave a donative to the troops and stopped the expensive subsidies that Zeno had been paying to his Isaurian comrades. Anastasius then married Ariadne on May 20, 491.[103] As with Pulcheria and Marcian, a "marriage coin" was issued showing Christ blessing their union.[104]

Anastasius was not a young man at his accession, probably around 60. Neither he nor Ariadne had children (although Anastasius did have three nephews, who would play a role later). Like Marcian, his age and lack of a male heir may have made him an attractive candidate to those who saw the opportunities that might be presented by another succession crisis. However, Anastasius proved to be surprisingly long-lived, giving the empire twenty-seven years of relative stability before he died at the age of eighty-eight in 518. Ariadne lived almost as long, dying in 515, almost sixty years after her father had initiated her family's dynasty. Although they endured wars, revolts (including a long revolt by disappointed Isaurians), invasions, major religious conflicts, and serious Hippodrome riots, Anastasius restored the military, fiscal, and economic health of the eastern empire to a level not seen since Leo's disastrous African expedition in 468.[105] In doing so, they laid the foundation for the empire's resurgence in the sixth century under Justinian.

Ariadne had chosen well, and the eastern Roman empire (unlike its western counterpart) would survive (in one form or another) for nearly another millennium.

---

[103] Evagrius, *HE*, III, 29; Theoph, *Chron.*, AM 5983; Const Porphyr. *De cer.*, I, 92; Malalas 16.1 (392); *PLRE* 2, Anastasius 4; Aelia Ariadne.
[104] Croke 2021:164.
[105] On Anastasius generally, Meier 2009; Haarer 2006. See also Elton 2018:246–53; Wickham 2009:89.

14

Conclusions

We began by asking why the eastern Roman empire survived the fifth century whereas the western Roman empire did not, even though there were significant similarities in their political situations and the threats they faced. Some historians have emphasized several advantages of the east Romans, such as a more favorable climate or geography, the strength of the defenses of Constantinople, the continuing economic health of a large part of the eastern empire, and the system of divided commands in the east Roman military.[1]

However, our focus has been on the political transformation of the Roman world, and it is there that the similarities seem most striking. In the mid-fifth century, both branches of the Theodosian dynasty faced similar succession crises. As a result, emperors with little or no dynastic claim came to the throne through the support of military commanders of non-Roman origin or descent. This led to struggles between these emperors and their military "generalissimos." Why did the emperors lose these struggles in the west and win in the east?

Earlier modern historians, sometimes reflecting the influence of nineteenth-century ideas about national identity, saw this as a conflict between ethnic factions, such as "Germans" v. "Romans" or "Germans" v. "Isaurians."[2] Others have stressed how charges of "barbarian" ancestry and/or "heretical" religious beliefs were used to define people like Stilicho and Aspar. While these models can be applied to both the eastern and western situations, neither explains why the outcomes were different. More recently, several scholars have come to understand these struggles, particularly in the east, as essentially a personal contest for power between key individuals or elite families rather than between "ethnic" groups.[3]

---

[1] See, e.g., Harries 1994:56–7; Kaegi 1981:19–24; Jones 1964: ch. 25, esp. 1064–8.
[2] See ch. II, *supra* on "German" as an anachronism. While Aspar may have identified as an "Alan" or as an "Arian," he primarily viewed himself as a "Roman." It is unlikely that he ever thought of himself as a "German," although he recognized an affinity with others of "barbarian" descent.
[3] Crawford 2019:87–92; McEvoy 2019a:117–25, 2016:501–6; Croke 2005:202–3, (rev. 2021:104–7).

I have tried to address three issues: First, how the succession crises of the mid-fifth century resulted in the further evolution of the "child-emperor" and "ceremonial ruler" concepts that had emerged in the late fourth century. Second, how the struggle between Aspar and Leo was essentially between two men (and families) with competing plans for the imperial succession.[4] Viewing their conflict in this way also shows the ebbs and flows of power and allows us to better understand the forces and strategies that were available at different points in their conflict. Third, I have explored how Aspar's personal history may have influenced the outcome of this struggle.

Beyond the "Child-Emperors"

McEvoy made a major contribution to studies of the dynasties of Valentinian and Theodosius by analyzing the frequent reigns of "child-emperors" in the west between 367 and 455.[5] She also explained how this phenomenon required a "transformation of the imperial office" in which the traditional image of the Roman emperor as a "soldier-emperor" became that of a "ceremonial ruler" who could rule in "partnership" with a military commander.

However, with the death of Theodosius II in 450 and then Valentinian III in 455, both branches of the Theodosian dynasty expired without a direct male heir. As we have seen, the situation in the east was temporarily resolved by the marriage of the Augusta Pulcheria to Marcian, an officer with no dynastic connection to the Theodosians. However, in 457 a "Theodosian-by-marriage" (Anthemius) was rejected in the east in favor of Leo I, an officer who had neither a dynastic nor a marital connection to the Theodosians. The choice of Leo marked the final extinction of Theodosian rule in the east. In the west, there were no Theodosians after 455 (except for 467–72, when two "Theodosian-by-marriage" emperors were provided by the east Romans).[6] There were also no further "child-emperors," with two very brief exceptions.[7]

---

[4] In discussing the conflict between Zeno and Illus, Burgess suggests that this was a struggle between two Isaurian families, not between Isaurian factions. Burgess 1992:878.
[5] McEvoy 2010:154–70, 2013:1–47, 305–29.
[6] Petronius Maximus may have tried to become a Theodosian by a forced marriage to the widow of Valentinian III. The later western "Theodosians" were Anthemius (whose wife's father had become a "Theodosian-by-marriage") and Olybrius (a "Theodosian-by-marriage").
[7] In the east, Leo II, and in the west, Romulus Augustulus (both of whom only reigned for a very short time).

I would like to suggest that this shows a further transformation of the imperial office, or perhaps an expansion of the "child-emperor" concept. Under this expanded concept, the choice of the new emperor was no longer limited to a child who had been named as an Augustus (if one existed) but could also be an adult who was willing to work in "partnership" with a military commander and was able to adequately perform the role of a "ceremonial" (and distinctly Christian) emperor.

The choices of Marcian and Leo illustrate this in the east. Both were adults who came from similar military and religious backgrounds, but neither were Theodosians by birth. In the case of Marcian, the novelty was blurred by his marriage to Pulcheria, who was able to provide a dynastic aura. However, in 457, Leo had no dynastic connection to the Theodosians and yet was chosen over a candidate who did. The support of Aspar was the most important factor in both cases, especially in the accession of Leo.

The rules of succession also seem to have expanded by acceptance of the inherent power of an Augusta to create a new (and unrelated) Augustus, something which perhaps had only occurred once in the fourth century.[8] However, in the fifth century there were several examples. The coronation of Marcian by Pulcheria was one example, as was that of Anastasius by Ariadne. However, the Augusta Verina did it (perhaps unwillingly) twice—once when she crowned her brother, Basiliscus, and a second time when she crowned the (totally unrelated) Leontius. Galla Placidia presents a more complex picture. She became an Augusta not by her birth but only after she had married and had children by the non-Theodosian emperor, Constantius III. Her son, Valentinian III, was not made an Augustus by her, but in a ceremony conducted by a representative of her nephew, the eastern Augustus Theodosius II. However, Placidia's unmarried daughter was later made an Augusta.

The desire for a dynastic connection between successive emperors had obviously not entirely died. It was clearly important that Pulcheria could provide this element for Marcian. While Leo had no dynastic credentials, he instead sought to identify himself and his family with the religious legacy of his Theodosian predecessors, especially Pulcheria. Aspar (like Stilicho earlier and Ricimer later) pursued his own dynastic ambitions by planning to have his son marry into Leo's family. However, while Leo's daughter Ariadne would in fact extend Leo's dynasty for over fifty years, neither of her marriages would include any member of Aspar's family.

---

[8] Philost. III.22. But even that example has been questioned. McEvoy 2021:119 n. 16; Omissi 2018:189; McEvoy 2016:154–79.

Ironically, it was Leo's lack of any dynastic or military legitimacy that made the ceremonial part of his role one of his most useful weapons in the struggle with Aspar. Because the ceremonial role had become so distinctly orthodox (e.g., the inclusion of the patriarch in Leo's coronation), and because "piety" had become a basis for legitimacy, Leo and his family were able to portray themselves as champions of orthodoxy. This was an area in which Aspar could not compete.

The Changing Nature of Aspar's Power

It is important to recognize that the fortunes of the Ardaburii changed over time. The Ardaburii were not always dominant in the eastern empire throughout the fifth century, and it would be a mistake to assume that they always had such power.

Although the Ardaburii enjoyed rising prominence from around 420 through the 430s, it was not yet "dominance." The support of others, such as Pulcheria and Plintha, was a major factor until well into the 430s. The period from 431 to 447 presents us with a more equivocal picture—Aspar and his family seem to have maintained their position in the east despite his mixed military results in Africa and the first war with the Huns. Thereafter, the period 447—50 represents a low point in Aspar's fortunes in which he was defeated by Attila and dismissed from his military (but not civil) office. Significantly, this was also a period in which Pulcheria's role was minimized by Chrysaphius and others at court, while Aspar faced competition from other generals, such as the first Zeno and Apollonius.

With Pulcheria's return to power in early 450, we see a resurgence in Aspar's prominence. In July, 450 he was at the bedside of the dying Theodosius II, but in his civilian role as *princeps senatus*. He was certainly a major player in the succession crisis that followed, and he succeeded in having the throne pass to Marcian, a man long associated with his family. However, this appears to have followed negotiations with Pulcheria, the first Zeno, and possibly others. Too often, historians conflate Aspar's role in the crisis of 450 with his much more dominant role in the crisis of 457.

Although many assume that Aspar immediately assumed a dominant role under Marcian, this may not have been the case. The year 453 appears to be a turning point. On one hand, the death of Zeno removed his major military rival and allowed Aspar to expand his influence within the east Roman army by obtaining the Antioch command for his son, Ardaburius the Younger. In addition, the aftermath of Attila's death in 453 resulted in Aspar's formation of a personal bond with the Thracian Goths, who would henceforth provide him with a source of military power outside the structure of the east Roman army. On the other hand, the death of Pulcheria in 453 deprived Aspar of his greatest ally at court. An important consequence of this was that it may have made it possible for Marcian to marry his daughter, Euphemia, to Anthemius, a member of a family whose imperial ambitions had supposedly concerned the Theodosians. After Pulcheria's death, Marcian appears to have become more independent of Aspar, probably grooming Anthemius to be his successor and creating a potential rival for the Ardaburii. The suggestion that Marcian may have been planning an attack on the Vandals at the time of his death may also point in this direction.

However, when Marcian died in 457, Aspar was strong enough to block the choice of Anthemius, and to place his nominee, the relatively undistinguished Leo, on the throne. Although Aspar appears to have had cordial relations with Leo until 465, Leo showed early signs of chafing under his domination; similarly, Aspar became impatient at Leo's failure to marry Ariadne to Patricius.

Things took a major turn in 465. The disclosure of Ardaburius' allegedly treasonous letters with the Persians abruptly shifted power away from the Ardaburii for the next several years. It also allowed Leo to advance Zeno, Basiliscus, and Jordanes to senior military positions. Most important, it allowed Leo to strike at Aspar's dynastic plans by marrying Ariadne to Zeno.

However, in 468 the colossal failure of Leo's effort to destroy the Vandal kingdom shifted the balance back in favor of the Ardaburii. With Basiliscus in disgrace, the Ardaburii were able to instigate Anagastes' revolt and force Zeno's effective exile to Antioch, all without any adverse consequences for themselves. In 470, despite religious objections, Leo was finally forced to make Aspar's son, Patricius, his Caesar. This was as close as Aspar would come to realizing his dynastic ambitions. However, apparently alarmed by word of a plot against him by Ardaburius, Leo reacted violently and murdered both Aspar and Ardaburius in 471.

This summary demonstrates the shifting nature of Aspar's power in fifth century politics at Constantinople. Although Aspar's descendants would continue to be wealthy and prominent in Constantinople into the sixth century, 471 marked the end of attempts by Aspar and his family to control the imperial succession.[9]

---

[9] McEvoy 2016a:492–4. The efforts of Theodoric Strabo and his son to "inherit" Aspar's *political* position ended in 484.

Tools of Persuasion

What resources and tools were available to Aspar and to Leo in their struggle for the future of the eastern Roman empire, and how did they use them?

Aspar's political power rested in large part on his military power, which came from two sources. One was the power that he exercised within the structure of the regular east Roman army as a *magister militum praesentalis*. This not only included troops under his direct command, but also troops commanded by his allies (e.g., when Ardaburius was *m.m. per Orientem*). His second source of military power came from soldiers who were *not* part of the regular east Roman army but who either served Rome as federates or Aspar as personal retainers. This seems to have become a more important component of Aspar's power from the 450s on. The most prominent source of these troops was the Thracian Goths, with whom Aspar was closely connected as both their imperial patron and likely by marriage into their royal family. Notably, both Aspar and Ardaburius maintained large groups of personal guards, largely of Gothic origin.

The power of Aspar's military position did not only come from commanding troops. Imperial generals received substantial salaries, and the Ardaburii had grown rich during the fifth century. Aspar is said to have been "generous" with his money, but his power went beyond direct gifts of money. As a senior general, Aspar could make other men wealthy by recommending or supporting them for promotion within the east Roman army. Of course, the emperor still had to approve these promotions, and as time went on this power was increasingly used by Leo to appoint his own partisans. Nonetheless, Aspar had been putting friends into key military positions for decades.

In addition to his military power, Aspar had a civilian role in the empire. He had been a consul in 434, and by 450 was the *princeps senatus* in Constantinople. In this capacity, he played a crucial role in the accession of Marcian in 450 and an even more prominent role in that of Leo in 457. This position allowed him to support his friends for positions within the civil government as well as the military.

Finally, in matters of religion, Aspar and his family were the main patrons of the Arian community in Constantinople. Just as Leo wanted to be seen as an orthodox champion, so the Ardaburii found it useful to defend the interests of the Arians. Given the intense anti-Arian sentiment in Constantinople, this may not have made him popular in some quarters, especially with the orthodox clergy and monks. However, given Aspar's ties to the Thracian Goths and the large number of Arian soldiers and civilians in Constantinople, this role may have been particularly valuable to him. The Ardaburii were still able to maintain good relations with at least some within the orthodox community, e.g., by obtaining relics for their churches or supporting certain bishops. Aspar's influence is also shown by his correspondence with leading bishops (including the Pope) on matters relating to the Orthodox Church.

Turning to Leo, one should remember that Leo's claim of legitimacy was extremely weak at his accession, his main claim being that he was the choice of Aspar. He was the first emperor in decades who could not claim any familial connection to the prior ruling dynasty. Nor was he a senior general (like Majorian) or a civil servant with extensive experience (like Anastasius).[10] His hold on the throne was potentially threatened from the outset by others who had a stronger dynastic claim, such as Anthemius and Olybrius. Although the prominent role of the patriarch in his accession ceremony was designed to bolster his claim of legitimacy, it also foreshadowed an important way in which Leo would develop a political base independent of the Ardaburii.

We have seen how Leo and his family repeatedly tried to associate themselves with the memory of Pulcheria, the great champion of orthodoxy, and with the growing cult of the Virgin.[11] Leo also found other ways to display his orthodoxy. These included his close relationship with Daniel the Stylite; obtaining relics (including those of the Virgin); and taking part in relic *adventus* processions in Constantinople. He was also skilled at staging public trials that would have pleased the orthodox by condemning pagans and heretics. When he was finally forced to make Patricius his Caesar, Leo was probably involved in the orthodox protest that ended with a promise of conversion by Patricius, yet another victory for the orthodox cause. Even his failed attempt to destroy the Vandals was portrayed as an effort to save the orthodox population of Africa from Arian persecution.

In short, Leo's best tool in the struggle with Aspar was his ability to portray himself and his family as champions of orthodoxy. It was the one area where the Ardaburii could not compete with him—unless they were willing to abandon their Arian faith, which (with the possible exception of Patricius) they had repeatedly shown they were not.

There were a few other weapons that could be used against the Ardaburii, some of which had existed long before the emergence of Leo. These were the

---

[10] Nor was he able to enhance his legitimacy by military victories. His memory was forever shadowed by the enormous failure of Basiliscus' expedition in 468.
[11] See ch. IX, *supra*.

accusations to which someone like Aspar would always be vulnerable—"unreliable barbarian" and "heretic."[12]

The "unreliable barbarian" trope was certainly used against Aspar by his opponents. However, it was difficult to really make it stick against a second-generation resident of Constantinople like Aspar who had become very culturally assimilated and who presented himself as a Roman consul, senator, and general. Of course, that did not stop some people—for example, Jerome did not hesitate to call Stilicho a "half-barbarian traitor" even though Stilicho's family had intermarried with the Theodosian imperial family. It also has to be recognized that Aspar sometimes found it useful to display the non-Roman side of his identity, and probably more so in the later part of his career with the Thracian Goths.[13] While such contacts may have given impetus to the slur that he was an "unreliable barbarian," many modern historians believe that Aspar's long service to the empire and his "Roman" lifestyle negated the "barbarian" charge for most Romans. The background of his opponents should also be considered—in Aspar's struggle with the Bessian Leo and the Isaurian Zeno, who was more likely to be perceived as the "barbarian"?[14]

The issue which did carry weight in fifth-century Constantinople was religion or, more particularly, Aspar's status as an Arian Christian. In the fifth century, there was intense popular opposition to Arians by the people of Constantinople and particularly by the Orthodox Church. This dated back to the anti-Arian pogrom that followed the overthrow of Gainas in 400, and it can be seen in the increasingly severe anti-Arian legislation under the Theodosians and Leo I. It erupted again in the demonstration against the choice of Patricius as Caesar, where the emphasis of the Hippodrome demonstrators was on Patricius' religion, not his ethnicity. Finally, we see it in our sources, such as the hostile comment by Marcellinus *comes* on the murder of Aspar, who he dismisses as "an Arian with his Arian brood."

Aspar was vulnerable to this type of attack, since he remained faithful to his Arian beliefs, and may have refused the offer of the throne in 457 for this reason. While Patricius might have promised to convert to orthodoxy in 470, neither Aspar nor Ardaburius ever compromised their religious beliefs in order to achieve imperial power. This was an issue that Leo was able to exploit to great effect.

---

[12] See ch. II, *supra*.
[13] Another question, which we cannot definitively answer, is whether Aspar's barbarian heritage (particularly his Arian religion but also his Alan ethnicity) might have been factors in his relations with Geiseric.
[14] Kaldellis 2019a:261 (Bessians and Isaurians as "distinct groups"); Arnold 2014:159–60.

However, both "barbarism" and "heresy" were essentially rhetorical tools used by Aspar's opponents.[15] They were not the real issue between Aspar and Leo. The real issue was controlling the imperial succession.[16]

A Conflict Between Individuals

History involves great forces—culture, religion, politics, economics, technology, climate, and disease.[17] However, the particular way in which events unfold often depends on the actions or choices of key individuals. And because individuals have complicated identities, their actions or choices may be determined in part by their identities. In the story of how the eastern Roman empire survived in the fifth century, Aspar was a key individual. It should therefore not be a surprise that he chose to emphasize different aspects of his own complex identity as and when it suited his purposes or that his choices would affect the course of events.

Others did the same, and lines were crossed when deemed necessary. A recent study of Sarus, an early fifth-century Gothic leader, emphasizes the fluctuating choices that were made by those who bestrode the line between being imperial officers and leaders of Gothic warbands.[18] Like Stilicho, Aspar seems to have always identified primarily as a Roman senator and general. Unlike Sarus or (at a later date) the two Theodorics, he did not frequently change from his imperial role and back again. Nonetheless, different aspects of Aspar's identity may have been prominent at different times and in different situations throughout his career.

A major theme of this book has been to reject assumptions about a struggle of ethnic "factions" in favor of a greater emphasis on individuals. As Elton says:

> Political survival and success in late antiquity (whether in civil, military, ecclesiastical, or court politics) depended on one's allies. Alliances of individuals, here described as factions, could be based on many factors, including regional origin, religion, common experience, patronage and marriage. Such alliances were flexible and mutating relationships in which no aspect was automatically dominant. An interpretation based on "ethnic" factions, Isaurians, Goths, Romans, should thus be rejected.[19]

---

[15] Arnold 2014:160 n. 79 concludes that the murder of the Ardaburii "does not seem to have been racially motivated ... [w]hat opposition there was to Aspar and Patricius appears to have been religiously motivated."
[16] McEvoy 2016a:503.
[17] See, e.g., Harper 2017.
[18] Wijnendale 2019b:489.
[19] Elton 2000:404; Amory 1997:5, 14–33, 314–20.

We have seen many examples in this book of unexpected alliances of individuals and changes in loyalty that crossed ethnic, religious, and political boundaries.

If one rejects the concept of warring ethnic factions, it has been suggested that the politics of the fifth century empire involved contests between rival "families."[20] However, while family ties were undoubtedly important, one can point to several cases where individuals sided against members of their own family. The family of Leo is particularly notorious, with Zeno, Verina, Basiliscus, and Armatus all busily intriguing against each other. Ariadne's own sister, Leontia, supported her husband's rebellion against Ariadne and Zeno.

Nor can one rule out differences between Aspar and his three sons. As we have seen, it is difficult to tell to what extent Aspar and Ardaburius the Younger were acting together after 457. While their goals were likely the same, their tactical approach may have been very different. As to Patricius, he may or may not have agreed to change his religion for the sake of the throne, something his father and older brother refused to do. Finally, as to Ermanaric, he seems to have had an unusually friendly relationship with Zeno, his father's and brothers' great enemy. For one thing, Zeno apparently removed him to safety to avoid the massacre of his family in 471. Our sources indicate that he may have later married an Isaurian woman from Zeno's family, revealed a conspiracy against Zeno, and commanded troops in Zeno's war against Illus. Finally, as McEvoy has shown, other members of the Ardaburii seem to have comfortably survived in Constantinople into the next century.[21]

Kaldellis has recently suggested that the rejection of politically powerful "barbarian" generals at Constantinople in the fifth century (a process from Gainas through Aspar and Zeno to the acclamation of Anastasius as a "Roman") can be attributed in part to the growing role of the city's people, a sort of Roman *plebs* or *populus* as a part of the "Byzantine republic."[22] However, this assumes a unitary identity for this *populus* rather than a more complex picture that accounts for cultural and religious cross-currents. A western example of such complexity is shown by the disparate reactions in Italy to the "Greek" emperor Anthemius.[23]

An issue that implicitly arises from an emphasis on individuals is age. Age has two aspects, one chronological and one generational. As to the first, both Croke and McEvoy have emphasized the advanced age of Aspar and Leo as a factor in

---

[20] McEvoy 2019:117–26; Croke 2005:149.
[21] McEvoy 2016:492–503–6.
[22] Kaldellis 2015:21, 106–8, 145; 2019:4–5.
[23] Arnold 2014; 16–20, 45, 125, 153, 179.

the ultimate outcome in the east. By 470, they were both elderly, which may have made their concerns about the succession more urgent. Aspar could only realize his goal by the marriage of his son, Patricius, to one of Leo's two daughters. For his part, Leo could only defeat Aspar if he was survived by a male heir who was not the product of marriage to Patricius.

Age also affected events through the emergence of a new generation more willing to take direct action to secure power. This seems to be particularly true of Aspar's son, Ardaburius.[24] If we knew more about events during the succession crisis in 457, we might have a better understanding of why Aspar declined the throne and how this might have affected Ardaburius. Was there a fundamental disagreement between them on strategy, with Aspar willing to wait for Leo to fulfill his promise about the marriage of Patricius while Ardaburius felt that his father had missed a chance? Did this remain a sore point between them as they saw increasing indications that Leo did not intend to fulfill his promise? If so, was this why Ardaburius began to engage in risky intrigues, such as the Persian letters in 465, the instigation of Anagastes' revolt in 469, and the attempt to assassinate Zeno (in 469) and possibly Leo (in 471)?

One should also consider the examples provided to Ardaburius by events in the west, such as the murders of Aetius and Valentinian III in 454–5, followed by Ricimer's overthrow of the emperors Avitus and then Majorian. The level of violence was rising. There are indications that in 471 Ardaburius was engaged in an intrigue involving Leo's guards, perhaps as a prelude to an attack on Leo himself. Now that the Ardaburii had achieved their goal of making Patricius a Caesar, were they planning to hasten matters by assassinating Leo? The *Suda* describes Leo as having "a streak of cruelty" and prone to anger. If such a man felt his life and his dynasty were at risk, it would not be surprising if he decided to strike first.[25]

A final question is whether we can connect elements of individual identity to specific choices or decisions by Aspar that affected the outcome of the struggle.

Although the crisis of 450 presented opportunities for the Ardaburii, I believe it should probably not be regarded as such an event. Although he succeeded in securing the throne for Marcian, Aspar had just returned to a position of influence and needed to contend with several other key parties. However, if there were any elements of his identity that played a role in the outcome, I would suggest two—his established ability to work as a "Roman" with the Theodosians

---

[24] It may also be true of Zeno, Basiliscus, Illus, and Strabo.
[25] See also the secret letter he supposedly sent to Anthemius, urging him to kill Ricimer, ch. XIII *supra*.

(mainly Pulcheria), and his preference for the negotiated solution. Another general in his position might have tried to force the issue, which could easily have led to a conflict with the first Zeno (who was supposedly "in revolt" at the time) and to civil war. However, that was not Aspar's way. For better or worse, he did not push things to their limit.[26]

A more compelling case can be made for the crisis of 457 as a moment when Aspar's identity did become crucial. It was probably the moment of Aspar's greatest "dominance." Yet, with fewer contenders, the most significant point was his apparent refusal of the throne for himself. Once again, this seems to be another example of his inclination towards compromise and not pushing things too far. If Leo could be a reliable "partner," as had generally been the case with Marcian, why did he need to "create a precedent"?

We can only speculate as to why he felt this way. One possibility was that his status as a "second-generation" Roman, who had absorbed Roman customs and tradition, might have inhibited him. Alternatively, was it the religious issue that kept him from taking this step? If Gibbon is right that Aspar could have become emperor if he would have been willing to "subscribe to the Nicene creed" was this what held him back?[27] It may be, since Aspar appears to have been sincere in his religious beliefs. Did his reluctance come from his political sense of how it would appear to "Romans" or how it would appear to other Arians? Perhaps he felt it would be a problem for both.

Once Aspar's struggle with Leo had commenced, there are two more occasions where things could have ended differently but perhaps did not because of Aspar. One was the reaction to the discovery of the Persian letters. The treachery of Ardaburius could and perhaps should have resulted in severe punishment or even execution. This might have forced Aspar to react in an extreme way and led to a bloody confrontation. Was it possible that Aspar and Leo agreed on a mere dismissal from office to avoid this outcome?

The other occasion was in 469, after Zeno had escaped the assassination attempt. Here, things were perhaps more evenly balanced. Ardaburius' incitement of Anagastes' revolt should have exposed him to punishment, but Leo had been weakened by the disgrace of Basiliscus and the flight of Zeno. It has been suggested that Aspar and Leo may have come to an agreement that Zeno would

---

[26] Other examples show the Ardaburii associated with treaties and negotiations, not smashing victories, e.g., Ardaburius the Elder and the Persians in 421; the compromise with Aetius after the fall of John; the treaty with the Vandals in 435; and the truce with Attila in 441.

[27] Gibbon, ch. XXXVI.

be sent to Antioch and the two sides would step down their hostility at Constantinople. A part of this détente may have been that Leo agreed to make Patricius his Caesar, perhaps in exchange for a promise that the Ardaburii would make no further attacks on Leo and Zeno.

Aspar's inclination was generally to wait. The marriage of Patricius to a daughter of Leo might in time give Aspar what he had always wanted. Perhaps this Zeno, like his predecessor of the same name, might die in Antioch. Or if Patricius and Leontia produced a male heir, there might be a contest for the succession with the son of Zeno and Ariadne. Although Leo would have pinned his hopes on Zeno's child, we have seen that Zeno was unpopular. With the support of the Ardaburii, Patricius might yet have succeeded and become the progenitor of a line of emperors in the east.

But history is about people. And Aspar's reluctance to push too far overlooked two people. One was his son, Ardaburius, who could not resist further intrigues that might hurry Leo's demise. The other was Leo, a man of "constant, inexorable anger" who had been pushed into a tight corner and feared for his life and his legacy. Neither had Aspar's preference for negotiation and patience.

In the struggle between Aspar and Leo for the eastern Roman empire, these qualities made a difference—for them, and for the fate of the eastern Roman empire.

Bibliography

Frequently Used Abbreviations

CAH XIII	Cameron, Averil, & P. Garnsey (ed.), *The Cambridge Ancient History*, vol. XIII, Cambridge: Cambridge Univ. Press, 1998.
CAH XIV	Cameron, Averil, B. Ward-Perkins, & M. Whitby (ed.), *The Cambridge Ancient History*, vol. XIV, Cambridge: Cambridge Univ. Press, 2000.
CLRE	R. Bagnall, Averil Cameron, S. Schwartz & K. Worp, *Consuls of the Later Roman Empire*, Atlanta: Amer. Phil. Assoc, 1987.
CSEL	*Corpus Scriptorum Ecclesiasticorum Latinorum.*
C. Th.	Pharr, C. (tr.) *The Theodosian Code*, Princeton: Princeton Univ. Press, 1952.
FCH	Blockley, R. C. (ed. & tr.), *The Fragmentary Classicising Historians of the Later Roman Empire*, vol. II, Cambridge: Francis Cairns, 1983.
GRBS	*Journal of Greek, Roman & Byzantine Studies.*
JLA	*Journal of Late Antiquity.*
JRS	*Journal of Roman Studies.*
LRE	Bury, J. B. *History of the Later Roman Empire, from the Death of Theodosius I to the Death of Justinian*, 2 vol, London: St. Martin's, 1923.
MGH AA	*Monumenta Germaniae Historica, Auctores Antiquissimi.*
Nov. Th.	"The Novels of the Sainted Theodosius Augustus," C. Pharr (tr.), *The Theodosian Code*, Princeton: Princeton Univ. Press, 1952.
ODB	A. P. Kazhdan, A.-M. Talbot, A. Cutler, T. E. Gregory & N. P. Sevcenko (ed.), *The Oxford Dictionary of Byzantium*, Oxford: Oxford Univ. Press, 1991.
ODLA	Nicholson, O. (ed.), *The Oxford Dictionary of Late Antiquity,* Oxford: Oxford Univ. Press, 2018.
PLRE 1	Jones, A. H. M., J. R. Martindale, & J. Morris (eds), *The Prosopography of the Later Roman Empire (Vol. 1, AD 260–395)*, Cambridge: Cambridge Univ. Press, 1971.
PLRE 2	Martindale, J. R. (ed.), *The Prosopography of the Later Roman Empire (Vol. 2, AD 395–527)*, Cambridge: Cambridge Univ. Press, 1980.
PLRE 3	Martindale, J. R. (ed.), *The Prosopography of the Later Roman Empire (Vol 3, AD 527–641)*, Cambridge: Cambridge Univ. Press, 1992.
RIC X	Kent J. P. C. *Roman Imperial Coinage, Vol. X*, London: Spink & Son Ltd, 1984.
TTH	Translated Texts for Historians.

Primary Sources

Ambrose, *De fide*, II, 16, in *Nicene and Post-Nicene Fathers*, 2d Series, Vol. 10 (de Romestin et al. tr.), Buffalo: Christian Lit. Publishing (1896).
Ambrose, *Explan.Psalm* 36, 25.2–4, *CSEL*, LXIV 91.
Ambrose, *Exposition evangelii secundum Lucam*, X, 10 (G. Coppa, tr,) Milan: Biblioteca Ambrosiana (1978).
Ammianus Marcellinus, *Res Gestae*, 3 vol., J. C. Rolfe (ed. & tr.), 3 vol. Loeb. Cambridge: Harvard Univ. Press (1935–40).
Arrian, *Acies contra Alanos*, in *Flavii Arriani*, vol. 2 (Ross & Wirth, ed.), Leipzig (1968).
Augustine, *Ep.* 220, 228–31 in *Nicene and Post-Nicene Fathers*, First Series, Vol. 1 (J. R. Knight, tr.), Buffalo: Christian Lit. Publishing (1887).
Ausonius, *Epitome de caesaribus*, 2 vol., H. G. White (ed. & tr.) Loeb, Cambridge: Harvard Univ. Press (1949–52).
Caesar, Julius, *Civil War*, C. Damon (ed. & tr.), Loeb, Cambridge: Harvard Univ. Press (2016).
Caesar, Julius, *Gallic Wars*, H. J. Edwards (tr.), Loeb, Cambridge: Harvard Univ. Press (1917).
Candidus, *Fragmenta*, in *FCH*, 464–73.
Cassiodorus, *Chronica*, T. Mommsen (ed.), *MGH AA 11.2*, Berlin: Weidmann (1894).
Cassiodorius, *Variae*, T. Mommsen (ed.), *MGH AA 12*, Berlin: Weidmann (1894); M. S. Bjornlie (tr.), Oakland: Univ. of California (2019).
Cedrenus, Georgius, *Historiarum Compendium* (ed. I. Bekker; 1838-39); also L. Tartaglia, trans., 2 vol., Roma: Academia Nazionale dei Lincei/ Bardi Edizioni, 2016.
Chron. Gallica, T. Mommsen. *MGH AA 9*, Berlin: Weidmann (1892); R. W. Burgess (tr., 2001); Murray (tr.), *From Roman to Merovingian Gaul*, Toronto: Univ. Toronto Press (2008).
Chron. Minora, T. Mommsen (ed.), *MGH AA 9, 11, 13*, Berlin: Weidmann (1894).
Chron. Paschale, Whitby & Whitby (tr.), Liverpool: Liverpool Univ. Press (1989).
Claudian, *In Rufinus*; *In Eutropium*; *Panegyrics on the Fourth and Sixth Consulates of Honorius*, *Panegyric to Stilicho*, in M. Plautner (ed. & tr.), *Claudian*, 2 vols., Loeb, Cambridge: Harvard Univ. Press (1922).
Constantine Porphyrogenitus, *De ceremoniis aulae Byzantinae*, J. J. Reiske (tr.), (1829–30); Bury, *LRE*, vol. 1, 314–16.
Damascius, *Damascii Vitae Isidori Reliquiae*, Zintzen (tr.), Hildesheim: Georg Olms Verlagsbuchhandlung (1967).
Ennodius, *Vita Epiphanii*, in Cook (tr.), *Life of St. Epiphanius by Ennodius*, Washington: Catholic Univ. Press (1942).
Ennodius, *Panegyric to Theodoric*, in Rota (ed. & tr.), *Magno Felice Ennodio, Panegirico del clementissimo re Teodorico*, Rome: Herder (2002).
Eunapius, *Testimonia*, in *FCH*, 6–150.

Eusebius, *Vita Constantini*, Averil Cameron & S. G. Hall (tr.), *Eusebius: Life of Constantine*, Oxford: Clarendon Press (1999).
Evagrius, *Historia ecclesiastica*, M. Whitby (tr.), *The Ecclesiastical History of Evagrius Scholasticus*, *TTH* 33, Liverpool: Liverpool Univ. Press (2000).
Gregory Nazianzus, *Orations*, in *Nicene & Post-Nicene Fathers*, 2d Series, vol. 7, (C. G. Browne & J. E. Swallow, tr.), Buffalo: Christian Lit. Publ Co. (1894).
Gregory of Tours, *The History of the Franks*, L. Thorpe, (tr.), London: Penguin (1974).
Herodotus, *The Histories*, de Selincourt (tr.), London: Penguin (1954).
Hydatius, *The Chronicle of Hydatius and the Consularia Constantinopolitana*, T. Mommsen, *MGH AA*, 11 (1894); R. W. Burgess (tr.), Oxford: Clarendon (1993).
Isidore of Seville, *Hist. Gothorum Wandalorum Sueborum*, T. Mommsen, *MGH AA* 11.2, Berlin: Weidmann (1894).
Jerome, *Letters*, I. Hilberg, *CSEL* 54-6 (1910-18); *Nicene & Post-Nicene Fathers*, 2d Series, vol. 6 (W. H. Freemantle et al. tr.), Buffalo: Christian Lit. Pub. Co (1893).
Jo. of Antioch, *Ioannis Antiocheni Fragmenta ex Historia chronica*, U. Roberto (ed. & tr.), Berlin: de Gruyter (2005).
Jo. Lydus. *De magistratibus*, R. Wuensch (ed.), Leipzig (1903); W. C. Bandy (tr.), *Ionnes Lydus, On Powers*, Philiadelphia: Amer. Philosophical Society Memoirs (1983).
Jo. Malalas, *Chronologia*, in E. Jeffreys, M. Jeffreys, & R. Scott (tr.)., *The Chronicle of John Malalas*, Byzantina Australiensa, Leiden: Brill (2017).
Jo. Malchus, *Testimonia*, in *FCH*, 402-62.
Jo. Nikiu, in R. H. Charles (tr.), *The Chronicle of John, Bishop of Nikiu*, London: Williams & Norgate (1916).
Jordanes, *Romana* and *Getica*, (Van Nuffelen & Van Hoof, tr.), Liverpool: Liverpool Univ. Press (2020).
Lactantius, *de Mortibus Persecutorum*, J. L. Creed (tr. & ed.), Oxford: Clarendon (1984); W. Fletcher (tr.), *Pre-Nicene Fathers*, vol. 7, New York: Cosimo (repr. of 1886); Lord Hailes (tr.), Merchantville: Evolution (repr. of 1792).
Marcellinus *comes, Chronicon*, T. Mommsen (ed.), *MGH AA* 11, 66, Berlin: Weidmann (1894); B. Croke (tr.) *The Chronicle of Marcellinus: A Translation and Commentary*, Sydney: Australian Assoc. for Byzantine Studies (1995).
Nestorius, *The Bazaar of Heracleides*, G. H. Driver & L. Hodgson (tr.), Oxford: Clarendon (1925).
Olympiodorus of Thebes, *Testimonium*, in *FCH*, 152-220.
Orosius, *Historia adversum paganos*, C. Zangemeister (ed.), *CSEL* 5 (1882,1889); R. J. Deferrari (tr.) *Paulus Orosius: The Seven Books of History Against the Pagans*, Washington D.C.: Catholic Univ. Press (1964).
Philostorgius, *Epitome of the Ecclesiastical History, compiled by Photius, Patriarch of Constantinople*, E. Walford (tr.), London: H. Bohn (1855).
Priscus of Panium, *Testimonia*, in *FCH*, 222-400.

Procopius, *Wars*, Dewing (tr.), 7 vols., Loeb, Cambridge: Harvard Univ. Press (1914–40); Kaldellis (tr.), *The Wars of Justinian*, Indianapolis: Hackett (2014).

Prosper Tiro of Aquitaine, *Prosper Tironis Epitoma Chronicon, Addamenta Africana*, a.446–55, T. Mommsen, MGH AA 9, 487, Berlin: Weidmann (1892); Murray (tr.) in *From Roman to Merovingian Gaul*, Toronto: Univ. of Toronto Press (2008).

Salvian, *On the Governance of God*, C. Halm (ed.), *MGH AA* 1 (1887); E. Sanford (tr.), New York: Columbia Univ. Press (1930).

Sidonius Apollinaris, C. Lutjohann (ed.), *MGH AA* 8 (1887); *Poems and Letters: Books 1–2* (vol.1), W. B. Anderson (tr.), Loeb, Cambridge: Harvard Univ. Press (1936).

Sozomen, *Historia Ecclesiastica*, E. Walford (tr.) London: H. Bohn (1855).

Socrates Scholasticus, *Historia Ecclesiastica*, E. Walford (tr.) London: H. Bohn (1853).

Suda, *Lexicon*, fragments in *FCH*, 474–82.

Synesius of Cyrene, *De regno*, in A. FitzGerald (tr.), *The Letters of Synesius*, London: Oxford Univ. Press (1926).

Synesius of Cyrene, *De Providentia (Egyptian Tale)*, in A. FitzGerald (tr.), *The Essays and Hymns of Synesius*, London: Oxford Univ. Press (1930).

Tacitus, *Annals*, in *Annals and Histories*, A. J. Church & W. J. Brodribb (tr.), New York: Knopf Everyman's (2009).

Tacitus, *Germania*, H. Mattingly (tr.), Penguin (2010).

The History of Zonaras From Alexander Severus to the Death of Theodosius the Great (T. M. Banchich & E. N. Lane, trans.), Abingdon: Routledge (2009).

Theodoret, *Historia eccelsiastica*, B. Jackson (tr.), *Writings of Theodoret*, New York: P. Schaff/Christian Literature Pub. Co. (1892).

Theophanes, *Chronographia*, C. de Boor, 2 vols., Leipzig: Teubner (1883–5); C. Mango & R. Scott (tr.), *The Chronicle of Theophanes Confessor*, Oxford: Clarendon (1997).

Fl. Vegetius Renatus, *Epitome Rei Militaris*, N.P. Milner (tr., *TTH*), Liverpool: Univ. of Liverpool (1993).

Vita Augustini (Possidius), H. T. Weiskotten (ed.), *The Life of Saint Augustine*, Princeton: Princeton Univ. Press (1919).

Vita Daniel Stylites in E. Dawes & N. H. Baynes (tr.), *Three Byzantine Saints*, Oxford: Blackwell (1948), 7–84.

Vita Hypatii (Callinicus), Seminarii Philologorum Bonnensis Sodales, Lipsia Teubner (1895).

Vita Marcelli, G. Dagron (tr.), *Anal. Boll.* 86, Louvain (1968), 287–321.

Vita Melaniae Iunioris, in E. A. Clark, *Melania the Younger*, New York: Oxford Univ. Press (2021), 199–239.

Victor of Vita, *Historia Persecutionis*, Halm *MGH AA* 3; J. W. Moorhead (tr., *TTH*), Liverpool: Liverpool Univ. Press (1992).

Zonaras, *Epitome Historiarum*, (ed. L. Dindorf; 1868–75).

Zosimus, *Historia Nova*, R. T. Ridley (tr.), Byzantina Australiensia, Leiden: Brill (1982).

Modern Scholarship

Alemany, A. *Sources on the Alans: A Critical Compilation*, Leiden: Brill, 2000.
Allen, P. "The Definition and Enforcement of Orthodoxy" in *CAH* XIV, 811–24.
Amory, P. *People and Identity in Ostrogothic Italy (489–554)*, Cambridge: Cambridge Univ. Press, 1997.
Anderson, P. *Passages From Antiquity To Feudalism*, London: Verso. 1974.
Andrade, N. J. *Zenobia: Shooting Star of Palmyra*, New York: Oxford Univ. Press, 2018.
Angelova, D. N. "The Ivories of Ariadne and Ideas About Female Imperial Authority in Rome and Early Byzantium," *Gesta* 43:1 (2004), 10–15.
Angelova, D. N. *Sacred Founders: Women, men, and gods in the discourse of imperial founding, Rome through Early Byzantium*, Oakland: Univ. of California, 2015.
Arnold, J. J. *Theoderic and the Roman Imperial Restoration*, Cambridge: Cambridge Univ. Press, 2014.
Arnold, J. J., M. S. Bjornlie, & K. Sessa (eds). *A Companion to Ostrogothic Italy*, Leiden: Brill, 2016. [Arnold 2016].
Babcock, M. A. *The Night Attila Died*, New York: Berkley, 2005.
Bachrach, B. S. *A History of the Alans in the West*, Minneapolis: Univ. of Minnesota Press, 1973.
Barker, J. W. *Justinian and the Later Roman Empire*, Madison: Wisconsin, 1966.
Barnes, T. D. *Constantine and Eusebius*, Cambridge: Harvard Univ. Press, 1993.
Barnwell, P. S. *Emperors, Prefects & Kings: The Roman West, 395–565*, Chapel Hill: Univ. of No. Carolina Press, 1992.
Basic, I. & J. Zeman. "What Can Epigraphy Tell Us about *Partitio Imperii* in Fifth-Century Dalmatia?" *JLA* 12:1 (2019), 88–135.
Beard, M. *SPQR*, New York: Norton, 2015.
Beard, M. *Twelve Caesars*, Princeton: Princeton Univ. Press, 2021.
Beers, W. "Faction Politics and the Transfer of Power at the Accession of Marcian," *Harvard Center for Hellenic Studies*, April 27, 2013.
Bleeker, R. A. "Aspar and Attila: The Role of Flavius Ardaburius Aspar in the Hun Wars of the 440s," *The Ancient World* 3:1 (1980), 23–8.
Blockley, R. C. *East Roman Foreign Policy*, Leeds: Francis Cairns, 1992.
Blockley, R. C. "The Dynasty of Theodosius," in *CAH* XIII, 111–37.
Börm, Henning. "Born to Be Emperor: The Principle of Succession and the Roman Monarchy," in Wienand 2015, 239–64.
Bowersock, G. W., P. Brown, & O. Grabar (eds). *Interpreting Late Antiquity*, Cambridge: Belknap, 2001. [Bowersock 2001].
Brather, S. "Ethnic Identities as Constructions of Archaeology: The Case of the *Alamanni*," in Gillett 2002a, 149–75.
Brooks, E. W. "The Emperor Zenon and the Isaurians," *Eng. Hist. Rev.* 8 (April 1893), 209–38.
Brown, P. *Augustine of Hippo*, Berkeley: Univ. of California Press, 1967 (rev. 2000).

Burgersdijk, D. "Creating the Enemy: Ammianus Marcellinus' Double Digression on Huns and Alans," *Bull. Inst. Classical Studies* 59:1 (2016), 112–32.

Burgess, R. W. "The accession of Marcian in the light of Chalcedonian apologetic and Monophysite polemic," *Byzantinische Zeitschrift* 86/87 (1994), 47–68.

Burgess, W. D. "Isaurian Factions in the Reign of Zeno the Isaurian," *Latomas* 51:4 (October–December 1992), 874–80.

Burns, T. S. *A History of the Ostrogoths*, Bloomington: Indiana Univ. Press, 1984.

Burns, T. S. *Barbarians Within the Gates of Rome: A Study of Roman Military Policy and the Barbarians, ca. 375–475 A.D.*, Bloomington: Indiana Univ. Press, 1994.

Burns, T. S. *Rome and the Barbarians*, Baltimore: Johns Hopkins, 2003.

Bury, J. B. *History of the Later Roman Empire, from the Death of Theodosius I to the Death of Justinian*, 2 vol, London: St. Martin's, 1923. [*LRE*].

Cain, A. & N. Lenski (eds). *The Power of Religion in Late Antiquity*, Burlington: Ashgate, 2009. [Cain & Lenski 2009].

Cameron, Alan. *Claudian*, Oxford: Oxford. Univ. Press, 1970.

Cameron, Alan. *Circus Factions,* Oxford: Oxford Univ. Press, 1976.

Cameron, Alan. "The Empress and The Poet: Paganism and Politics at the Court of Theodosius II," *Yale Classical Studies* 27 (1982), 217–89.

Cameron, Alan. "Flavius: A Nicety of Protocol," *Latomus*, 47:1 (Jan–March 1988), 26–33.

Cameron, Alan. *The Last Pagans of Rome*, Oxford: Oxford Univ. Press, 2011.

Cameron, Alan. "City Personifications and Consular Diptychs," *JRS* 105 (2015), 250–87.

Cameron, Alan & J. Long. *Barbarians and Politics at the Court of Arcadius*, Berkeley: Univ. of California Press, 1993.

Cameron, Averil. *The Mediterranean World in Late Antiquity, AD 395–600,* London: Routledge, 1993a.

Cameron, Averil. *The Later Roman Empire*, Cambridge: Harvard Univ. Press, 1993b.

Cameron, Averil. "Vandal and Byzantine Africa," in *CAH* XIV, 552–69.

Cameron, Averil & P. Garnsey (eds). *The Cambridge Ancient History*, vol. XIII, Cambridge: Cambridge Univ. Press, 1998. [*CAH* XIII].

Cameron, Averil, B. Ward-Perkins, & M. Whitby (eds). *The Cambridge Ancient History*, vol. XIV, Cambridge: Cambridge Univ. Press, 2000. [*CAH* XIV].

Canepa, M. P. *The Two Eyes of the Earth*, Berkeley: Univ. of California Press, 2009.

Chew, K. "Virgins and Eunuchs: Pulcheria, Politics, and the Death of Theodosius II," *Historia* 55:2 (2006), 207–27.

Clark, E. A. *The Life of Melania the Younger*, New York: Oxford Univ. Press, 1984.

Clark, E. A. "The Lady Vanishes," *Church History* 61:1 (1998), 1–31.

Clark, E. A. *Melania the Younger: From Rome to Jerusalem*, New York: Oxford Univ. Press, 2021.

Clover III, F. M. "Geiseric the Statesman: A Study of Vandal Foreign Policy," PhDdiss., Univ. of Chicago (T13276), 1966.

Clover III, F. M. "Geiseric and Attila," *Historia* 22 (1973), 104–17 (repr. in Clover, *The Late Roman West and the Vandals*, Routledge, 1993).

Clover III, F. M. "The Family and Early Career of Anicius Olybrius," *Historia* 27:1 (1978), 169–96.

Cohen, S. "Religious Diversity," in Arnold 2016, 503–32.

Collins, R. "The Western Kingdoms," in *CAH* XIV, 112–34.

Conant, J. P. *Staying Roman*, Cambridge: Cambridge Univ. Press, 2012.

Conant, J. P. "Romaness in the Age of Attila," in Maas 2015, 156–72.

Courtois, C. *Les Vandales et L'Afrique*, Paris: Arts & Metiers Graphiques, 1955.

Crawford, P. *Roman Emperor Zeno*, Barnsley: Pen & Sword, 2019.

Croke, B. "The Date and Circumstances of Marcian's Decease (A.D. 457)," *Byzantion* 48 (1978), 5–9.

Croke, B. "Two Early Byzantine Earthquakes and their Liturgical Commemoration," *Byzantion*, 51 (1981), 122–47.

Croke, B. *Count Marcellinus and His Chronicle*, Oxford: Oxford Univ. Press, 2001.

Croke, B. "The imperial reigns of Leo II," *Byzantinische Zeitschrift* 96 (2003), 559–76 (revised in Croke 2021, 134–52).

Croke, B. "Dynasty and Ethnicity: Emperor Leo I and the Eclipse of Aspar," *Chiron* 35, (2005), 147–203 (revised in Croke 2021, 51–107).

Croke, B. "Leo I and the palace guard," *Byzantion* 75 (2005a), 117–51 (revised in Croke 2021, 108–33).

Croke, B. "Dynasty and Aristocracy in the Fifth Century," in Maas 2015, 98–124 (revised in Croke 2021, 29–50).

Croke, B. "Ariadne *Augusta*: shaping the identity of the early Byzantine empress," in Dunn, G. R. & W. Mayer (eds), *Christians Shaping Identity from the Roman Empire to Byzantium*, Leiden: Brill (2015a, 293–320) (revised in Croke 2021, 153–68).

Croke, B. *Roman Emperors in Context: Theodosius to Justinian*, Abingdon: Routledge, 2021. [Croke 2021].

Cromwell, R. S. *The Rise and Decline of the Late Roman Field Army*, Shippensburg: White Mane, 1998.

Davenport, C. *A History of the Roman Equestrian Order*, Cambridge: Cambridge Univ. Press, 2019.

Demandt, A. "Der spatromische Militaradel," *Chiron* 10, (1980), 609–36.

Demandt, A. *Der Fall Roms*, Munich: C. H. Beck, 1984.

Dillon, J. N. "The Inflation of Rank and Privilege: Regulating Precedence in the Fourth Century," in Wienand 2015, 42–66.

Drijvers, J. W. "The *divisio regni* of 364: The End of Unity?" in Dijkstra, van Poppel and Slootjes (eds), *East and West in the Roman Empire of the Fourth Century*, Leiden: Brill (2015), 82–96.

Drijvers, J. W. & N. Lenski. *The Fifth Century: Age of Transformation: Proceedings of the 12th Biennial Shifting Frontiers in Late Antiquity Conference*, Bari: Edipuglia, 2019. [Drijvers & Lenski 2019].

Drinkwater, J. F. "The Revolt and Ethnic Origin of the Usurper Magnentius," *Chiron* 30 (2000), 131–59.

Elton, H. "Illus and the Imperial Aristocracy Under Zeno," *Byzantion* 70:2 (2000), 393–407.

Elton, H. *The Roman Empire in Late Antiquity: A Political and Military History*, Cambridge: Cambridge Univ. Press, 2018.

Errington, R. M. *Roman Imperial Policy from Julian to Theodosius*, Chapel Hill: Univ. of No. Carolina Press, 2006.

Escribano Pano, M. V. "The Social Exclusion of Heretics in Codex Theosianus XVI," in Aubert & Blanchard, *Droit, religion, et societe dans le Code Theodosian*, Univ. of Neuchatel, 2009, 39–66.

Ferrill, A. *The Fall of the Roman Empire: The Military Explanation*, New York: Thames & Hudson, 1986.

Fournier, Eric. "Review of Moderan 2014," in *Bryn Mawr Classical Review*, 2015.07.09.

Fowden, G. *Empire to Commonwealth: Consequences of monotheism in late antiquity*, Princeton: Princeton Univ. Press, 1993.

Frend, W. H. C. *The Rise of the Monophysite Movement*, Cambridge: Cambridge Univ. Press, 1972.

Gaddis, M. *There is no crime for those who have Christ: Religious violence in the Christian Roman Empire*, Berkeley: Univ. of California Press, 2005.

Gauthier, E. -F. *Genseric: Roi des Vandales*, Paris: Payot 1935, 217–71.

Geary, P. J. "Ethnic Identity as a Situational Construct in the Early Middle Ages," *Mitteilung der anthropologischen Geselschaft in Wien*: 113 (1983), 15–26.

Geary, P. J. *Before France & Germany: The Creation & Transformation of the Merovingian World*, Oxford: Oxford Univ. Press, 1988.

Geary, P. J. "Barbarians and Ethnicity," in Bowersock 1999, 107–29.

Gehn, U. "Aspar Inscription at Stara Zagora," Posting on *Europeana Eagle Project*. May 4, 2015; www.eagle-network.eu/story/ardabur-aspar/

Gibbon, E. *The Decline and Fall of the Roman Empire*, J. B. Bury ed., 7 vol., London: Methuen, 1909.

Gillett, A. "The date and circumstances of Olympiodorus of Thebes," *Traditio* 48 (1993), 1–29.

Gillett, A. "Rome, Ravenna, and the Last Roman Emperors," *Papers of the British School at Rome* 69 (2001), 131–67.

Gillett, A. (ed.). *On Barbarian identity: Critical Approaches to Ethnicity in the Early Middle Ages*, Turnhout: Brepols, 2002. [Gillett 2002a].

Gillett, A. "Was Ethnicity Politicized in the Earliest Medieval Kingdoms?" in Gillett 2002a, 85–121. [Gillett 2002b].

Gillett, A. *Envoys and Political Communication in the Late Antique West, 411–533*, Cambridge: Cambridge Univ. Press, 2003.

Goffart, W. *Barbarians and Romans: The Techniques of Accomodation*, Princeton: Princeton Univ. Press, 1980.

Goffart, W. *Barbarian Tides: The Migration Age and the Later Roman Empire*, Philadelphia: Univ. of Pennsylvania Press, 2006.

Goffart, W. "The Technique of Barbarian Settlement in the Fifth Century: A Personal, Streamlined Account with Ten Additional Comments," *JLA* 3:1 (2010), 65–99.

Gordon, C. D. *The Age of Attila*, Ann Arbor: The Univ. of Mich. Press, 1960.

Greatrex, G. "The Two Fifth-Century Wars Between Rome and Persia," *Florilegium* 12 (1993), 1–14.

Greatrex, G. "Justin I and the Arians," *Studia Patristica* 34 (2001), 72–81.

Greatrex, G. "Government and Mechanisms of Control, East and West," in Maas 2015, 26–43.

Greatrex, G. "The Emperor, the People, and Urban Violence in the 5th and 6th Centuries", in J. H. F. Dijkstra & C. R. Raschle (ed.), *Religious Violence in the Ancient World*, Cambridge: Cambridge Univ. Press, (2020), 389–405.

Grig, L. & G. Kelly (eds). *Two Romes: Rome and Constantinople in Late Antiquity*, Oxford: Oxford Univ. Press, 2012. [Grig & Kelly 2012].

Gruen, E. S. *Rethinking the Other in Antiquity*, Princeton: Princeton Univ. Press, 2011.

Haarer, F. *Anastasius I: Politics and Empire in the Late Roman World*, Cambridge: Francis Cairns (2006).

Halsall, G. "The Techniques of Barbarian Settlement in the Fifth Century: A Reply to Walter Goffart," *JLA* 3:1 (2010), 99–113.

Halsall, G. "Two Worlds Become One: A 'Counter-Intuitive' View of the Roman Empire and 'Germanic' Migration," *German History* 23:4 (2014), 515–32.

Halsall, G. "The Ostrogothic Military," in Arnold 2016, 173–99.

Handley, M. A. "Two Hundred and Seventy-Four Addenda and Corrigenda to Prosopography of the Later Roman Empire from the Latin-Speaking Balkans," *JLA* 3:1 (2010), 113–58.

Harper, K. *The Fate of Rome*, Princeton: Princeton Univ. Press, 2017.

Harries, J. *Sidonius Apollinaris and the Fall of Rome*, Oxford: Clarendon, 1994.

Harries, J. "Men Without Women: Theodosius' Consistory and the Business of Government," in Kelly 2013, 67–89.

Haynes, I. *Blood of the Provinces: The Roman Auxilia and the Making of Provincial Society from Augustus to the Severans*, Oxford: Oxford Univ. Press, 2013.

Heather, P. *Goths and Romans*, Oxford: Oxford Univ. Press, 1991.

Heather, P. *The Goths*, Oxford: Blackwell, 1996.

Heather, P. "The Western Empire, 425–76," in *CAH* XIV, 1–32.

Heather, P. *The Fall of the Roman Empire*, Oxford: Oxford Univ. Press, 2006.

Heather, P. "Why Did the Barbarians Cross the Rhine?" *JLA* 2:1 (2009), 3–29.

Heather, P. *The Restoration of Rome: Barbarian Popes and Imperial Pretenders*, Oxford: Oxford Univ. Press, 2013.

Heather, P. *Rome Resurgent*, Oxford: Oxford Univ. Press, 2018.

Hebblewhite, M. *Theodosius and the Limits of Empire*, Abingdon: Routledge, 2020.

Hekster, O. *Caesar Rules: The Emperor in the Changing Roman World*, Cambridge: Cambridge Univ. Press, 2023.

Herrin, J. *Unrivalled Influence*, Princeton: Princeton Univ. Press, 2013.

Herrin, J. "Late antique origins of the 'Imperial Feminine': Western and eastern empresses compared," *Byzantinoslavica* 74: 1-2 (2016), 5-25.

Holum, K. "Pulcheria's Crusade," *GRBS* 18 (1977), 153-72.

Holum, K. *Theodosian Empresses*, Berkeley, Univ. of California Press, 1982.

Humphries, M. "Valentinian III and the City of Rome (425-55)," in Grig & Kelly 2012, 161-82.

Humphries, M. "Family, Dynasty, and the Construction of Legitimacy From Augustus to the Theodosians," in Tougher 2019, 13-27.

Isaac, B. *The Limits of Empire: The Roman Army in the East* (rev.ed.), Oxford: Oxford Univ. Press, 1992.

Isaac, B. "The Eastern Frontier," in *CAH* XIII, 437-60.

Jacobsen, T. C. *A History of the Vandals*, Yardley: Westholme, 2012.

James, E. *Empresses and Power in Early Byzantium*, Leicester Univ. Press, 2001.

Jones, A. H. M. *The Later Roman Empire (284-602): A Social, Economic, and Administrative History*, 3 vol., Oxford: Oxford Univ. Press, 1964.

Kaegi, W. E. "Arianism and the Byzantine Army in Africa 533-46," *Traditio* 21 (1965), 23-53 (repr. in *Army, Society, and Religion in Byzantium*, 1982).

Kaegi, W. E. *Byzantine Military Unrest, 471-843: An Interpretation*, Amsterdam: Hakkert, 1981.

Kahloss, M. *Religious Dissent in Late Antiquity, 350-450*, New York: Oxford Univ. Press, 2020.

Kaldellis, A. E. *The Byzantine Republic*, Cambridge: Harvard Univ. Press, 2015.

Kaldellis, A. E. "Leo I, Ethnic Politics, and the Beginning of Justin I's Career," *Institute for Byz. Studies* 55 (2018), 9-17.

Kaldellis, A. E. *Romanland: Ethnicity and Empire in Byzantium*, Cambridge: Belknap, 2019a.

Kaldellis, A. E. "Byzantium's Belated Hegemony," in P. Van Nuffelen (ed.), *Historiography and Space in Late Antiquity*, Cambridge, 2019b, 14-35.

Kaldellis, A. & M. Kruse *The Field Armies of the Eastern Roman Empire*, Cambridge: Cambridge Univ. Press, 2023.

Kaperski, R. "Ethnicity, Ethnogenesis, and the Vandals," *Acta Poloniae Historica* 112 (2015), 201-42.

Keenan, J. G. "The Names Flavius and Aurelius as Status Designations in Later Roman Egypt," in *Zeitschrift Papyrologie und Epigrafek* [*ZPE*], 13 (1974), 285-304.

Kelly, C. *Ruling the Later Roman Empire*, Cambridge: Belknap, 2004.

Kelly, C. *The End of Empire: Attila the Hun & the Fall of Rome*, New York: Norton, 2009.

Kelly, C. (ed.). *Theodosius II: Rethinking the Roman Empire in Late Antiquity*, Cambridge: Cambridge Univ. Press, 2013. [Kelly 2013].

Kelly, C. "Rethinking Theodosius," in Kelly 2013, 3–64.
Kent, J. P. C. "*Aureum Monetam ... Cum Signo Crucis*," *The Numismatic Chronicle & Numismatic Society*, Sixth Series, 20 (1960), 129–32.
Kent, J. P. C. *The Roman Imperial Coinage*, vol X, London: Spink, 1994.
Klassen, M. "The *Fasti Parisini*," *JLA* 5:1 (2012), 145–65.
Kosinski, R. "Leo II: Some Chronological Questions," *Palamedes* 3 (2008), 210–11.
Kulikowski, M. "Nation v. Army: A Necessary Contrast?" in Gillett 2002a, 69–84.
Kulikowski, M. *The Triumph of Empire*, Cambridge: Belknap, 2016.
Kulikowski, M. *The Tragedy of Empire*, Cambridge: Belknap, 2019.
Lacey, J. *Rome: Strategy of Empire*, Oxford: Oxford Univ. Press, 2022.
Langford, J. *Maternal Megalomania: Julia Domna and the Imperial Politics of Motherhood*, Baltimore: Johns Hopkins, 2013.
Laniado, A. "Aspar and his *phoideratoi*: John Malalas on a special relationship," in Roberto & Mecella 2015: http://books.openedition.org/efr/2805.
Lee, A. D. "The Eastern Empire: Theodosius to Anastasius," in *CAH* XIV, 33–62.
Lee, A. D. *From Rome to Byzantium AD 363 to 565*, Edinburgh: Edinburgh Univ. Press, 2013.
Lee, A. D. "Theodosius and His Generals," in Kelly 2013, 90–108.
Lee, A. D. "Emperors and Generals in the Fourth Century," in Wienand 2015, 100–18.
Lee, A. D. "Food Supply and Military Mutiny in the Late Roman Empire," *JLA* 12:2 (2019), 277–97.
Lenski, N. "Assimilation and Revolt in the Territory of Isauria," *J. Econ and Soc. History of the Orient* 42 (1999), 413–65.
Lenski, N. *Failure of Empire: Valens and the Roman State in the Fourth Century A.D.*, Berkeley: Univ. of California Press, 2002.
Lenski, N. "Valens and the Monks," *Dumbarton Oaks Papers* 58 (2004), 93–117.
Lenski, N. *Constantine and the Cities*, Philadelphia: Univ. of Penn, 2016.
Liebeschuetz, J. H. W. G. "Review of 'Theodosian Empresses,'" *The Classical Review* 35:1 (1985), 146–7.
Liebeschuetz, J. H. W. G. *Barbarians and Bishops: Army, Church, and State in the Age of Arcadius and Chrysostom*, Oxford: Clarendon Press. 1990.
Liebeschuetz, J. H. W. G. "Making a Gothic History," *JLA* 4:2 (2011), 185–216.
Linn, J. "The Roman Grain Supply, 442–55," *JLA* 5:2 (2012), 298–321.
Lintott, A. *Cicero as Evidence*, Oxford: Oxford Univ. Press, 2008.
Lot, F. *The End of the Ancient World and the Beginnings of the Middle Ages*, Paris: La Renaissance du Livre, 1927 (Harper Torchbook ed. 1961).
Luttwak, E. *The Grand Strategy of the Roman Empire,* Baltimore: Johns Hopkins, 1976 (2d. ed., Johns Hopkins, 2016).
Luttwak, E. *The Grand Strategy of the Byzantine Empire*, Cambridge: Belknap, 2009.
Maas, M. (ed.). *The Cambridge Companion to the Age of Attila*, New York: Cambridge Univ. Press, 2015, [Maas 2015].
MacGeorge, P. *Late Roman Warlords*, Oxford: Oxford Univ. Press, 2002.

Macmullen, R. *Voting on God in Early Church Councils*, New Haven: Yale, 2006.
Maenchen-Helfen, O. J. *The World of the Huns,* Berkeley: Univ. of California Press, 1973.
Mango, C. "The Date of the Studius Basilica at Istanbul," *Byz. & Modern Greek Studies IV* (1978), 115–22.
Mathisen, R. W. "Resistance and Reconciliation: Majorian and the Gallic Aristocracy After the Fall of Avitus," *Francia* 7 (1979), 597–627.
Mathisen, R. W. "Patricians as Diplomats in Late Antiquity," *Byz. Zeitschrift* 79:1 (1986), 35–49.
Mathisen, R. W. "Leo, Anthemius, Zeno, and Extraordinary Senatorial Status in the Late Fifth Century," *Byz. Forschungen* 17 (1991), 191–222.
Mathisen, R. W. "Sigisvult the Patrician, Maximinus the Arian, and Political Strategems in the Western Roman Empire, 425–40," *Early Medieval Europe* 8: 2 (1999), 173–96.
Mathisen, R. W. "*Peregrini, Barbari,* and *Cives Romani*: Concepts of Citizenship and the Legal Identity of Barbarians in the Later Roman Empire," *Amer. Hist. Rev.* (Oct. 2006), 1011–40; basis for "Becoming Roman, Becoming Barbarian: Roman Citizenship and the Assimilation of Barbarians in the Later Roman Empire," in U. Bosma et al. (ed.), *Migration and Membership Regimes in Global and Historical Perspective*, Leiden: Brill (2013), 191–217.
Mathisen, R. W. "Ricimer's Church in Rome: How an Arian Barbarian Prospered in a Nicene Word," in Cain & Lenski 2009, 307–26. [Mathisen 2009a].
Mathisen, R. W. "Provinciales, gentiles and marriages between Romans and barbarians in the Late Roman Empire," *JRS* 99 (2009), 140–55. [Mathisen 2009b].
Mathisen, R. W. "The End of the Western Roman Empire in the Fifth Century CE: Barbarian Auxiliaries, Independent Military Contractors, and Civil Wars," in Drijvers & Lenski 2019, 137–56.
Mathisen, R. W. & D. Shanzer (eds). *Romans, Barbarians and the Transformation of the Roman World*, Abingdon: Routledge, 2016. [Mathisen & Shanzer 2016].
Mathisen, R. W. & H. S. Sivan (eds). *Shifting Frontiers in Late Antiquity*, Aldershot, 1996. [Mathisen & Sivan 1996].
Matthews, J. *Western Aristocracies and Imperial Court*, Oxford: Oxford Univ. Press, 1975.
Matthews, J. *The Roman Empire of Ammianus Marcellinus*, Baltimore: Johns Hopkins, 1989.
Matthews, J. *The Journey of Theophanes,* New Haven: Yale Univ. Press, 2006.
Matthews, J. "The *Notitia Urbis Constantinopolitanae*," in Grig & Kelly 2012, 81–115.
McCormick, M. *Eternal Victory: Triumphal Rulership in Late Antiquity, Byzantium, and the Early Medieval West*. Cambridge: Cambridge Univ. Press, 1986.
McEvoy, M. "Rome and the transformation of the imperial office in the late fourth—mid-fifth centuries AD," *Papers of the British School at Rome* 78 (November 2010), 151–92.
McEvoy, M. *Child Emperor Rule in the Late Roman West,* AD *367–455*, Oxford: Oxford Univ. Press, 2013.

McEvoy, M. "Between the Old Rome and the New: Imperial co-operation ca. 400–500 CE" in Dzino, D. & Parry, K. (eds). *Byzantium, Its Neighbours and Its Cultures*, Brisbane: Byzantina Australiensis, (2014), 245–67.

McEvoy, M. "Becoming Roman? The Not-So-Curious Case of Aspar and the Ardaburii," *JLA* 9:2, (2016), 483–511. [2016a].

McEvoy, M. "Constantia: The Last Constantinian," *Antichthon* 50 (2016), 154–79. [2016b].

McEvoy, M. "Celibacy and Survival in Court Politics in the Fifth Century A.D.," in Tougher 2019, 115–34. [2019a].

McEvoy, M. "Leo II, Zeno, and the Transfer of Roman Imperial Rule from a Son to his Father in 474 CE," in Drijvers & Lenski 2019. [2019b].

McEvoy, M. "Orations for the First Generation of Theodosian Imperial Women," *JLA* 14:1 (2021), 117–41.

McLaughlin, M. "Bridging the Cultural Divide: Libanius, Elleblichus, and Letters to 'Barbarian Generals,'" *JLA* 7:2 (2014), 253–79.

Meier, M. *Anastasios I, Die Entstehung des Byzantinischen Reiches*, Stuttgart (2009).

Meier, M. "A Contest of Interpretation: Roman Policy Towards the Huns as Reflected in the 'Honoria Affair,'" *JLA* 10:1 (2017), 42–61.

Merrills, A. & R. Miles. *The Vandals,* Oxford: Blackwell, 2010.

Millar, F. *The Roman Near East: 31 B.C.–A.D. 337*, Cambridge: Harvard Univ. Press, 1993.

Millar, F. *A Greek Roman Empire: Power and Belief Under Theodosius II, 408–50*, Berkeley: Univ. of California Press, 2006.

Moderan, Y. *Les Vandales et l'Empire romain* (M.-Y. Perrin, ed.), Aries: Editions Errance, 2014.

Moorhead, J. *Theodoric in Italy*, Oxford: Clarendon Press, 1992.

Moralee, J. "Maximinus Thrax and the Politics of Race in Late Antiquity," *Greece & Rome* 55, no.1 (2008), 55–82.

O'Donnell, J. J. *The Ruin of the Roman Empire*, New York: HarperCollins, 2008.

O'Flynn, J. M. *Generalissimos of the Western Roman Empire*, Edmonton: Univ. of Alberta Press, 1983.

Omissi, A. *Emperors and Usurpers in the Later Roman Empire: Civil War, Panegyric, and the Construction of Legitimacy,* Oxford; Oxford Univ. Press, 2018.

Oost, S. I. "Aetius and Majorian," *Classical Philology* LIX, (1964), 23–9.

Oost, S. I. *Galla Placidia Augusta: A Biographical Essay*, Chicago: Univ. of Chicago, 1968.

Ostrogorski, G. *History of the Byzantine State*, New Brunswick: Rutgers Univ. Press, 1969.

Pickett, J. "A Social Explanation for the Disappearance of Roman *Thermae*", *JLA* 14:2 (2021), 375–414.

Potter, D. *Constantine the Emperor*, Oxford: Oxford Univ. Press, 2013.

Previtte-Orton, C. W. *The Shorter Cambridge Medieval History*, 2 vol., Cambridge: Cambridge Univ. Press, 1952.

Roberto, U. "Aspar e il suo gruppo: integrazione dei barbari e lotta politica nell Oriente romano di V secolo," Lecture at AST Naples, (2009).

Roberto, U. & L. Mecella (eds). *Governare e riforme l'impero al momento della sua divisione: Oriente, Occidente, Illirico*, Publications de l'Ecole francaise de Rome, Dec. 8, 2015. [Roberto & Mecella 2015]l; www.books.openedition.org/eft/2788

Rubin, Z. "The Mediterranean and the Dilemma of the Roman Empire in Late Antiquity," *Mediterranean Hist. Rev. 1* (1968), 13–62.

Salisbury, J. E. *Rome's Christian Empress: Galla Placidia Rules at the Twilight of the Empire*, Baltimore: Johns Hopkins, 2015.

Salway, B. "What's In A Name?" *JRS* 84 (1994), 137–41.

Salzman, M. R. *The Falls of Rome*, Cambridge: Cambridge Univ. Press, 2021.

Schor, A. "Performance and Social Strategy in the Letters of Theodoret," *JLA* 2:2 (2009), 274–99.

Schrier, O. J. "Syriac Evidence for the Romano-Persian War of 421–22," *GRBS* 33 (1992), 75–86.

Scott, L. R. "Aspar and the Burden of Barbarian Heritage," *Byzantine Studies/Etudes Byzantines* 3:2 (1976), 56–69.

Scott, R. "Byzantine Chronicles," *The Medieval Chronicle* 6 (2009), 31–57 (repr. in R. Scott, *Byzantine Chronicles and the Sixth Century*, Routledge (2012)).

Scott, R. "From propaganda to history to literature: The Byzantine stories of Theodosius' apple and Marcian's eagle," in R. Macrides (ed.), *History as Literature in Byzantium*, Farnham: Ashgate, 115–32 (2010) (repr. in R. Scott, *Byzantine Chronicles and the Sixth Century*, Routledge, (2012)).

Shaw, B. "Bandit Highlands and Lowland Peace: The Mountains of Isauria-Cilicia," *J. of Social and Economic History of the Orient* 32:2, 199–233; and 33:3, 237–70 (1990).

Shaw, B. "War and Violence," in Bowersock 1999, 130–69.

Shaw, B. *Sacred Violence: African Christians and Sectarian Hatred in the Age of Augustine*, Cambridge: Cambridge Univ. Press, 2011.

Sivan, H. S. "Was Theodosius I A Usurper?" *Klio* 78:1 (1996), 198–211.

Sivan, H. S. "Why Not Marry a Barbarian? Marital Frontiers in Late Antiquity (The Example of *CTh* 3.14.1)," in Mathisen & Sivan 1996: 135–45.

Sivan, H. S. *Galla Placidia: The Last Roman Empress*, Oxford: Oxford Univ. Press, 2011.

Snee, R. "Gregory Nazianzen's Anastasia Church: Arianism, the Goths, and Hagiogaphy," *Dumbarton Oaks Papers* 52, (1998), 157–86.

Southern, P. & K. R. Dixon. *The Late Roman Army*, New Haven: Yale Univ. Press, 1996.

Stephenson, P. *New Rome: The Empire in the East*, Cambridge: Belknap, 2022.

Stewart, M. E. "The First Byzantine Emperor? Leo I, Aspar, and the Challenges of Power and *Romanitas* in Fifth-century Byzantium," *Porphyra* 11:22 (December, 2014), 4–17.

Stoneman, R. *Palmyra and Its Empire: Zenobia's Revolt Against Rome*, Ann Arbor: Univ. of Michigan, 1992.

Swain, B. "Goths and Gothic Identity in the Ostrogothic Kingdom," in Arnold 2016, 203–33.

Testa, R. L. "Mapping the Church and Ascetism in Ostrogothic Italy," in Arnold 2016, 480–502.

Thompson, E. A. "The Isaurians Under Theodosius II," *Hermathena* 68 (1946), 18–31.

Thompson, E. A. "The Foreign Policies of Theodosius II and Marcian," *Hermathena* 76 (1950), 58–75.

Thompson, E. A. *Romans and Barbarians: The Decline of the Western Empire*, Madison: Univ. of Wisconsin, 1982.

Thompson, E. A. *The Huns*, Oxford: Blackwell (rev. ed 1996).

Tougher, S. (ed.). *The Emperor in the Byzantine World*, Abingdon: Routledge (2019). [Tougher 2019].

Traina, G. *428 A.D.: An Ordinary Year at the End of the Roman Empire*, Princeton: Princeton Univ. Press, 2009.

Tsatsos, M. *Empress Athenais-Eudocia*, Brookline: Holy Cross Orthodox Press, 1977.

Van Hoof, L. & P. Van Nuffelen. *The Fragmentary Latin Histories of Late Antiquity*, Cambridge: Cambridge Univ. Press, 2020.

Van Nuffelen, P. "Playing the Ritual Game in Constantinople (379–57)," in Grig & Kelly 2012, 183–200.

Van Nuffelen, P. "Olympiodorus of Thebes and Eastern Triumphalism," in Kelly 2013, 130–52.

Van Nuffelen, P. "A Wise Madness: A virtue-based model for crowd behaviour in late antiquity," in C. DeWet & W. Mayer (eds), *Reconceiving Religious Conflict*, London: Routledge (2018), 234–58.

Waldron, B. "Diocles the Timid," *JLA* 14:1 (2021), 29–49.

Watts, E. "Theodosius II and His Legacy in Anti-Chalcedonian Communal Memory," in Kelly 2013, 269–84.

Whitby, M. "The Balkans and Greece, 420–662," in *CAH* XIV, 701–30.

Whitmarsh, T. *Battling the Gods*, New York: Knopf, 2015.

Whittaker, C. R. *Frontiers of the Roman Empire: A Social and Economic Survey*, Baltimore: Johns Hopkins, 1994.

Wickham, C. *Framing the Middle Ages*, Oxford: Oxford Univ. Press, 2005.

Wickham, C. *The Inheritance of Rome*, New York: Viking Penguin, 2009.

Wickham, C. *Medieval Europe*, New Haven: Yale Univ. Press, 2016.

Wienand, J. (ed.). *Contested Monarchy: Integrating the Roman Empire in the Fourth Century*, Oxford: Oxford Univ. Press, 2015. [Wienand 2015].

Wijnendaele, J. W. P. *The Last of the Romans: Bonifatius–Warlord and Comes Africae*, London: Bloomsbury, 2015. [2015a].

Wijnendaele, J. W. P. "Review of Salisbury 2015," *Bryn Mawr Classical Review*, 2015.11.32. [2015b].

Wijnendaele, J. W. P. "The early career of Aetius and the murder of Felix (*c.* 425–30 CE)," *Historia* 66:4 (2017), 1–20. [2017a].

Wijnendaele, J. W. P. "The Career and 'Revolt' of Gildo," *Latomus* 76:2 (2017), 1–18. [2017b].

Wijnendaele, J. W. P. "The Manufacture of Hercalianus' Usurpation," *Phoenix* 71:2 (2017), 138–56. [2017c].

Wijnendaele, J. W. P. "Late Roman Civil War and the African grain supply," *JLA* 12:2 (2019), 298–28. [2019a].

Wijnendaele, J. W. P. "Sarus the Goth: From imperial commander to warlord," *Early Medieval Europe* 27:4 (2019), 469–93. [2019b].

Williams, D. *Romans and Barbarians*, New York: St. Martin's, 1998.

Williams, S. & G. Friell. *Theodosius: The Empire at Bay*, New Haven: Yale Univ. Press, 1994.

Williams, S. & G. Friell. *The Rome That Did Not Fall: The Survival of the East in the Fifth Century*, London: Routledge, 1999.

Wolfram, H. *The Roman Empire and Its Germanic Peoples*, Berkeley: Univ. of California Press, 1997.

Wolfram, H. *History of the Goths (rev.2d ed.)*, Berkeley: Univ. of California Press, 1998.

Wood, I. "Barbarians, Historians, and the Construction of National Identity," *JLA* 1:1 (2008), 61–81.

Wood, P. "Multiple Voices in Chronicle Sources: The Reign of Leo (457–74) in Book Fourteen of Malalas," *JLA* 4:2 (2011), 298–14.

Woods, D. "The Constantinian origin of Justina," *Classical Quarterly* 54 (2004), 325–7.

Zaccagnino C., G. Bevan, & A. Gabov. "The *Missorium* of Ardabur Aspar: New Considerations of Its Archaeological and Historical Contexts," *Archaeologia Classica LXIII* (2012), 419–54.

Zuckerman, C. "L'empire d'Orient et les Huns: Notes sur Priscus," *Travaux et Memoires Byz.* 12 (1994), 159–82.

Index

Adrianople, Battle of, 10, 25, 68, 79
Aegidius, 143–4
Aelurus, Timothy, 125, 164 n.40
Aetius, Flavius, 46–7, 51, 55–6, 57, 69, 205
Africa, 50, 52, 107
   Vandals enter, 52–5
   campaign of 431–5, 55–9
   campaign of 441, 61, 65–7, 149
   campaign of 468, 148–9, 153–5
   see also Geiseric, Vandals
age, role of, 134, 150, 168, 204–5
Alans, 23–5, 53–4, 61, 68
Alaric, 27
Alexandria, 125, 145, 164, 166
Anagastes, revolt of, 157–9, 205
Anastasius, Emperor, 109, 193 n.101, 194, 197
Anatolius, *m.m.*, 66, 71, 81
Anatolius, Patriarch, 111, 118
Anthemius, PPO, 33
Anthemius, Emperor, 107, 109–10, 112, 113–14, 120, 146–7, 149, 162, 183–4, 199
Anthusa, 133
Antioch, 133–4, 160, 162, 168
Apollinaris, Sidonius, 113
Apollonius, *m.m.*, 72, 104, 112–17
Arcadius, Emperor, 1, 27–9
Arcadius, son of Theodosius II, 83, 84
Ardaburius the Elder, 17, 23–5, 25–6, 29, 30–1, 36, 37–40, 48–9, 61, 90
Ardaburius the Younger, 17–18, 21, 86, 103, 105, 107, 116, 124, 131–5, 143, 158–62, 169–70, 198–9, 204–7
Areobindus, *m.m.*, 14, 39, 71, 78
Ariadne, Empress, 22, 192–4, **192**
Arianism, 15–16, 24–5, 31, 35–6, 61, 63, 126, 167, 173
Armatus, *m.m.*, 152, 163, 185–6
Arnegliscus, *m.m.*, 76 n.71, 78, 80, 157

Aspar, Flavius Ardaburius, 2, 4–6, 14
   accession of Leo I, 93, 111–18
   accession of Marcian, 93–102
   African campaign of, 55–9
   Alan heritage, 23–5, 61
   Ardaburius the Younger, relations with, 134–5, 158–60, 168–70, 204–5
   Arianism and, 14, 16, 61, 115, 167, 200–1
   birth and family, 17, 13–14, 21–2, 26, 106, 204–5
   civil role, 125–7, 200
   consulate, 17–18, 26, 49, 59
   death of, 170–5
   dynastic plans, 116–17, 139–40, 197
   Hun wars, 71, 73–6, 78–82, 86, 87
   imperial candidacy of, 99, 114–16
   Italian campaign, 44–7
   missorium of, 17–21
   name, 19–20
   Persian War (421/22), 38–40
Asterius, 54
Attila, 63
   death, 104
   Hun war of 441–2, 75
   Hun war of 447, 76–82
   Marcian's policy, 103–4
   murder of Bleda, 76
   negotiations with, 87–8, 90–1
   rise of, 69–70, 73
   see also Huns
Augustine of Hippo, 55, 56

Barbarians, 2, 8–14
   anti-barbarian sentiment, 9–10, 14, 81–2, 202–3
   as emperors, 10–12
   assimilation of, 10, 13
   identity, 7–8, 13–14
   intermarriage with and among, 12, 13–14

invasions, 4–5
recruiting of, 5, 9, 10, 25
religion, 15
Roman fears of, 9–10
Basiliscus, emperor, 122–3, 124, 131, 140, 148–55, 157, 161–2, 168, 172, 182, 184–5, 187–91, 197, 199, 206–7
Berichus, 81–2
Bleda, 69–70, 75, 76
Boniface, *m.m.*, 47, 51–2, 55, 56, 57

Caesar, as title, 162–3
Candidianus, 45
Carthage, 17, 50, 56, 57, 58, 65, 66, 66–7, 72, 148, 153
Castinus, *m.m.*, 43–7, 46, 54
ceremonial rulership, 4, 117, 196, 197, 198
Chalcedon, Council of, 35, 61, 93, 102, 108, 109
Charaton, 69
child-emperors, 3, 5, 11–12, 196, 196–8
Chrysostom, John, bishop of Constantinople, 28, 35, 74
Chrysaphius
 and Aspar, 90
 fall of, 89, 90–1, 98
 influence over Theodosius II, 81, 89
 negotiations with Attila, 88
 rise of, 72, 84, 85, 86
 theological battles, 88–9
coinage, 1, **34**, **48**, **83**, 102, **147**
Constantia, 74
Constantinople, 17–18, 25, 27–9, 31, 85, 204
 church of St. Gregory Nazianzus, 133–4
 circus factions, 78
 Cistern of Aspar, 126
 Column of Marcian, 102
 earthquake, 447, 77–8
 fire, 464, 126–7
 Pulcheria's statue, 34
Constantinople, First Ecumenical Council of, 15
Constantius I, Emperor, 2, 88
consuls and consulship, 17–18, 22, 48–9, 59, 119–20, 121–2, 124, 131, 138–9, 158
court factions, 135
Cyrus of Panopolis, 85

Dagalaifus, consul, 119
Daniel the Stylite, 120, 121, 122, 132, 133, 137, 138, 191, 193
Dengizich, 141–3, 157
dynastic principle, 96, 197

earthquake of 447, 77–8
empress, the, role of, 33–4, 97
Ephesus, Second Council of, 35, 89, 94, 108
Ermanaric, 21, 22, 106, 124, 131, 170, 178, 204
Ernach, 141
ethnicity, 7–8, 8–14, 203–4
ethnogenesis, 7–8
Eudocia, Empress, 12, 28, 31, 33, 37, 43–7, 72, 82–6, **83**, 109, 112, 121
Eugenius, 26
Eutropius, 27, 28
Eutychean controversy, 89

Felix, Flavius Constantine, 51, 55
Fravitta, 29
Frigidus, Battle of, 26

Gainas, *m.m.*, 16, 26–31, 68, 136
Galla Placidia, Empress, 12, 17–18, 40, 40–9, **42**, 50–3, 55–6, 57, 58, 97, 109, 197
Geiseric, 25, 54, 56 n.34, 58–9, 66–7, 96, 183
 and Aspar, 58–63, 71, 154
 birth and character, 54
 capture of Carthage, 65
 and the Huns, 67n. 11, 103
 leads Vandals to Africa, 54–5
 Leo's campaign against (468), 148–55
 marries son into imperial family, 122
 and Olybrius: 122, 183
 peace negotiations (435), 58–9
 religious views, 54
 and Ricimer, 143, 144, 145, 183
Gennadius, Patriarch, 166
Goths, 27, 28–9, 30, 31, 40–1, 68, 105–6, 123, 127–8, 141–3, 171–2, 177–8, 187–91, 199
Gundobad, 184
Guntharic, 54

Heraclius of Edessa, 149, 188
heretics, 8, 15–16

Hippo Regius, 55, 56, 57
Honoria affair, the, 97, 103, 104
Honorius, Emperor, 1, 40–1, 42
Huneric, 122
Huns, 157–8
    Aetius and, 46–7, 57
    early history in Europe, 67–8
    predecessors of Attila: Uldin, Charaton, Octa & Ruga, 68–9
    Marcian and, 103–5
    Dengizich, son of Attila, 141–3, 157–8
    see also Attila

identity, 7–8, 13, 14, 21, 124–5, 136, 180, 195–6, 203–6
Illus, 185–7, 191
Illyricum, 27, 75, 76
imperial legitimacy, 2–3, 95, 96, 102, 126, 177, 181, 198, 201
Isaurians, 81, 135–40, 180, 192–3
Isocasius, trial of, 165–6

Jerome, 12
Jerusalem, 84, 86
John, usurper, 43–7
John the Vandal, 60, 157
Jordanes, 54, 69, 136–7, 140, 158, 161

legitimacy, 2–3, 95, 96, 102, 126, 177, 181, 198, 201
Leo, Pope, 125
Leo I, Emperor, 15, 96, **147**, 196, 197
    accession of, 93, 111–17
    Arians, legislation against, 173
    background, 117
    Byzantine memory of, 173–5
    death of, 178–9
    dynastic strategy of, 120–1, 131, 162–3, 167–8, 177, 179, 207
    family, 22, 116–17, 120–1, 123
        (*see also* Ariadne, Leo II, Leontia, Verina)
    Isaurians and, 135–40
    Isocasius, trial of, 165–6
    Menas, trial of 164–5
    Patricius Caesar and, 162
    political theater and, 164–7
    religion, 126, 164–7
    Tatianus/Vivianus dispute, 138–9
    Vandal campaign (468), 143–55
    Zeno and, 135–40, 168 (*see also* Zeno)
Leo II, Emperor, 179, 181, 182, 183
Leontia, daughter of Leo I, 117, 163, 168, 204
Leontius, usurper, 186–7
Longinus, 191–2

Magnentius, Emperor, 11
Majorian, Emperor, 119, 128–9, 143–4, 144
Marcellus, St., 164, 166, 170
Marcia Euphemia, daughter of Marcian, 110
Marcian, Emperor, 59–61, 62, 65, 127–8, 138, 197, 198, 199
    accession, 93–102
    achievements, 108–9
    age, 101
    background, 101
    coronation, 102, 118
    death, 107, 109, 111–12
    dynastic issues, 108–10
    foreign policy, 103–5
    legitimacy, 95, 102
    military policy, 105–8
    miracle stories, 101–2
    religious policies, 108, 109
Marcianopolis, sack of, 80
Marcianus, 181, 190
Margus, bishop of, 74–5
Marsus the Isaurian, 149
Maurianus, 191
Maximinus, ambassador, 38–40, 81–2
Maximinus Thrax, Emperor, 10–11
Melania the Younger, 83, 98
Menas, trial of, 164–5
military commands, 70
missorium of Aspar, 17–22, **19**, **20**, 49

Nedao, Battle of the, 105
Nepos, Julius, 181
Nestorius, 80
Nicaea, First Council of, 15
Nisibis, siege of, 37, 38
Nomus, 81

Olybrius, Anicius, 96–7, 121–2, 183–4
Orthodox Church, 8, 14–15, 16, 31, 108, 115, 122, 134
Ostrys, *comes*, 172–3

paganism, 165–6
patricius, title of, 21
Patricius, 21, 21–2, 116, 119, 120, 121, 123, 131, 139, 162, 204, 207
   claim to throne, 167–8
   death, 170–1
   elevation to Caesar, 162–4
Paulinus, 85
Persian Letters, the, 131–5, 135, 138, 146, 168, 199
Persian War, 421/22, 26, 36–40, 101
Philippopolis, siege of, 79
Placidia, daughter of Valentinian III, wife of Olybrius, 121–2
Plintha, 13–14, 17, 30, 35, 49, 63, 69, 72, 76, 90
Pulcheria, Augusta, 31, 61, 196, 198
   and the accession of Marcian, 93–4, 102
   coinage, **34**
   at the Council of Chalcedon, 93
   cult of, 121, 126, 172, 201
   death, 109, 199
   Eudocia, 82, 84
   execution of Chrysaphius, 98
   and fall of Chrysaphius, 89
   imperial candidacy, 97–9
   influence, **34–6**
   marriage to Marcian, 102
   and military policy, 35–6
   and the Persian War, 421/22, 36–7, 38n36
   re-emergence of, 90, 91
   role, 82, 93–4
   vow of virginity, 33, 97, 98–9

Ratiaria, fall of, 77
Ravenna, 41, 43, 45, 45–6, 51
Recitach, son of Strabo, 190
Ricimer, 128–9, 143–7, 149, 155, 183–4
Roman army, 10
   barbarian recruits, 9, 10, 25
   barbarian troops, 5
   rise of barbarian commanders, 10–11
Roman Empire
   c. 400 AD., xii–xiii
   cooperation between parts, 1
   division of, 1

Rome, Vandals sack, 109, 121
Rufinus, 1, 26, 27

Salona, 44
Sarus, 203
Sassanid Persian Empire, 4, 36–40
Saturninus, 86
Sebastianus, 57
Serdica, 160
Sicily, 30, 65, 66, 149, 153, 155
Sigisvult, *m.m.*, 55, 66
Silvanus, Emperor, 11
spiritual marriages, 98–9
Stilicho, 1, 11–12, 26–7, 40–1
   dynastic approach, 2–4
Synesius of Cyrene, 9, 28, 30

Tatianus, 107, 138–9, 145
Theoderic Strabo, 62, 106, 172, 177–8, 181, 186, 187–90
Theoderic the Amal, 106, 114, 127–8, 188–91
Theodoret, 125
Theodosiopolis, siege of, 37
Theodosius I, Emperor, 1, 2–3, 9, 10, 12, 15, 17–18, 23–5, 25, 26–7
Theodosius II, Emperor, 30, 33, 43–7, 82, 95
   and Chrysaphius, 86, 89
   death, 35, 91, 93, 196
   earthquake of 447, 78
   foreign policy, 88
   and Galla Placidia, 41–2
   marriage to Eudocia, 35, 82–6
   and the Persian War, 421/22, 37–8
   succession crisis, 35, 65, 91, 93–102, 111, 205–6
   and Vandal threat, 66
   Western succession crisis (424/425), 43–4, 47
Thessalonica, 44
Thrace, 73, 75
Triarius, 22, 106, 172
Tribigild, 28

Uldin, 68–9

Valentinian I, Emperor, 2
Valentinian II, Emperor, 12

Valentinian III, Emperor, 40, 44, 45, 83, 87, 197
  and the accession of Marcian, 94–7
  assassination of, 104, 107, 109, 128, 196, 205
  investiture, 47–8
  recognition of Marcian, 103–4
Vandals, 24, 107, 128
  campaign against (431–5), 55–9
  campaign against (441), 61, 65–7, 149
  campaign against (468), 143–55
  enter Africa (429), 52–5
  inaction against by Marcian, 107
  Leo I and, 143–55
  Leo's truce with, 168–9
  raids, 65
  sack Hippo Regius, 57
  sack Rome, 109, 121
  see also Africa, Geiseric
Varahram V, King of Persia, 36
Verina, Augusta, 120, 122, 125, 150 n.62, 152, 168, 179, 181–2, 186–7
Vivianus, 120, 138–9

Western Empire
  Aspar offered throne, 49
  collapse, 1–2, 182–4
  cooperation with Eastern, 1
  Huns arrival in, 46–7
  Leo I relations with, 128–9
  succession crisis, 40–9
  Vandal problem, 143–7

Yezdegerd I, King of Persia, 36, 37
Yezdegerd II, King of Persia, 66

Zeno, *m.m.*
  and the accession of Marcian, 94, 100–1
  death, 105, 198
  Hun war, 447–8, 81
  influence, 104
  Marcian foreign policy, 103
  negotiations with Attila, 88
  revolt threat, 90
  rise of, 81
Zeno, emperor, 174, 179–82, 184–92
  background, 135–6
  Balkans, 187–91
  co-Augustus, 163
  death, 192
  internal exile, 161–2, 199, 206–7
  Isaurian identity, 136, 180
  legitimacy, 181
  Leo summons, 168
  marries Leo's daughter, 139–40, 168
  and the Persian Letters, 132, 135
  plot against, 159–62
  relationship with Leo, 135–40
  religious views, 180–1
  and revolt of Anagastes, 158–9
  rise of, 131–40, 152
  succession, 191–4
  temporary overthrow, 181–2
  unpopularity, 180–1
Zercon, 73

www.ingramcontent.com/pod-product-compliance
Lightning Source LLC
Chambersburg PA
CBHW062148300426
44115CB00012BA/2039